T0330325

Configured by Consumption

For our grandchildren from the youngest to the oldest:
Mikayla Kam, and Silas, Griffin, Jethro, Imogen, Joshua and
Marina Rimmer

Configured by Consumption

How Consumption–Demand Will Reshape Supply Chain Operations

Booi Hon Kam

College of Business and Law, RMIT University, Melbourne, Australia

Peter J. Rimmer AM

ANU College of Asia and the Pacific, Australian National University, Canberra, Australia

 Edward Elgar
PUBLISHING

Cheltenham, UK • Northampton, MA, USA

Published by
Edward Elgar Publishing Limited
The Lypiatts
15 Lansdown Road
Cheltenham
Glos GL50 2JA
UK

Edward Elgar Publishing, Inc.
William Pratt House
9 Dewey Court
Northampton
Massachusetts 01060
USA

A catalogue record for this book
is available from the British Library

Library of Congress Control Number: 2022932629

This book is available electronically in the **Elgar**online
Economics subject collection
http://dx.doi.org/10.4337/9781789905731

ISBN 978 1 78990 572 4 (cased)
ISBN 978 1 78990 573 1 (eBook)

Printed and bound by CPI Group (UK) Ltd, Croydon, CR0 4YY

Contents

Preface

The unanticipated arrival of the COVID-19 pandemic interrupted our writing of *Configured by Consumption*. Our original plan was to demonstrate that supply chain operations over the last few decades have been configured by changing consumption patterns underpinned by technological advancements. The imposition of travel restrictions and social or physical distancing rules following COVID-19 lockdowns forced many brick-and-mortar operations to go online. The ensuing changes in consumption patterns followed by a corresponding shift in supply chain operations vindicated our contention. We regrouped to take our cues from fresh evidence surfacing unremittingly from the COVID-19 pandemic, redesigned some chapters, and updated our narratives as new insights into logistics and supply chain operations unfolded during what has become known as the 'digital pandemic'.[1]

Since the mid-2010s business operations have become increasingly enmeshed in an evolving digital ecosystem under Industry 4.0. As the trend grows more prominent during the COVID-19 pandemic, we sense that a totally new dimension is emerging. We expect, and continue to witness, digital technologies advancing in quantum leaps under Industry 4.0. This has prompted us to contemplate where such mind-boggling changes will take logistics and supply chain operations beyond the already predictable higher levels of automation, use of robotics and artificial intelligence.

We started to explore this new dimension by asking the question: How will all these changes affect business and consumers? More specifically, how do we make sense of these changes from a supply chain and logistics operations perspective? Our attempt to understand the conceptual underpinnings of these changes became more pressing once the term Supply Chain 4.0 gained traction during the COVID-19 pandemic. We pondered: Does Supply Chain 4.0 really signal a paradigm shift in logistics and supply chain operations? Or, is it merely a fanciful way of encapsulating the supply chain changes occurring under the Industry 4.0 ecosystem?

---

[1]   Steve Davis and Precious Matsoso (2020). 'COVID-19 as a digital pandemic', *Think Global Health*, 7 July. Available at www.thinkglobalhealth.org/article/covid-19 -digital-pandemic (accessed 17 July 2020).

These issues we intended to unravel in *Configured by Consumption* had their roots in our earlier book *Consumer Logistics: Surfing the Digital Wave*.[2] There we argued that consumer demand and technological advancements will drive new logistics innovations, instanced by the rise of Uber Eats and the emergence of omnichannel retailing. We proposed an 8th R (enlisting the *right* consumer) to be added to the time-honoured 7Rs of logistics management – getting the *right* goods, at the *right* quantity, to the *right* consumer, at the *right* time, at the *right* place, in the *right* condition, and at the *right* price — to emphasize the role of technology in speeding up the fulfilment of the 7Rs.

Our quest for answers to the issues raised took us back to the five waves of change uncovered in *Consumer Logistics*. We zoomed into the triggers of change, asking why those drivers have forced a change in the operational trajectory of logistics and supply chain processes. We concluded that supply chain operations, in their relentless pursuit of cost-efficiency and customer responsiveness to gain competitive advantage, have been looking towards, or influenced by, technological advancements to achieve process innovations, which, in turn, have been shaped by changes in consumption patterns and consumer purchasing journeys. Also, we observed that technologies are a double-edge sword. On the one hand, as demonstrated by the use of robots in warehouses, they have provided the means for process automation to boost operational efficiency. On the other hand, as exemplified by the rise of social commerce, they have offered a medium for consumers to share their purchasing experience and mould their consumption patterns. The socialization of technology suggests that supply chain operations bent on embracing technologies to enhance extant processes will always play a 'catch-up' game. Exploring how supply chain operations ought to capitalize on technological advancement under Industry 4.0 to meet evolving consumer demand has propelled us to write *Configured by Consumption*.

As in *Consumer Logistics*, we again adopt a historical approach to explore how, first, logistics, followed by supply chain operations, have evolved as a discipline and practice through the combined lens of accommodating technological advancement and supporting consumption. Our primary aim in writing this book, therefore, is to dig deeper into the theoretical underpinnings of changes in supply chain configurations as business logistics morphs into supply chain operations under an evolving business landscape: from trade globalization through e-commerce and m-commerce, before mutating into omnichannel retailing and social commerce. We want to make sense of the configurational

---

2   Peter J. Rimmer and Booi Hon Kam (2018). *Consumer Logistics: Surfing the Digital Wave*. Cheltenham, UK and Northampton, MA, USA: Edward Elgar Publishing.

changes that have occurred in product supply chains over the past five to six decades and, in doing so, develop a general theory of supply chain operations, or, in Clayton Christensen's words, 'a statement of causality'.[3]

As anticipated, covering the historical evolution of a discipline is, in practice, an enormous task. It is fraught with twists and turns in terms of direction and thrust. Partly, this is due to the voluminous, yet fragmentary, information available. Also, it is partly attributable to the rapid pace of change occurring in supply chain practices under the digital landscape of Industry 4.0 technologies referred to as Supply Chain 4.0. A case in point was our initial disproportional attention to 3D printing, which, we believed, had the greatest potential of fulfilling the mission of 'product on demand' until, despite the hype, our desk research showed otherwise.[4] Thus, *Configured by Consumption* chronicles the three-way interactions between technological development, the evolution of logistics and supply chain operations, and post-Second World War changes in consumer purchasing behaviour and consumption patterns.

    [3]   Dina Gerdeman and Clayton Christensen (2016). 'Author Interview: Clayton Christensen: *The Theory of Jobs to Be Done*', Working Knowledge: Business Research for Business Leaders, Harvard Business School, 3 October.
    [4]   Matthias Heutger and Markus Kückelhaus (2020). *Logistics Trend Radar*, 5th Edition. Deutsche Post DHL Group: Bonn DE. Available at www.dhl.com/cn-en/home/insights-and-innovation/insights/logistics-trend-radar.html (accessed 10 November 2020).

Acknowledgements

Over the past 18 years our collegial work has been achieved through reciprocal visits between our respective workplaces in Australia's state of Victoria and the Australian Capital Territory. However, COVID-19 affected our *modus operandi* and this process has not been possible. As this manuscript goes to press, Booi has been in lockdown on six occasions in Melbourne and Peter twice in Canberra. Our interactions have been confined to Skype and telephone calls. Therefore, we need to outline our separate tasks in producing this book and thank people in our respective domains before writing our joint appreciations.

Booi supplied the idea for this study, scoped and structured its contents and provided contributions to individual chapters. He thanks past and present students, academic colleagues and practising professional friends, including those met during research leave in China, the United Kingdom and South Korea during 2019, whose perceptions are reflected in this study. Special mention must be made of two former colleagues in the School of Business IT and Logistics (now the School of Accounting, Information Systems and Supply Chain) at RMIT University, Melbourne: Professor Caroline Chan, University of Newcastle, Australia, for constant support and Dr Leon Kok Yan Teo of Australia Post for insights into Industry 4.0 technologies and supply chain analytics. On a more personal note, his appreciation is extended to his wife Shirley and their children Tritia, Noreen, Nicholas and his wife Jocelyn, and Christopher for their unconditional love and encouragement of his intellectual activities. Their permanently online presence, social media and social commerce activities, and relentless click-and-mortar purchases have provided the consumer backdrop and fuelled his contributions to this study.

Peter has managed the writing process, researched and drafted the chapters, compiled the bibliography and drawn the accompanying figures. He thanks colleagues in the School of Culture, History and Language in the College of Asia and the Pacific, Australian National University, especially its Director Professor Simon Haberle for continuing support; staff at the university's library and the National Library of Australia; and his cartographic advisors Sandy Potter, Jenny Sheehan and Karina Pelling at CartoGIS Scholarly Information Services ANU and Kay Dancey, former head of CartoGIS. For their unfailing love and support of his academic endeavours he is indebted to his wife, Sue, and their children and respective partners, Joseph and Belle, Matthew and Susan and Rachel and Arunas.

Our collective thanks are due to those individuals and organizations facilitating permission to use illustrations: Barbara Candelas, World Economic Forum; Gary Farachi, WPG Holdings; Emily Fisher, Linux Foundation; Markus Krisetya, TeleGeography; Nicole Lavender, AmerisourceBergen World Courier; Erin O'Shea, BBC; Sheila Seles, Fast Radius; and Frank Stockhausen, Deutsche Post DHL Group. Open access to information provided by the National Health Service England and Our World in Data is much appreciated.

Further, thanks are due to Dr Sue Rimmer for editing the text and her insights into consumerism; Professor Tessa Morris-Suzuki, School of Culture History and Language, Australian National University, for her comments on Chapter 2; and Dr Matthew Rimmer, Professor, Intellectual Property and Innovation Law, Queensland University of Technology, Brisbane, for his wide-ranging advice extending from Industry 4.0, through vaccination supplies and vulnerable supply chains, to legal matters.

Also, at Edward Elgar Publishing our gratitude extends to Alex Pettifer, Editorial Editor, Alex O'Connell, Senior Supervising Editor, Karen Jones, Managing Editor and Finn Halligan, Assistant Editor, who have been an unfailing source of assistance. On this occasion, we have benefitted from their infinite patience in allowing us the extra COVID-related time to bring this project to a conclusion. Also at Edward Elgar, Barbara Pretty, Senior Desk Editor, has orchestrated production with Andy Driver developing the cover, Dawn Preston providing copy editing, Sarah Cook providing proofreading and Victoria Chow supplying the index.

This book is dedicated to our respective grandchildren, who give us immense pleasure. We hope that they will inherit a better and peaceful 'new normal' marking the end of COVID-19.

Permissions

Figure 2.8 Gary Farachi, WPG Holdings

Figure 2.9 Gary Farachi, WPG Holdings

Figure 4.2 Deutsche Post DHLGroup

Figure 4.4 Hyperledger, CC-by 4.0

Figure 5.8 AmerisourceBergen World Courier

Figure 6.7 Fast Radius

All icons are from the Noun Project (https://thenounproject/com/).

All base maps in this study are subject to permission being given by Carto GIS Scholarly Information Services ANU (sis.cartogis@anu.edu.au).

The boundaries and names shown and the designations used on the figures in this study do not imply official endorsement or acceptance.

1. Introduction to *Configured by Consumption*

The novel coronavirus-19 (COVID-19) pandemic has accelerated the digital transformation of work and play. As governments in infected countries legislated lockdown and called for social, or more appropriately, physical distancing, any activity that could be performed in cyber space was literally moved to an online environment. These included teaching and learning, medical consultation (telehealth) and gymnasium instruction among many activities. While online shopping is not new, its frequency and intensity surged during COVID-19 (Australian Associated Press, 2021). Australia Post, for instance, recorded a doubling of parcel volumes within four weeks of the country's cities going into lockdown in March–April 2020 (Durkin, 2020). 'Online department store purchases are up 473 per cent,' reported Kirsten Robb and Ashlynne McGee (2020), 'while fashion purchases have trebled (up 203 per cent).' To cope with this unprecedented increase in demand and despite the fact that most air freight services in Australia were grounded, Australia Post has had to retrain 2,000 motorcycle 'posties' to process and deliver parcels and charter extra planes to minimize delivery delays.

In the United States, data sourced from 10,000 retailers by Signifyd Inc., an e-commerce security and fraud prevention vendor, showed that e-commerce sales for seven categories of goods rose an average of about 40 per cent between 26 May and 1 June 2020, compared with the pre-pandemic week of 24 February–1 March 2020 (Berthene, 2020). Signifyd's data also revealed that buy-online-pick-up-in-store orders increased 248 per cent during the week 25–31 May 2020 against the pre-pandemic week (24 February–1 March 2020).

The COVID-19 pandemic also witnessed radical changes in the manufacturing sector. General Motors, an automobile manufacturer, was reported to be converting its idle facilities in Kokomo, Indiana, to build ventilators in partnership with Ventec Life Systems in addition to also producing Level 1 surgical masks at its Warren, Michigan, manufacturing facility (GM, 2020). Likewise, Ford, another iconic automobile manufacturer, worked with 3M to develop a new generation of 'powered air-purifying respirator' masks and collaborated with GE Healthcare to make ventilators (Valdes-Dapena, 2020). In Australia, distilleries around the country, including the Queensland distilleries of Bundaberg Rum and Beenleigh Rum, Western Australia's Tender

Rum and New South Wales' Earp Distilling, either donated ethanol or turned to producing hand sanitizer as normal supplies failed to meet surging demand (Hegarty et al., 2020).

For many companies, the COVID-19 pandemic provided a context in which transformation was not a choice but a necessity. Manufacturers and suppliers scrambled to reduce the number of stock-keeping units they were making, by refitting their factories to produce, and warehouses to store, only high-demand products. Supply chains feverishly improvised collaborative arrangements to create opportunities for faster end-to-end redesign, production and distribution of critical products. With cities the world over in lockdown mode, e-commerce became the only option to trade. Digitization came directly under the spotlight, offering a ready-made solution.

COVID-19 has amplified a long-recognized relationship between supply chain operations and patterns of product consumption. This is expected since the primary mission of logistics and supply chain management is to meet customer expectations, encapsulated in the so-called 7 Rights – getting the *right* product, in the *right* quantity, in the *right* condition, at the *right* place, at the *right* time, to the *right* customer, at the *right* price. Yet, studies of supply chain management practices have paid scant attention to the effects that product consumption patterns have had upon supply chain configurations.

This raises a series of issues. How will changes in the way consumers purchase goods affect the configuration of supply chains operated by manufacturers? How will embracing Industry 4.0 technologies provide the answer to building a consumption-directed supply chain? How will the role of logistics and supply chain management be cast in a digital ecosystem powered by artificial intelligence that runs Big Data and advanced analytics to respond to consumer demand in real time?

In this book, we seek answers to these issues by taking a broad sweep at the historical discourse on logistics and supply chain management. We trace the advent of logistics operations in trade, commerce and industry through various lenses: industrialization, technological advances and consumer movements. Then we build the link between the evolution of supply chain configurations and changes in consumption habits to reveal transformations observed at the both the firm (micro) and industry and country (macro) levels.

THE CURSE OF PRODUCTION

Relentless growth of materialistic consumption is changing the configuration of supply chains. The insatiable desire to consume has given rise to existing product distribution channels – physical stores, mobile phones, e-commerce and online marketplaces – being integrated to offer consumers a seamless shopping experience. Omnichannel retailing and the omnicommerce experience allow consumers to simultaneously search for product information across all channels to decide how to purchase and where to pick up or have their purchase delivered.

Paradoxically, this escalation of consumption patterns has been neglected by logisticians. They have been preoccupied with the fourth stage of industry development – Industry 4.0: Cyber-Physical Systems – and linked supply chain management operations embodied in Supply Chain 4.0's Total Network Integration (Figure 1.1). But they have ignored the associated changes in product consumption. As a result, Industry 4.0 and Supply Chain 4.0 have become contemporary catchwords. Consumerism 4.0 is a little-known entity.

This neglect of consumerism raises a second series of issues because its occurrence has been a pervasive feature of three earlier stages in the development of Industry 1.0 (mechanization), Industry 2.0 (mass production), and Industry 3.0 (automation), which is aligned with Logistics 3.0 (business

Date	Industrial development	Logistics and supply chain management (SCM)	
2020s	Industry 4.0 Digitization	Logistics 4.0 Intelligent logistics systems	SCM 4.0 Total network integration
2010s			
2000s	Industry 3.0 Automation	Logistics 3.0 Business logistics	SCM 3.0 Integration between two channels
1990s			
1980s			
1970s		Logistics 2.0 Physical distribution management	SCM 2.0 Isolated decision-making
1960s	Industry 2.0 Mass production		
1950s		Logistics 1.0 Mechanization	
1900s			
1890s	Industry 1.0 Mechanization		
1790s			
1780s			

Source: Based on information from Frazzon et al. (2019) and Rodrigue (2020a).

Figure 1.1   *Alignment of industry and logistics and supply chain management*

logistics) and Supply Chain 3.0 (the first phase of supply chain management). How have these four stages of industrial development been represented? Why have the associated aspects of consumerism been ignored in this representation? How can the four stages in the culture of product consumption be articulated? More particularly, how have digital technologies reshaped the supply chain process, particularly during the COVID-19 pandemic? How have Industry 4.0 technologies and the COVID-19 pandemic given rise to the production-on-demand phenomenon? How is this phenomenon triggering the merger of industry and distribution under Industry 4.0 technologies? And finally, how has this union of product and distribution been incorporated into the supply chain process?

These issues are explored in this book. Before identifying how the book is structured to address them, it is important to elaborate on why this book is needed.

WHY THIS BOOK?

To the corporate world, artificial intelligence technology and machine learning, in particular, will be creating an economy so big that it will be like the rise of a second China (Cross, 2020). Instead of millions of factories, it will be zillions of algorithms processing Big Data, powering a vast range of services – search engines, facial recognition and voice typing – that were once domains that only human inputs could accomplish. More significantly, artificial intelligence technology holds the promise to undertake them faster and more effectively than human processing. The scope of this promise seems endless – like a genie emerging out of a bottle.

With 'all things digital' paving the way to a post-COVID-19 'next normal', we are witnessing the overwhelming effects of digital technologies on consumer behaviour. To the public-at-large, these observations have reached a level where eventually digital technologies and artificial intelligence will take over all jobs. Logistics and supply chain operations will be run autonomously – at a new height that only imagination could portray.

We are not debating whether this will be the ultimate future. In this book, we argue that for supply chain operations to run autonomously, interactions between humans and technologies cannot be ignored. While artificial intelligence technology will drive the next generation of supply chains, human interactions with technology will shape the configuration of supply chain processes. We build our argument on the inseparable relationship between supply chain operations and human consumption that has been made blatantly obvious during the COVID-19 pandemic. This effort is mirrored in the book's structure, which highlights its theme of giving a broad overview of the correspondence between industrialization, the evolution of logistics and the supply

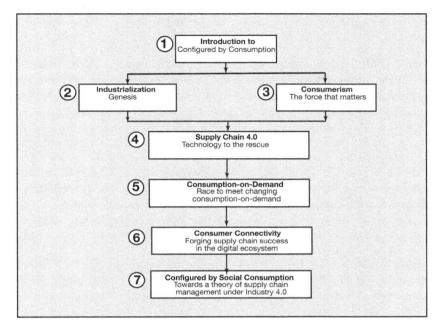

Figure 1.2   The book's structure

chain, and consumerism (Figure 1.2). Our focus in addressing this task has been to string a coherent thread through significant events in logistics and supply chain practices over time.

THE BOOK'S STRUCTURE

Chapter 2 argues that industrialization is the root of logistics and supply chain operations, having created the need for the efficient handling and movement of raw materials, which has led to the birth of logistics management. Subsequent progress is reflected in a history of industrialization, which traces the successive production-consumption cycles as the economic growth engines moved from Industry 1.0 through Industry 2.0 and 3.0 to 4.0. What is missing from this analysis is any discussion of the four waves of product consumption, because they do not correspond exactly to the stages of industrialization until the fourth stage.

Chapter 3 analyses how product consumption since the Second World War has changed with the advent of containerization, followed by the birth of the World Wide Web and the invention of the smart phone, before it marched into the suite of intelligent Industry 4.0 technologies with digitization. We characterize these changes that have shaped logistics and supply chain processes as transformation, progression, evolution and revolution, and associate the corresponding adjustments in consumption patterns as Consumerism 1.0, 2.0, 3.0 and 4.0. We argue that the moves from brick-and-mortar through multichannel to omnichannel retailing have transformed supply chain management from a production-based operation to a consumption-centred process.

Chapter 4 investigates the conceptual underpinnings of Supply Chain 4.0 practices. This study seeks to make sense of how the mind-boggling changes occasioned by the introduction of smart Industry 4.0 technologies are transforming consumer purchasing journeys and offering opportunities for supply chain operations to innovate or reinvent themselves. We outline the possibilities, summarize the vision, assess the realities and speculate on the challenges Supply Chain 4.0 operations will confront as new possibilities unfold.

Chapter 5 draws evidence from the monumental impacts, including both supply disruptions and demand shifts, the unprecedented international border closure, prolonged city, regional and national lockdowns, and worldwide travel restrictions that the COVID-19 pandemic has generated. These further illustrate our notion of how supply chain operations have been configured by consumption with the help of Industry 4.0 technologies.

By Chapter 6 our analysis converges to provide an understanding that supply chain success under the digital ecosystem of Industry 4.0 will be centred upon consumer connectivity. With apps becoming the epicentre of social interaction, and with social shopping and social commerce driving consumption, we identify, based on that premise, six network types arising from the merger of production and distribution, which we have termed *productribution* – a portmanteau term derived from the words production and distribution. This recognition allows us to argue that network connectivity will determine supply chains' competitive advantage under the hegemony of the digital ecosystem.

Finally, Chapter 7 concludes the book by synthesizing the findings of the foregoing chapters to produce a theory of supply chain management under Industry 4.0.

2.   Industrialization: genesis

Our overarching focus in this book is the three-way interactions between technological development, the evolution of logistics and supply chain operations, and changes in consumer purchasing behaviour over the past six decades. We contend that the cause of this dynamic is rooted in industrialization. The evolutionary journey of logistics and supply chain operations, as a practice and an academic discipline, began with mechanization, which triggered the first industrial revolution. This chapter is, therefore, designed to explore the broad linkages between industrialization, technological innovations and demand for goods and services (an indication of consumption) as manufacturing moved through four industrial revolutions — Industry 1.0, Industry 2.0, Industry 3.0 and Industry 4.0 (Figure 2.1).

Our attention in describing these linkages over the four phases is directed primarily to the innovations, stemming from mechanization through mass production and automation to cyber-physical systems, and the economic drivers, arising from substitution through the economies of scale and value adding to digitization. We highlight how each phase has created its own distinctive structure from industrial cities, industrial regions, global production arenas to the global cyber web, and the associated range of logistics responses to changes in demand and customer expectations. We view the linkages between the drivers and structures through the lens of a series of production-consumption cycles as the four phases of industrial revolution transition from one to the next.

This focus gives rise to a series of key issues. How have individual recursive cycles evolved within each industrial revolution? How has this process led to the origins and changes in logistics and supply chain practices? And how in the grand scheme of things have certain attributes played a key role in the transition from one industry revolution to the next?

In addressing these issues, we first examine how each industrial revolution created a production-consumption cycle and its link to technological innovation and demand for logistics and supply chain operations. The first three stages are treated summarily, whereas the fourth stage is elaborated in more detail. This allows a deeper exploration of the new field of innovations brought about by the proposition that Industry 4.0 will not only modify production processes but also consumer purchasing journeys. We then tie together our analysis of the four stages by discussing how each has transitioned to the next and to pinpoint recurrent features.

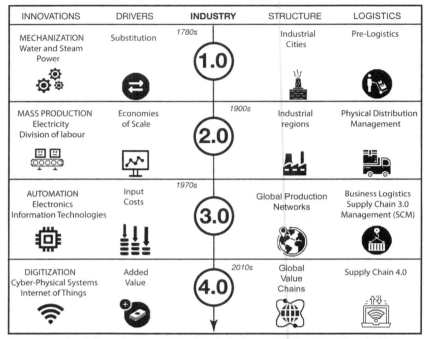

Source: Based on information from Rifkin (2016), Venkumar (2019) and Rodrigue (2020a).

Figure 2.1   *Representations of Industry 1.0, Industry 2.0, Industry 3.0*
               and Industry 4.0

THE FIRST THREE INDUSTRIAL REVOLUTIONS

Before the 1780s the production of food, clothing, dwellings, tools and weapons relied upon manual labour and was often orchestrated by a landed aristocracy. Consumption was largely food based and, given the state of transport, heavily reliant on either self-provisioning from the immediate local area and subject to recurrent famines. Energy was provided either by hand, animal or wind power; mobile transport was supplied by animal-driven vehicles or a variety of waterborne craft; and communication was by messenger.

By 2010 three industrial revolutions had occurred with each one building upon and advancing past production-consumption cycles in progressively replacing human labour by machinery to manufacture goods. The production aspects are best discussed by drawing upon Jeremy Rifkin's (2016) description of their three prime characteristics, namely: (1) new sources of energy to *power* economic activity more efficiently; (2) new modes of transport to *move* goods and people more efficiently; and (3) new communication technologies to *manage* economic activity more effectively. Purchases of newly produced goods for immediate consumption have prompted focus on the middle class – 'traders, inventors and managers' – rather than the upper class or lower class (McCloskey, 2016: xii). Arguably, the propensity of the middle class to demand greater political accountability has resulted in higher salaries that created a stable demand for goods and services (EC, 2020; Amaranto et al., 2010). Indeed, their repeated, but differing, role in each of the three industrial revolutions has stemmed from, and contributed to, higher economic growth.

Industry 1.0: Mechanization

The Industry 1.0 production-consumption cycle stretched from the mid-eighteenth century to the late nineteenth century and encompassed the shift from an agricultural to an industrial society in Britain (Figure 2.2). Associated with the mechanization of production and mechanical power generation, this society was marked by the transition from artisanal (craft) production in cottages meeting a customized demand to industrial production in factories with owners, managers and employees organized to produce a higher volume that met the expanding demand for the low variety of goods available. Energy was supplied first by waterpower and then by steam drawing upon abundant coal resources; transport was provided initially by canals before they were progressively superseded by national railway systems, later complemented by steamships replacing sailing ships, allowing the movement

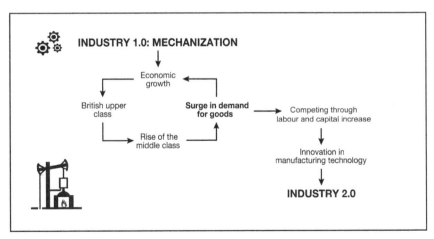

Figure 2.2   The Industry 1.0 production-consumption cycle

of both people and goods over greater distances and less subject to the vagaries of the weather; and communications were marked by steam-powered printing and the telegraph.

The sustained increase in labour productivity driven by the famous steam-based technological innovations may have been overestimated, but it did mark the onset of 'modern' economic growth (Crafts, 2004). The increased human productivity, rising real wages and resultant increase in consumption were typified by developments within Britain's cotton textile industry in Lancashire pivoted on the important commercial and industrial city of Manchester, which became a provincial centre and world marketplace for cotton (Rodgers, 1960). Industrial development within Lancashire, as in other parts of Britain, was aided and abetted by the upper class. Despite their ostentatious consumption and some opposition to technological innovations, the landed aristocracy played a key role in promoting the early take-off not only of agriculture but also of mining, manufacturing and transport improvements in Britain (Raybould, 1984).

This aristocratic influence was less marked in Manchester itself where a commercial and industrial middle class emerged and took advantage of new forms of transport to escape the inner city for tree-lined suburbs (Kidd, 1985). There their wives indulged their predilections for domestic calicoes in their clothing and furnishings, notably curtains and upholstery, and displayed bric-a-brac in their homes originating from the Empire and foreign lands (Joshi, 2010). In turn, while retaining their business connections with Manchester, the more eminent families among the new merchant and industrial aristocracy left their suburban mansions and the city's environs for other parts of Britain (Rodgers, 1962).

Such developments gave rise to a wider surge in customer demand for goods that not only led to further economic growth but also the transition to a consumer economy, especially after the Long Depression of 1893–97 (Rummelt, 2008). By then there was competition for both labour and capital, particularly as the productivity from high-priced steam power, even from the railways, was small and long delayed in the 'simple market' of Adam Smith's *Wealth of Nations* where price adjusted any mismatches occurring between supply and demand (Yin et al., 2018). This shortfall in productivity provided the impetus for innovations in manufacturing technology to be brought to the market to overcome the shortage of supplies. A new industrial revolution was imminent, which offered higher productivity factor growth by going beyond mechanization and 'adding precision, standardization, interchangeability, synchronisation and continuity' (Rae, 1965: 54). These desiderata were fulfilled in the United States.

Industry 2.0: Mass Production

The Industry 2.0 production-consumption cycle covered the period between the end of the railway boom to the termination of the post-war boom around 1970. This period within the United States era was marked by a centralized electricity system and cheap oil supplying energy to power individual stationary and portable machines; transport typified by trans-continental railways and automobiles on national road systems; and communications delivered by telephone, radio and television. Industry was characterized by: (1) mass production providing a greater volume and variety of goods, (2) the application of Frederick Taylor's *Principle of Scientific Management* to optimize the productivity of workers and workplace operations and (3) the rise of a new middle class (Figure 2.3).

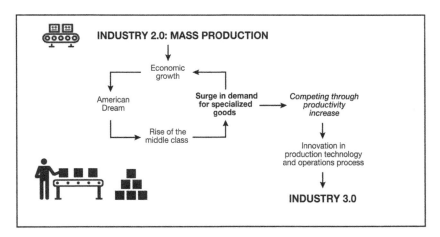

Figure 2.3   *The Industry 2.0 production-consumption cycle*

The mass production of goods using assembly lines, coupled with the division of labour, boosted productivity and increased output to meet market demand. This style of production was introduced into the American automobile industry in which Henry Ford (1863–1947) transformed the conveyor belt employed in a Chicago slaughterhouse into an assembly line to produce a single and uniform product: the black Model T automobile (Rae, 1965). Subsequent developments by the Ford Motor Company and fellow automakers General Motors and the Chrysler Corporation led to the greater production and variety of automobiles at low cost and the introduction of physical distribution management to facilitate deliveries. Also, their co-location confirmed the Midwest of the United States as the country's prime manufacturing belt pivoted upon Chicago.

This mass production system underpinned the growth of the consumer economy after the Great Depression of the 1930s, which, through mass marketing, offered a greater volume of product without necessarily taking the end user into account (Rummelt, 2008). Nevertheless, the resultant economic growth gave rise to the 'American Dream' in history, politics and fiction – the idea that if you worked hard enough anything was possible (Jillson, 2016). If successful you were able to afford cars, houses with white picket fences, healthcare, college costs and a family vacation to Disneyland. This dream was marked by a surge in demand for specialized consumer goods such as air conditioners, refrigerators and washing machines for what businesses perceived as a single-class market highlighting the importance of the housewife as consumer.

In turn, the 'American Dream' gave rise to the explosion of the middle class in the United States during the immediate post-Second World War era. This development was generated by an increase in real income and a more even distribution of wealth, incorporating both white-collar and blue-collar workers. Not only did this demand reflect the pervasiveness of consumer capitalism but also it reinforced economic growth. Originating in the 1960s counterculture movements challenged this white and male American middle class rooted in education and upward mobility, eventually reflected in the emergence of a black middle class (Samuel, 2014). By the 1970s this consumerist way of life embodied in the 'American Dream' was in decline versus the alternative 'gospel of wealth', which emerged when institutions in the United States became less effective in regulating society (Vogel, 1979; Daleiden, 1999; Garfinkle, 2006). Consequently, the middle class was struggling to survive sandwiched between a powerful and sparsely populated upper class and a politically weak and increasingly populated underclass.

This decline of the middle class coincided with American industry in the original core manufacturing areas having difficulty competing in terms of productivity with Japan, especially in the automobile industry. The just-in-time material system or lean manufacturing concepts pioneered in 1978 by Japan's Taiichi Ohno as the Toyota Production System improved both quality and output, reduced production costs by minimizing resource waste and offered customers a greater variety of automobile products. These developments were the harbinger of the offshore outsourcing of automobile production and other manufactured items to take advantage of cheaper sources of labour in Asia and elsewhere. The shift enabled corporations domiciled in the United States, exemplified by General Motors, IBM, Oracle and Cisco Systems, to take advantage of the greater productivity per unit cost by moving their activities across international borders. Such offshoring has been attributed to the subsequent loss of trade, wealth and jobs by the United States and other developed Western economies (Davey, 2012).

The resultant disappearance of tradeable middle-class manufacturing jobs in old industrial core areas of America was compounded by innovations in production technology and the operations process in Japan, which triggered the more flexible manufacturing system embodied in Industry 3.0 aimed at enhancing quality and shortening delivery times. Nevertheless, doubt has been cast by Henning De Haas and others (2021) as to whether supply chain management could advance beyond the Toyota Production System during Industry 3.0. Wage rises during this high growth period not only spurred the search by United States, Japanese and other developed country firms for cheaper sources of labour through overseas investment but also for labour-saving sources of automation.

Industry 3.0: Automation

The Industry 3.0 production-consumption cycle (Figure 2.4) extending from the late 1970s to the first decade of the twenty-first century propelled first Japan and then the entire East Asian region into prominence (Vogel, 1979, 1991; Holloway, 1991). The cycle was epitomized by the introduction of electronic devices stemming from technological innovations such as the conversion from analogue to digital, and the switch from integral-to-modular architecture (e.g. from desktop computers to game software). Initially embodying transistors and later integrated circuits, these devices automated individual machines and processes used in office and factory work (Morris-Suzuki, 1988).

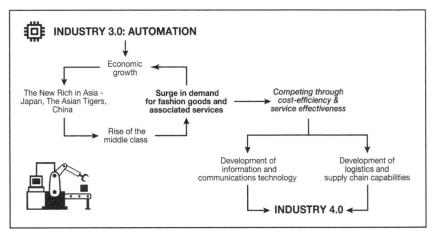

Figure 2.4   The Industry 3.0 production-consumption cycle

These enhanced communications provided by computing and the Internet in an emerging information society were underpinned by renewable energy and automated transport guided by digitalized global positioning systems. During the 1970s many micro-electronic technology innovations supported by venture capital occurred in new information communications technology clusters in the United States, notably in northern California's Silicon Valley and Boston's Route 128 in Massachusetts (Rogers and Larsen, 1984). A decade later Route 128 had lost its competitive edge as personal computers replaced workstations and Silicon Valley chip makers relinquished the semi-conductor market to Japan (Saxenian, 1994).

This loss gave impetus to Japan becoming a new centre of economic dynamism that brought once peripheral economies in Northeast Asia and Southeast Asia into a regional production network incorporating a flexible management system to reduce average product life cycles in electrical goods and automobiles (Hatch and Yamamura, 1996). During the 1980s the 'Asian Tigers' of Hong Kong, Singapore, South Korea and Taiwan were also ensnared within Japan's economic arena, which allowed the component parts for transistor radios, cassette players, stereo players and coloured televisions to be sourced across borders before assembling them at a preferred location (Vogel, 1991; Rimmer, 1995; Partner, 1999). Within Japan a more responsive assembly line system than Toyota's had been deployed by Canon and Sony using mini-assembly units or *seru* (Yin et al., 2018).

By the early 1990s Japan's boom was over and its economy lapsed into a prolonged recession. Nevertheless, the 'flying geese' phenomenon that incorporated the 'tiger cub' economies into an East Asian network continued, as Toyota's gas engines were produced in Indonesia, steering gears in Malaysia, transmissions in the Philippines and diesel engines in Thailand (Coe et al., 2007). During the first decade of the new millennium this dynamism had reached China, India and Vietnam, orchestrated in varying degrees through their national governments playing a strong directive role and by returnees hailing from companies in Silicon Valley.

The resultant rapid, high-capitalist economic growth generated by electronic commerce led to the emergence of Asia's 'new rich' characterized by throngs of customers at McDonald's, omnipresent mobile phones and increasingly sophisticated computer games (Robison and Goodman, 1996). This phenomenon spread from Japan where per capita income in the late 1980s exceeded that of the United States (McCormack, 1996; Francks, 2009: 183–217). During the 1990s the spread of the new rich had continued through South Korea, Taiwan and Southeast Asia (Pinches, 1999). By the 2000s it had reached the well-educated and newly affluent in China and India (Jaffrelot and van der Veer, 2008). Not only did Asia's new rich provide additional markets for Western products such as computer software, film, processed foods and television soaps and its own pop culture, but also generated a stream of new tourists and students to boost foreign economies and educational institutions and expand the overseas Chinese, Japanese and Korean diaspora.

Over time a new and very different middle-class consuming public in Asia emerged from the improved incomes, accumulated wealth and material prosperity that was more than a mere transplantation of their American counterparts. Initially, purchases had begun with basic household durables such as gas stoves, rice cookers and refrigerators within a milieu previously distinguished by Third World material deprivation (Dick, 1985). With increased income and leisure time derived from industrial change, the wish list extended to golf, resorts and theme parks (Rimmer, 1992, 1994). Later, the wanted list moved to cars and designer fashion goods from Lacoste polo shirts to Calvin Klein fragrances, which were manifested in a rash of controlled shopping malls that reflected the industrialization of consumption (Chua, 2000; Rimmer and Dick, 2009). Eventually, the list extended to the range of real estate services underpinning the expansion of housing consumption.

Besides reinforcing economic growth, this surge in demand highlighted the need for entrepreneurs to compete through cost-efficiency and service effectiveness. This new requirement resulted in material requirement planning being superseded by enterprises resource planning, which tracked frequently purchased quality products through the factory to meet the premium put on quicker delivery. In turn, this led to the further development of logistics capabilities to meet the new emphasis on delivery time, which resulted in the introduction of supply chain management concepts to address any malfunctioning flow lines in a volatile market.

Meanwhile, there was further growth in the development of personal computers, which saw Asian producers working in tandem with those in the United States (Rosenberg, 2002; Saxenian, 2006). By then Silicon Valley had recovered from the global financial crisis of 2008–2009 and restored its position in what had become a global economy. This recovery had been aided by the birth of the smart phone – the most important information and communications technology device – which led to mobile commerce (m-commerce) and omnichannel retailing and the associated proliferation of apps prior to the onset of Industry 4.0.

THE FOURTH INDUSTRIAL REVOLUTION

The fourth industrial revolution was first proposed as a 'promising technological framework' at the beginning of the twenty-first century's second decade (Xu et al., 2018). Such an epochal change based on advances in digital technologies shortly after the establishment of the third industrial revolution has not been universally accepted as the prime means of driving economic and social transformation. Ambivalence with the new revolutionary concept has on the one hand seen it resulting in optimistic generalizations redolent of an emerging techno-utopia and on the other triggering adverse social risks and outcomes (Hirsch-Kreinsen, 2016). Indeed, the latest revolution is regarded as 'conjecture in advance of the real practice', especially given the uncertainty over consumer dimensions and the likely architecture of electric vehicles (André, 2019: 1).

Before these reservations can be addressed in discussing the extension of the 'fourth industrial revolution' discourse into supply chain and logistics operations, the immediate task is to detail the revolution's key technological components under the Industry 4.0 rubric. Industry 4.0's production-consumption cycle is designed to propel the hyper-customized, smart manufacturing program of the future. Not only will this stem from the potential of today's digital technologies in creating new forms of industrial goods and marketing them, but also from the prospect of creating customized objects at a greater array of locations. In the process the aphorism 'made in the East and sold in the West' may no longer be appropriate in a more complex world.

Industry 4.0: Digitization

The Industry 4.0 production-consumption cycle is initially focused upon two pivotal technological innovations that have been regarded by Jeremy Rifkin (2016) as key components of Industry 3.0 (Figure 2.5). They are the Internet of Things and the accompanying three-dimensional (3D) printing model. These technologies are detailed as the prime indicators of Industry 4.0's production system and their ramifications are discussed before the full technical axis is considered later.

The Internet of Things network involves a system of interconnected unique identifiers embodied in everyday devices such as automatic teller machines, autonomous vehicles and sensors, which connect them to the Internet and digitalized technologies (e.g. Big Data analytics and wireless networks) and allows them to send or receive data without human or human–computer interaction. These data assist enterprises in examining their environmental conditions so that machines can take autonomous action to avoid the failure of equipment, interruptions in the manufacturing process and bottlenecks in logistics. The performance of products and their use can be monitored, software upgrades programmed and data chains leveraged to create new business models and to drive growth through the adoption of a consumer-centric approach (Rifkin, 2016). Besides having global application to manufacturing processes on the plant floor, the Internet of Things is applicable to the automotive industry, energy and utilities, and transport and logistics activities and is expected to transform them all.

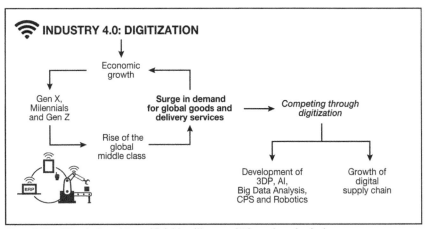

Note: 3DP – 3D printing; AI – artificial intelligence; CPS – cyber-physical systems.

Figure 2.5   The Industry 4.0 production-consumption cycle

Three-dimensional (3D) printing has accompanied the emergence of the Internet of Things economy. The 3D printing process is an additive manufacturing process, which uses software derived from a computer-aided design model to direct molten material from new or recycled sources in a layer-by-layer process that generates little environmental waste and creates a final fully formed and manoeuvrable product when it emerges from the printer. This is contrary to the traditional subtractive waste-generating manufacturing process that machines, cuts, drills and discards raw materials before assembly into the final product. Thus, 3D printing and additive manufacturing can simplify product design, enhance customer service, reduce time to market and warehousing costs and permit mass customization by channelling the individual requirements of a diverse range of customers.

As shown in Figure 2.6, these benefits can be achieved by allowing: (1) prosumers in the sharing economy to manufacture and consume their own products; and (2) subcontractors in additive manufacturing to create prototypes of a product in on-site computers using licensed designs – a process affected by difficulty in establishing intellectual property rights (Mendis et al., 2020). Within the market economy engineers are working to move beyond prototyping to integrate additive processes into their expanding manufacturing portfolio covering aerospace, automotive, health (medical), consumer goods, energy, tooling and construction industrial sectors. By 2018 three-quarters of major automotive manufacturers in the United States and Germany were

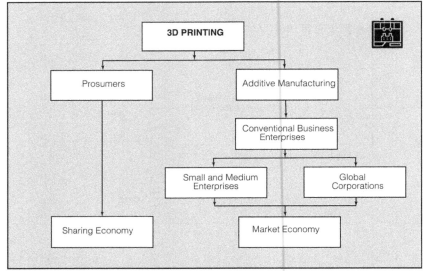

Source: Based on information in Rifkin (2016).

Figure 2.6   Structure of the 3D printing process

employing 3D printing for end-use purposes (3D Hubs, 2019: 3). Since then, for example, Desktop Metal headquartered in Burlington, Massachusetts has collaborated with Audi, BMW and Ford Motor Company to develop new metal 3D printing technologies to mass produce spare parts for the automotive industry's aftermarket for consumers (3D Hubs, 2019). By 2019 70 per cent of online 3D printing orders were in the United States, the United Kingdom and the Netherlands, but its expanding use in China was not reflected in these figures (3D Hubs, 2020). Although 3D printing may not be able to supersede traditional manufacturing processes such as computer numerical control machining or injection mouldings, it can be used alongside them in a digital ecosystem to transform production methods, especially given its capability to print geometric structures (Varotsis, 2019).

This digital ecosystem based on the Internet of Things and 3D printing holds the potential to generate the productive gains to meet the promises of Industry 4.0. Already there is evidence that companies involved gain 3.5 per cent in productivity compared with 0.5 per cent among those adhering to traditional modes (André, 2019: xxiv). In turn, this enhanced productivity is expected to contribute to economic growth.

The anticipated income gains will provide a greater range of opportunities manifested in the entrenched consumer habits of the three generations following the baby boomers (1945–64). Generation X (1965–79) grew up with cassettes, CDs, the Walkman and calculators, but are now, given their spending power, purchasers of high-cost brand-name durables such as cars and luxury articles (Howe and Strauss, 2000). The millennials (1981–96), less reliant on social media and brand-owned messaging, have been splurging upon travel and luxury hotels while still maintaining their spending on material goods such as premium apparel and shoes (Tulgan and Martin, 2001; Kruman, 2019). Generation Z (1997–2012) in North America, guided by social media, are using any device or channel to shop at physical stores in search of the latest unique product and enrich their everyday lives through hobbies and entertainment (Francis and Hoefei, 2018; Bhargava et al., 2020). Their generation Z cousins in the Asia-Pacific region, now moving into adulthood during a global pandemic, exhibit similar patterns of reliance on social media, especially video content, in preferring brands that reflect their personality and uniqueness, and, without necessarily being willing to pay for it, an environmental consciousness (Kim et al., 2020).

Collectively, the three groups and their regional variants have contributed to the rise of a global middle class. Although a precise definition is elusive, the middle-class social category is broadly based around the world covering an estimated population of 3.8 billion in 2018 (Kharas and Hamel, 2018). The middle class in the advanced economies of America and Europe comprises a quarter of the world's total, but many of their number have been finding it increasingly difficult to withstand an economic shock – illness or unemployment – without descending into the vulnerable group below (EC, 2020). This has resulted in a pronounced shift towards China and India, which, together with Brazil and Russia, now account for two-fifths of the world's middle class, leaving developing countries contributing the balance of the habitual users of the Internet or 'netizens' (Miao, 2017).

The rise of a global middle class has led to a surge in the demand for online goods and improved delivery services orchestrated by advances in information and communications technology. Under this regime there is a wider emphasis upon standardization and interoperability of interfaces between a greater array of technologies to create added value (Topleva, 2018). Spurred by the birth of the smart phone, these advances have included the emergence of mobile commerce (m-commerce) and omnichannel retailing that have triggered a surge in demand for online purchases.

This dramatic increase in online purchases has led to Amazon.com, Alibaba.com, Jingdong.com and other e-tailers growing into behemoths at the expense of the traditional retail giants. These giants have struggled to survive the prolonged 'retail apocalypse' since the mid-2019s in both developed and develop-

Table 2.1   Trends in the failures of United Kingdom retail businesses,
*   2015–21*

Year	Companies failing	Stores affected	Employees affected
2015	25	728	6,845
2016	30	1,504	26,110
2017	44	1,383	12,225
2018	43	2,594	46,014
2019	43	2,051	46,506
2020	54	5,214	109,407
2021*	10	1,668	24,199

Note: Excludes restaurants, cafes and food services; * until May 2021.
Source: CRR (2021b).

ing countries. While Walmart (2018), the world's largest retailer in sales, has responded by extending its activities online and acquiring a 77 per cent holding in Flipkart, the Indian e-commerce website, other United States retailers have been less fortunate. An examination of 117 bankruptcies by CB Insights (CBI, 2021a) in the United States between January 2015 and September 2020 reveals that they were not only due to competition with Amazon.com but also to mounting debt and lack of adaptability. Since the COVID-19 pandemic competition between companies has been mainly fought online, which has reduced shopping mall traffic and accelerated the demise of departmental stores with both Neiman Marcus and JCPenney being among the 28 firms filing for bankruptcy between April and September 2020 (CBI, 2021a).

These company failures have been repeated in the United Kingdom's high streets with 2020 being what the Centre for Retail Research (CRR, 2021a) described as a 'perfectly horrid year' that included the demise of 22 outlets and a further 28 outlets projected for closure operated by the department store Debenhams (Table 2.1). Also, in Australia, Retail Oasis (RO, 2020) suggested 933 retail stores, especially those selling fashion goods, had closed in 2020, a trend likely to be continued with many big retailers such as David Jones, Mosaic, Myer and Target with plans to reduce their floor space or close some or all of their stores. Nevertheless, despite these setbacks, some brick-and-mortar companies have remained afloat by reducing their floor space and switching to in-store retail technologies (CBI, 2021b).

Besides the industrial Internet of Things and 3D printing/additive manufacturing, Industry 4.0's cutting-edge technologies, according to Sniderman and others (2016), include artificial intelligence, autonomous robots-collaborative robots (cobots), autonomous vehicles, augmented reality, Big Data analytics, cloud computing, cyber security, cyber-physical systems, nanotechnology and advanced materials, sensors, simulation/digital twins, and system integration (Figure 2.7). The application of these technologies and innovations to business make manufacturing execution systems, shop-floor control and product life-cycle management possible, and promise an architectural change from integrated to modular in manufacturing electric vehicles (Crandall, 2017a, 2017b). Also, their fusion blurs the boundaries between physical, digital and biological spheres, and contributes to a systemic change in national economies with wide-ranging disruptive effects not only on workforces and industries but also upon the environment, governance and society.

Indeed, countries have been seeking to accommodate Industry 4.0 to their individual strengths and weaknesses by choosing which of the new cutting-edge technologies and innovations in Figure 2.7 to incorporate into their national programmes (Speringer and Schnelzer, 2019). In 2011 the German Federal Government became the acknowledged leader by announcing at the Hannover Fair 'Platform Industrie' – a synonym for the cyber-physical system in manufacturing – in a bid to safeguard its core engineering, information technology and logistics industries in the world market (Kagermann, 2015; Vogel-Heuser and Hess, 2016; Rojko, 2017). Germany's Industry 4.0 incorporated artificial intelligence, cloud computing, the Internet of Things and machine learning into customized solutions to deliver 'greater consumer value using fewer resources' (Christopher, 2021: 2).

By 2012 both the United States' 'smart manufacturing plant', incorporating artificial intelligence, robotics and 3D printing, and Japan's 'Society 5.0' had countered by drawing up their own versions of Industry 4.0 in a bid to protect their market share. Nevertheless, Germany's program, driven by the country's computer scientists, innovation policy actors and entrepreneurs, had become, when it was finalized in 2013, the 'high-tech' template, outlined in Table 2.2, for Australia and 12 other countries (Hirsch-Kreinsen, 2016). By 2016 Klaus Schwab (2016), founder and executive chairman of the World Economic Forum, had endorsed and promoted the idea of a 'fourth industrial revolution'. Also, in 2016, the People's Republic of China had become the leader among emerging industrialized countries following Beijing's enunciation of 'Made-in-China 2025' (Ma, 2016; Petri and Dollar, 2020). This program has spurred Beijing to integrate a range of technologies and complex systems to build fifth-generation wireless networks, create smart cities and accelerate smart manufacturing in an effort to challenge for global leadership (Doshi, 2020). The interaction between the proposed technologies and innovations within an integrated digital industrial ecosystem will have significant implications for e-business models and consumer purchasing patterns. Another evolution in production-consumption patterns is inevitable.

According to Gary Farachi's (2020) vision of an integrated digital industrial ecosystem, its configuration will feature a manufacturing process drawing

INDUSTRY 4.0 (I4.0)

ADDITIVE MANUFACTURING

Elimination of scrap
Mass customization
Rapid prototyping

ARTIFICIAL INTELLIGENCE

Decreased costs
Optimized travel
Environmentally friendly

AUTONOMOUS VEHICLES

Decreased costs
Optimized travel
Environmentally friendly

BLOCKCHAIN

Distributed ledger
Captures digital product
memories
Transparent supply chain data
Increases trust

CYBER SECURITY

Stronger protection for
Internet-based manufacturing
Technology products with
longer life cycle

INDUSTRIAL INTERNET OF THINGS

Object tagging
Internet-object communication
via low powered radio
Real time data capture
Optimized stock

SENSORS

Zero default deviation
Reactivity
Traceability
Predicatbility

ADVANCED ROBOTICS

Real time automomy
Productivity
Full transpatency on data
reporting

AUGMENTED REALITY

Increased equipment uptime
Increased maintenance efficiency
Improved training
Object visualization

BIG DATA

Makes sense of complexity
Creativity
Collaborative manfacturing

CLOUD COMPUTING

Network of remote servers
hosted on Internet to store,
manage and process data
rather than on server
or personal computer

CYBER-PHYSICAL SYSTEMS (CPS)

Numerical command
Full automation
Totally interconnected systems
Machine-to-machine
communications

NANOTECHNOLOGY

Smart value added products
Technical differentiation
Connectivity

SIMULATION

Digital Twin
Trial then launch
Can predict failures

Note: Portable Wi-Fi and radio frequency identification are, on occasion, included in this list of technologies but they should be regarded as belonging to Industry 3.0.
Source: List derived from a diagram by Gary Farachi (2020).

Figure 2.7   Industry 4.0's main components

Table 2.2   Characteristics of Germany's Industry 4.0 platform

Transformative technologies	Key drivers	Benefits
Advanced automation and robotics (including collaborative robots or 'cobots')	Rising data volumes, computational power and connectivity	Better connectivity between customers and supply chains through real-time access to production information, logistics and monitoring
Sensor technology and data analytics	Improvements in transferring digital instructions to the physical world, such as robotics and 3D printing	
Machine-to-machine and human-to-machine communication	Emerging analytics and business intelligence capabilities	Greater flexibility for businesses to produce differentiated products and services to tap unmet consumer demands, compete in global markets and capture emerging opportunities
Artificial intelligence and machine learning	New forms of human–machine interaction, such as touch interfaces, augmented and virtual reality systems	Enhanced workplace safety, production and improvements across the entire value chain

Source: Australian Government (2018a, 2018b).

upon additive production/3D printing, advanced manufacturing systems, nano-technology and advanced materials, robots and autonomous vehicles (Figure 2.8). Designed to produce added value by responding to customer demand for both variety and shorter delivery times, this selection of technologies is supported by an overarching superstructure comprising the advanced manufacturing system, Big Data, cloud computing, cyber security and advanced sensors. The key element in advanced manufacturing is the cyber-physical system, which integrates computation, networking and physical processes embedded in computers and networks. This system monitors and controls the feedback loops between the physical processes and computations (Ptolemy Project, 2018). Besides incorporating the cyber-physical system, the advanced manufacturing system includes numerical commands offering full automation, totally interconnected systems and machine-to-machine communication.

There is no set Industry 4.0 ecosystem featuring the smart factory and smart products being pursued by companies such as General Electric and Siemens in the operational procedures underpinning their production systems. Juggling and repositioning the digital technologies can create a different alignment, which is shown in the next representation, where it occurs under the canopy of cyber security and system integration (Figure 2.9). These two technologies are designed to provide stronger protection for the industrial Internet of Things to

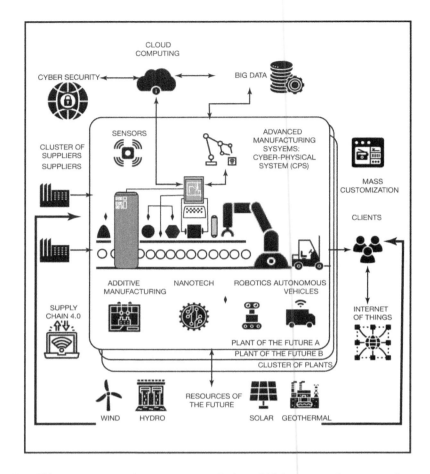

Note: This ecosystem recognizes mass consumerization, which is a strategy that creates value through company–consumer interaction and supplies customized products. The upper level of the representation is the information level; the middle level is the physical system supplying the product; and to the left and right of the physical system are the suppliers and customers, respectively.
Source: Based on a diagram by Gary Farachi (2020).

Figure 2.8   Industry 4.0 ecosystem of the future

guarantee a longer life for technology products, safeguard personal and customer data and provide communication between both information technology
and operations technology and the manufacturing execution system. In this
version real-time orders to suppliers are generated through the flexibility and

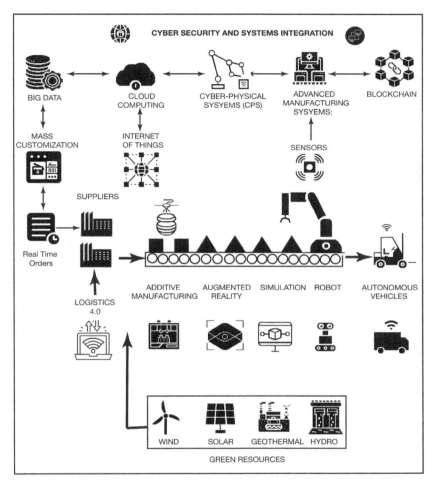

Note: This representation comprises the top layer of data collection and communication devices, the middle layer the smart factory's physical structures and the bottom layer green energy sources. The left column shows that the end user's opinion is the starting point of customized production operations for smart products such as smart phones that comprise physical, smart and connectivity modules (e.g. electrical components, sensors and networks).
Source: Based on a diagram by Gary Farachi (2020).

Figure 2.9   *Industry 4.0 ecosystem: the smart value version providing the key to implement mass customization under Industry 4.0*

modularity of mass customization, which is interconnected with Big Data, cloud computing/industrial Internet of Things, the industrial cyber-physical system, advanced manufacturing drawing upon sensors offering supervisory control and data acquisition, computerized maintenance and management system and the blockchain. In this process additive manufacturing has been complemented by augmented reality, simulation and collaborative robots (cobots) before autonomous vehicles are required to move the finished product.

A key role is afforded to Logistics 4.0 in both representations of smart manufacturing plants and agri-food supply chains of the future, and personalized customization of products and services (Ponnambalam et al., 2019; Ali et al., 2021). Automated data exchange will streamline transit inventories and improve demand forecasting to contribute to a logistics company's competitiveness.

While businesses still need Logistics 4.0 to bring goods to the market, this activity has not been seen as value adding. Indeed, meeting the burgeoning demand occasioned by online retailing costs US$12–15 per US$100 of sales compared with $US3–5 per $100 for brick-and-mortar retailing (Dekhne et al., 2019). Much emphasis, therefore, has been placed by the 'growth performers' among logistics companies, notably Deutsche Post DHL (DPDHL, 2016), on investing in automation technologies in smart warehouse operations, which assist the movement and handling of goods to minimize costs in e-commerce (Hausmann et al., 2021). Driven by the rising tide in consumer expectations and service needs, these technologies include augmented reality, autonomous vehicles, conveyor systems, drones and, above all, robotic picking systems, according to a DHL survey (Harrington, 2020). Also, automated data exchange will streamline transit inventories and improve demand forecasting to contribute to a logistics company's competitiveness. Some of these Warehousing 4.0 technologies could also be used to automate some aspects of the supply chain.

Digital supply chain management (SCM 4.0) will be able to mitigate risk and ensure synchronized deliveries between supplier and clients by both cloud computing and cyber-physical systems allowing the linking of production sites (Hinds, 2019). The synchronization of deliveries will be influenced by mass customization, which will be marked by customer intimacy driven by marketing, on-demand manufacturing and flexibility. These attributes will ensure a perfect match between the customer's needs for production efficiency and speed and great service. Nevertheless, hyper-customization remains an ongoing challenge for supply chain management given the need to heed and respond to customers speedily (Strauss, 2021). Further improvements will be sought in real-time factory connections and the digitization of both products and processes.

INTERLINKING THE FOUR INDUSTRIAL REVOLUTIONS

This broad overview has interpreted the four industrial revolutions by focusing on their production-consumption cycles. Given the detailed nature of these interactions, the analysis has concentrated upon the progressive increase in automation between Industries 1.0–3.0 before dealing with the higher degree of technicality involved and projected in Industry 4.0. As this analysis has

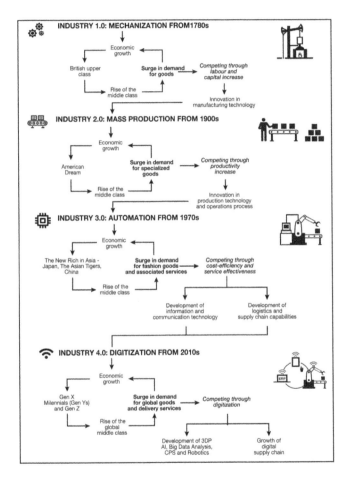

Note: 3DP – 3D printing; AI – artificial intelligence; CPS – cyber-physical systems.

Figure 2.10   Industries 1.0–4.0

occurred at the expense of showing how Industries 1.0–4.0 are interlinked, it is now opportune to look at the process in its entirety and highlight recurrent features (Figure 2.10).

The primacy of economic growth has been the key feature of the entire disruptive process of one technological mode supplanting another. This recurrent feature has given rise to different manifestations of the middle class from its origins in Britain through the 'American Dream' and the new rich in Asia to a global version encompassing generations X, Y and Z. Of critical importance is the transformative effect of the resultant middle class upon the surge in consumer demand across Industries 1.0–4.0, which has ranged through goods, specialized goods, fashion goods and associated services to global goods and delivery services. Not only has this demand reinforced economic growth, but it has also propelled new and different ways of competing. These have extended from increasing labour and capital, productivity to cost-efficiency and service effectiveness, before resorting to digitization. In turn, this competition has given rise to innovations in manufacturing technology and the operations process, the development of both information and communications technology and logistics and supply chain capabilities before an array of new and disruptive technologies have had to be considered under Industry 4.0.

CONCLUSION

The broad linkages between industrialization, technological innovations and the demand for goods and services have been identified over four industrial revolutions by focusing on their production-consumption cycles. This analysis has centred on how the process has speeded up: the first industrial revolution took approximately 120 years, the second 70 years and the third 40 years before the fourth was declared in the 2010s. Attention now needs to shift from these technological advances to the four waves of consumption that have coursed across the globe since the end of the Second World War in 1945. Given the preoccupation with production when detailing Industries 1.0–4.0, the significance of consumption has been underplayed and worthy of study in its own right (Chapter 3).

3. Consumerism: the force that matters

Novel coronavirus-19 (COVID-19) has plunged supply chain operations into a tailspin. Operational disruption is an understatement. From early 2020 with its entrenchment in Wuhan, China, to its progressive spread and heavy toll on human life across the globe in subsequent months, COVID-19 has upended global supply chain operations in form, magnitude, scale and scope far greater than the collective disruptions triggered by Cyclone Tracy that devastated Darwin, Australia, between 24 and 26 December 1974, the 11 September 2001 attacks in the United States, the Indian Ocean earthquake and tsunami on 29 December 2004 and the eruptions of Iceland's Eyjafjallajökull volcano in April 2010. During those calamities, only supply sources were disrupted. Global demand remained intact. Alternatives were available. Their occurrence was also episodic and transient in nature.

In sharp contrast, the pandemic created by COVID-19 has simultaneously shattered both supply sources and altered demand patterns. The joint effects of supply disruption and demand shift have created unprecedented chaos: some businesses have been forced to close, while others have scrambled to seek alternatives, ventured into new forms of production and modified their supply chains. Equally significant, the scale of disruption is global in scope, and the disturbances have been scattered both in time and over space, rattling one after another like raging spot-fires across the globe. The effect is unprecedented and devastating. Indeed, it is a veritable supply chain apocalypse.

As global supply chains have crumbled under the weight of COVID-19's lockdowns and border closures, the juxtaposition of production and consumption locations have been significant. The innovative features created under the banner of the global supply chain such as offshoring, and collaborative forecasting, planning and replenishment have suddenly become inoperable. As e-commerce and online trading surge into prominence, the physical processes of organizing goods flowing along the linear supply chain from suppliers through manufacturers, distributors and retailers to consumers have been hurriedly thrown back to the drawing board.

Evidence emerging from the pandemic has shown that businesses capable of sailing through the storms of the COVID-19 lockdowns were agile in reconfiguring their supply chains through improvisation of untested options. They include exploring supply substitutions, remodelling production facilities to manufacture products with immediate demand and offering last-mile delivery choices within the constraints of physical distancing. The conceptual underpinning of these adjustments is apparent: businesses adapt their supply chain operations according to changes in product demand and consumer purchasing behaviour.

We argue that this improvisation of supply chain operations occasioned by the pandemic is not unexpected but an extension of four waves of consumerism – transformation (Consumerism 1.0), progression (Consumerism 2.0), evolution (Consumerism 3.0) and revolution (Consumerism 4.0) (see Figure 3.1). Central

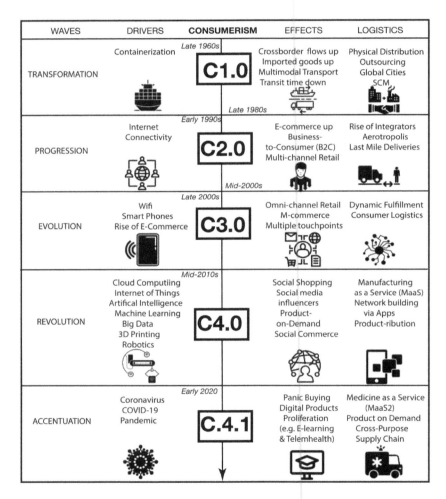

Figure 3.1   *The four waves of consumerism and the accentuation of the fourth wave*

to the four waves of consumerism is the notion that changes in logistics practices and supply chain operations are closely tied to consumer purchasing behaviour and consumption patterns. Given that the tenet of this dictum has been abundantly demonstrated during the COVID-19 pandemic, we call it Consumerism 4.1 – Accentuation.

Discussing these changes in logistics and supply chain configuration from the perspective of consumerism is, therefore, an essential counterpoint to Chapter 2's examination of shifts in production. While industrialization took off in the late eighteenth century with the mechanization of production, consumerism, in terms of acquiring goods manufactured in another country, only came on stream in the late 1960s with the advent of the shipping container, which Arthur Donovan and Joseph Bonney (2006) call 'the box that changed the world'. In short, Consumerisms 1.0–4.0 did not march in tandem with Industries 1.0–4.0 over their evolutionary trajectories. The two sets of movements have dissimilar roots and triggers, though both have cast a long shadow over the evolution of global consumption and logistics and supply chain operations.

In this chapter, we examine the key drivers, economic effects and influence on supply chain and logistics operations of each wave of consumerism in turn by looking back over five decades of research. We then extend the discussion to the effects of the COVID-19 pandemic on supply chain and logistics operations as an accentuation (Consumerism 4.1) of the revolutionary fourth wave.

CONSUMERISM 1.0: TRANSFORMATION

A transformation of consumerism occurred between the late 1960s and the late 1980s. Prior to the late 1960s the human desire to consume finished goods from overseas locations was hampered by transport and logistical constraints. This situation stemmed from the economies of scale achieved from purpose-built carriers of coal, iron ore and oil being difficult to replicate for general cargo handled by liner shipping. Major ports used thousands of dock workers to load, stack and discharge a diverse array of goods in barrels, boxes, sacks and wooden crates, which comprised thousands of lines on the ship's manifest. This slow and cumbersome labour-intensive break-bulk process was subject to damage, delays, leakages and theft, particularly in the reciprocal transfer of items between sea and land transport.

Stacking boxes and sacks on forklift pallets was a practical improvement, but bottlenecks at major ports continued for general cargo. Hence, in 1961 cargo liners wholly engaged in New Zealand–United Kingdom trade did not complete two round voyages a year (PBSUC and NZTSC, 1964: 39). Containerization has progressively transformed this situation by linking the manufacturer with the ultimate consignee and eliminating as many as 12 separate piece-by-piece freight handlings (Hodd, 1970: 19).

The real dawn of containerization occurred in 1956 when Malcolm McLean's Sea-Land organization demonstrated the feasibility of putting general cargo into steel boxes and shipping them along the Atlantic coast of the United States of America in the converted tanker *Ideal X* (Cudahy, 2006). This gave rise to the concept of 'intermodalism', which allowed the same container, with its entire contents, to be transported seamlessly between ship, truck and railroad cars for the entire journey without having to be unpacked. By 1959 the first generation of purpose-built containerships with specialized cranes had entered service. During the early 1960s containerization had been established between the United States and Alaska, Hawaii and Puerto Rico. In 1966 Germany, the Netherlands and the United Kingdom had all adopted containerization. By 1970 a container standard of 8 feet wide, 8 feet high and 10, 20, 30 and 40 feet long had been designated by the International Organization for Standardization and second-generation containerships carried 1,500 20 foot equivalent units (TEUs). During the early 1980s the third-generation container ship had reached over 4,500 TEUs and 122 out of 157 countries around the world had adopted container facilities in port or on rail (Bernhofen et al., 2016: 48). The benefit was not so much reduced ocean shipping rates, which actually increased because of escalating fuel prices, but reduced door-to-door transit time, insurance and inventory costs through more efficient intermodal transportation (Hummels, 2007).

Containerization has long been regarded by historians Marc Levinson (2006, 2016) and Daniel Headrick (2009) as the key driver of international trade and globalization rather than the effects of free trade agreements espoused by trade economists. Using econometric estimates this proposition was tested by Daniel Bernhofen and others (2016), who concluded that between 1962 and 1990 containerization was a large driver of international trade within the industrial world. In particular, they derived the cumulative effects of containerization on North–North trade by abstracting 22 industrialized countries from the total of 157 countries over a shorter 15-year period (1968–83). Based on a panel of product-level bilateral trade flows it was estimated that the 22 industrialized countries had grown at 1,240 per cent compared with 900 per cent for all 157 countries. This result suggests that the long-term effects of the container revolution on developing countries engaged in North–South and South–South trades were relatively smaller during this early period of containerization because they lacked the industrial world's better port and railway infrastructures.

These findings on containerization's role as the driver of twentieth-century economic globalization underpinned the critical role of logistics as a distinctive practice and field of study separate from marketing in transforming consumerism within the industrial world (La Londe, 1969). Nevertheless, the connection of containerization with the study and practice of logistics has been underplayed in documenting the business task of getting the *right* goods to the *right* place at the *right* time for the minimum total cost (Ballou, 2007: 333). With the onset of containerization during the early 1960s these desiderata were incorporated in the concept of physical distribution management that encompassed the outbound flow of finished articles in containers and on pallets from the manufacturer to the user. The concept was fashioned and streamlined at Michigan University in the United States' Midwest Industrial Belt by Edward Smykay and others (1961) and expanded to include the suppliers of raw materials. The application of physical distribution management then diffused rapidly within the rest of the industrial world as a marketing concept (Heskett et al., 1964; Gilmour, 1974; Mentzer et al., 1989). During the 1980s, much to George Gecowets' (1979) displeasure, physical distribution management was progressively superseded by 'business logistics' to incorporate the efficiency of activities within the firm. This move was designed to take advantage of the globalization of markets and dispel any lasting connection with military logistics associated with procuring, maintaining and transporting facilities, materiel and personnel.

During the mid-1990s supply chain management, coined in 1982 by Keith Oliver as the 'chain of supply' in a bid to unify the strategies of fragmented multinational corporations, was poised, in turn, to supersede business logistics (Alfalla-Luque and Medina-López, 2009). By the late 1990s research into the supply chain concept had solidified to demonstrate that the integration of the upstream and downstream linkages between the focal firm's multitiered suppliers and customers delivered superior value to customers at less cost and risk (Lambert et al., 1998). As shown in Figure 3.2, the supply chain is a linear flow structure that commences with the raw material suppliers on the supply side and ends with the consumers, or the end customers, on the demand side, with the latter only being accessible to the retailers. The underlying rationale is to distribute products to retailers at the lowest possible cost and the highest possible level of customer responsiveness. In 1985 this proposition was echoed in the introduction of the Quick Response Strategy within the United States' apparel industry whereby retailers transferred sales information directly from their point-of-sale scanning systems to distributors and manufacturers (Kincade et al., 1993). Also, the strategy integrated marketing information on promotion, discounts and forecasts into the manufacturing and distribution plan that was later incorporated into the efficient customer response practices and continuous replenishment programme (Lummus and Vokurka, 1999). With consumers enjoying quicker responses and increasingly wider choices of goods within the flourishing global trade made possible by containerization, the ultimate aim of supply chain management has been to meet the expanded

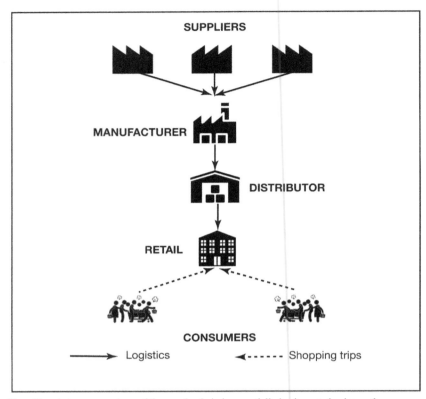

Note: Flow between members of the supply chain is essentially business to business; the business-to-consumer movement only exists with retailers.

Figure 3.2   *The single-channel brick-and-mortar linear supply chain*

desiderata of the end consumers encapsulated in the 7Rs: getting the *right* product, in the *right* quantity, in the *right* condition, at the *right* place, at the *right* time, to the *right* customer at the *right* price.

This supply chain activity was focused upon the major container ports in the international maritime trade. By 1985 the top container hubs in the industrial world housed cargo owners and logistics operators that determined supply chain routing, which, in turn, created jobs and prosperity for coastal communities. Eight of the top 25 container hubs were in the United States' orbit, six in Europe, nine in East Asia and one each in the Middle East and Australia (Figure 3.3). Those on the United States mainland, Europe and Australia had the added advantage of being able to reach inland concentrations of business

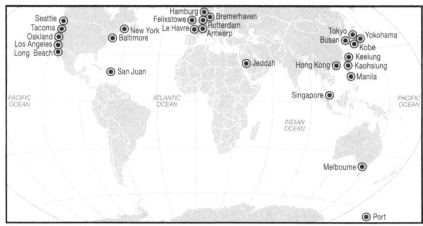

Source: Information derived from Lambert (1987).

Figure 3.3   *The top 25 container ports*

and population by rail or inland waterway before stuffing or destuffing their containers (Johnson and Garnett, 1971). Conversely, their East Asian and Middle Eastern counterparts had to undertake these tasks within the port's confines because of the absence of rail in their poorly connected intermodal systems and road congestion within adjacent urban areas. By the end of the 1980s the first wave of containerization was over, and consumerism was ready to progress to the second wave.

CONSUMERISM 2.0: PROGRESSION

The second wave of consumerism emerged in the 1990s and continued into the mid-2000s when companies sought to complement high-speed transport with advanced information technology to source parts globally, minimize inventories and respond quickly to the needs of consumers worldwide. This advanced information technology wave was triggered by the birth of the World Wide Web, which led to the initiation of electronic commerce, or e-commerce, that had repercussions on the nature of supply chain configuration. The Web, invented by Sir Tim Berners-Lee in 1989 at the Conseil Européen pour la Recherche Nucléaire near Geneva, is a system grafted onto the then rarefied military and academic Internet network using Uniform Resource Locators, Hypertext Transfer Protocol and Hypertext Markup Language standards to identify documents and access information. In 1993, at Berners-Lee's request, the European organization put the Web into the public domain to facilitate interaction between scientists, without fees or permission being required. This opened the opportunity for everyone to enter cyberspace via the Internet and interact, play and live in a different world from their own.

During 1993 advancement in the Web's commercial use quickened when the National Center for Supercomputing Applications (NCSA, 2021) at the University of Illinois at Urbana-Champaign released the Mosaic Browser, which allowed pictures and media to be displayed simultaneously with text. In 1994 Marc Andreessen, a former student at the National Center, established the Mosaic (later changed to Netscape) Communications Corporation with James Clark in Mountain View California, which produced the browser, Netscape Navigator. Meanwhile, the National Center had licensed its Mosaic Browser to Spyglass, which, after further development, extended it to other companies, notably the Microsoft Corporation that used it as the basis for the introduction of Internet Explorer. Not only did this ignite the 'first browser war' between Microsoft and Netscape, but resolution of these issues paved the way for the further development of e-commerce and the prospect of an alternative way of retailing (Lohr, 1998). Already telephone and mail orders had expanded the retailing landscape by offering an alternative to brick-and-mortar retailing that bypassed retailers and created an additional interface between product supply chains and consumers.

E-commerce originated in the 1960s with the development of electronic data interchange in transport and some retail organizations, involving the exchange of business documents from one computer to another in a standard format (Tian and Stewart, 2006; Becker, 2008). Nevertheless, the diffusion of information and communications technology was slow due to its expense and persistent technical issues. The term e-commerce did not come into popular use for commercial transactions via the Internet and the transfer of money and data to complete them until the Web's inception. This was marked by the first recorded sale on 11 August 1994, when a compact disc by the artist Sting was retailed through the website NetMarket (Arcand, 2019). By 1995 commercial applications on the Internet were manifest in the appearance of the world's largest online bookstore and auction site operated by Amazon and eBay, respectively. In 1996 these Internet companies (e-tailers) featured among more than 257,000 websites and 77 million users, which not only extended the alternative to brick-and-mortar retailing but also gave rise to e-commerce and created multichannel retailing (ILS, 2018). By then Dell had begun to sell personal computers direct to consumers on the Internet with its made-to-order model.

The Dell example gave consumers the opportunity to switch from buying computers from a brick-and-mortar store to an online website. This transformed Dell into a multichannel seller. Other alternatives have involved consumers ordering either by catalogue, interactive television, mail or tele-

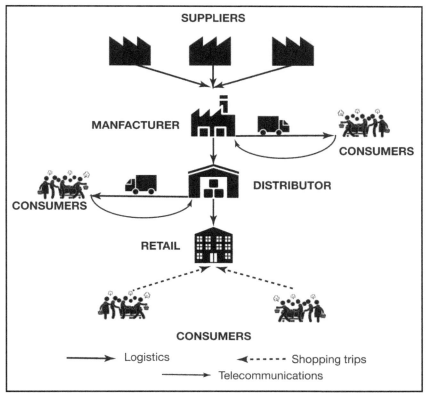

Note: Business-to-consumer flows are possible between manufacturer, distributor (wholesaler) and retailer.

Figure 3.4   *The multichannel supply chain*

phone or through comparing different shopping sites. The injection of online shopping into multichannel retailing allowed customers to buy goods in different ways but this process did not bring about any integration of the process. Nevertheless, the addition of online ordering to multichannel retailing shifted attention away from the physical store, changing the supply chain configuration from one where business-to-consumer interactions only occurred at the retailer to one where business to consumer could also take place at the manufacturer and distributor, as shown in Figure 3.4. The ability of the manufacturer and distributor to engage directly with the consumer offered increased flexibility in the delivery process and reduced cycle time. Since the early 1990s this process has been underpinned by the emergence of dedicated third-party logistics service providers, including CEVA Logistics, DHL, FedEx, Kuehne and Nagel, Schenker, TNT and UPS (Hesse, 2002; Lieb and Miller, 2002). These developments have popularized home delivery in retailing (Thorby, 2007).

The online addition to the multichannel framework was immediately successful, as many companies built their Web presence and intensified their transactions online. This was typified by travel industry participants, notably Booking.com, Expedia and TripAdvisor, that expanded online at the expense of traditional outlets (Verhoef et al., 2015). By 1999 business-to-consumer sales had grown in the United States to almost US$7 billion (Kasarda, 2000). Also, Internet retailers shipped 166 million packages of which 70 per cent required express delivery. During Christmas 1999 retailers could not fulfil their orders. Before this could be remedied, the dot.com boom burst resulting in the demise of many innovative Internet companies. At the beginning of the downturn the share prices of Amazon and eBay plummeted by 30 and 28 per cent, respectively, between 14 March and 20 April 2000 (Cassidy, 2002: 292–293). Nevertheless, the new economy was not killed off and commercial transactions on the Internet continued to grow unchecked.

Most of the explosive growth was expected to occur in the business-to-business sector. By 2003 it was forecast that Internet retailers would ship 1.1 billion packages valued at US$7 trillion in 2004 (Forrester, 2000; Kasarda, 2000). As these transactions involved high value-to-weight items such as automobile components, fashion clothing, optics and pharmaceuticals, air cargo became the preferred mode of transport to meet the importance of speed in order fulfilment. This prerequisite has resulted in e-commerce distribution centres being developed near airports that offered extensive flight networks. These centres accommodated the emergence of sophisticated logistics providers that, in turn, heightened the importance of the 'last-mile delivery'.

Much of the air commerce activity to ensure rapid order fulfilment was initially centred within 5 km of existing airport cities, notably London's Heathrow, Los Angeles International, Miami International, New York's Kennedy and Paris' Charles de Gaulle airports. These airport cities are contrasted with the emergence of the aerotropolis. The latter is a regional development model that has been detailed by John Kasarda and Greg Lindsay (2011) and designed to accommodate time-sensitive manufacturing and commerce within a 25 km radius of the airport. In 2005 Singapore was the only one in operation but elsewhere in East Asia another six were under development in Bangkok, Beijing, Hong Kong, Kuala Lumpur, Seoul (Incheon) and Shanghai together with Amsterdam in Europe, Dubai in the Middle East and Belo Horizonte in South America (Figure 3.5). Also in the mid-2000s, another was planned at Guangzhou in Asia together with two in the United States at Denver and Detroit with three others in Dallas/Fort Worth, Memphis and

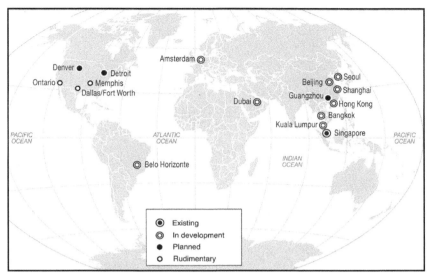

Source: Information derived from Lindsay (2007).

Figure 3.5   Distribution of aerotropolises, c. 2005

Ontario being still at a rudimentary stage of development. Already, Memphis was a freight mega-hub operated by FedEx, which like its counterpart operated by UPS in Louisville could be regarded as a mini-aerotropolis. Along with the European-based DHL and TNT, these freight integrators in the United States offered next-day delivery within their respective continental spheres of operation for orders delivered by midnight. Not only did these integrators arrange the delivery of goods like a freight forwarder but they also owned the necessary assets (aeroplanes, rail wagons, ships and trucks).

By the mid-2000s the 'big four' freight integrators – DHL, FedEx, TNT and UPS – had captured the bulk of global air cargo at the expense of traditional freight forwarders that organized deliveries on behalf of clients through regular airline services. Much emphasis was placed by the integrators upon the product's journey from the terminal to the consumer's doorstep in congested urban areas. Not only could this last-mile delivery of online shopping in e-commerce logistics be the most expensive and time-consuming component of the shipping process for an e-tailer, but it could also be the key to consumer satisfaction (Xu et al., 2008). Much of the dissatisfaction was attributed to the household being unattended, which resulted in a network of delivery points being developed from which consumers could pick up their deliveries. This issue was addressed during the next phase in the development of consumerism.

CONSUMERISM 3.0: EVOLUTION

The third wave of consumerism evolved between the late 2000s and the early 2010s when the further development of search engines such as Google, the expansion of Internet bandwidth across international borders and the birth of smart phones gave consumers increased access to product information. As the ease of information access continued to grow, consumers switched progressively from a reliance upon advertisements and salespeople to undertaking their own research, gaining more autonomy in making their purchasing decisions using their smart phones.

The smart phone's development dramatically altered the nature of consumerism. By 2010 the technology had progressed from IBM's Simon Personal Communicator available from 1992 with a one-hour battery life, through cell phones connected to the Internet (3G) network from 2001 to the most influential iPhone developed by Steve Jobs and team at MacWorld from 2007 (Tocci, 2020). The birth of the iPhone heralded a new generation of smart phones, which has become a must-have for consumers. Not only did it allow consumers full access to the Internet 24/7 anywhere with a mobile signal but also an ability to browse the Web that gave rise to social networks typified by Facebook, LinkedIn and Twitter.

This process was underpinned by the rise of smart phone mobile applications (apps) and their monetization. Mobile apps provided the software that ran on cell phones and tablets, which can be downloaded from a range of distributive platforms such as Android, Blackberry, IOS (Apple) and Windows. Also available on computers and laptops, these apps were either free or for payment to an online store. The latter offered advertisers a new arena to develop content and generate income.

The buying or selling of goods and services through wireless handheld devices such as smart phones and tablets gave rise to mobile commerce, or m-commerce. This process has enabled users to access online platforms for banking, paying and shopping without needing to use a desktop computer or laptop.

The process has allowed the creation of an omnichannel environment, which through the use of advanced technologies has offered a sales and marketing approach 'merging touch-and-feel information in the physical world with the online' (Brynjolfsson et al., 2013: 24). This has prompted online and offline retailers to adopt new and innovative means of competing by using the physical channel to satisfy basic needs and serve as the showroom, leaving the omnichannel for niche items (Chopra, 2018).

In the process a new dimension – the e-commerce giant – has been added to the existing commercial landscape, which has revolved around maximizing

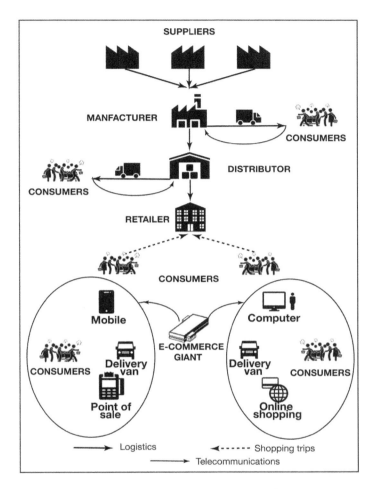

Figure 3.6   The omnichannel supply chain network

consumers' value rather than the products (Figure 3.6). The giant e-commerce powerhouses are typified by the American behemoth Amazon (Rodrigue, 2020b) and China's Alibaba Group Holdings (Jia and Kenney, 2021). They have created a seamless shopping experience for consumers across their brands by removing boundaries between e-commerce's multiple sales and marketing channels to transform them into a unified and integrated experience (Mishra et al., 2020). Interactions with consumers are made through an array of touch points – Web, email, mobile, in-store and social media – that expose them to the necessary offline information, online product content and funds to drive their engagement within a single transaction process. These touch points, coupled with mobile apps, have been critical in building up long-term customer relationships.

Once the consumer has made the decision to purchase through the omnichannel portfolio – face to face, in-store or remotely online – the e-giant's supply chain and logistics network will allow the acquired item to be picked up in-store, at an intermediate point of sale, or through rapid home delivery organized by the e-commerce giant to satisfy the prevailing 'right-now' culture. Also, the faster the delivery time, stemming from the employment of robots, drones and artificial intelligence, the more positive response received from online consumers and the greater positive spill-over effects upon the physical store (Fisher et al., 2019). In the process customer behaviour has been transformed and has prompted a major reconsideration of the ruling 4Ps marketing aphorism dating back to 1960 when marketers were dominant.

The enduring 4Ps of marketing – Product, Price, Place and Promotion – coined by E. Jerome McCarthy (1960), have been superseded by the preponderance of digital life embodied in the experiential economy derived from purchasing boats, cars, designer furniture, smart phones and tablets (Danziger, 2019). Initial rethinking of this traditional marketing mix had resulted in juggling the persistent and well-known aphorism by promoting Place above the other 3Ps to recognize that the cost of transport could be higher than the item itself. Then Ogilvy and Mather's Brian Fetherstonhaugh (2009) sought to replace the entire set with a new one – the 4Es: Experience, Everyplace, Exchange and Evangelism – by recognizing that the consumer had seized control, audiences were fragmented and sliced, products lasted minutes not years and the new ecosystem was unstructured and hinged upon billions of one-to-one and peer-to-peer conversations.

Thus the product had been transformed into a personal Experience for the consumer. Place had become Everyplace by consumers being able to follow their own paths and purchase their brands at home, in-store, online or by phone. Price had been replaced by Exchange to engage with the brand's value beyond its cost. Promotion had turned into Evangelism, as consumer logistics have been engaged to promote the brand.

This process of delivering on the promise to the consumer has involved managing the complexity of dynamic fulfilment (i.e. the successful transfer or allocation of products to satisfy consumer demand). A distinction has been made in fulfilling this task between distributed order management and dynamic fulfilment. The former had sought to 'satisfy customer demand requests by executing a series of filters seeking the first identified feasible source', whereas the latter considered 'the full view of the ever changing, continuously updating and progressing end-to-end supply chain system' (Solvoyo,

2014). Under the first process retailers have not been afforded the data at the time of demand to comprehend if the transaction's fulfilment had been profitable and, therefore, unable to determine the decision's effect on future demand. Conversely, under the second process of dynamic fulfilment a platform underpinned by real-time data makes it possible to determine the costs of retaining or allocating the inventory and its status relative to future demand and the service implications of fulfilment. As dynamic fulfilment realizes the full potential of the supply chain infrastructure, it is seen as superior to the distributed management approach in maximizing revenue and profit, minimizing cost and providing the best service.

The heightened interest in dynamic fulfilment has been accompanied by the development of consumer logistics. This concept stems from an initial use of the term by Kent Granzin and Kenneth Bahn (1989) to highlight the neglected role of the consumer in industrial logistics. This role was reflected in their contribution to the supply chain process by bagging groceries and engaging in food takeaways. The further development of this concept beyond a process model of stages in consumer logistics decision-making has been used to reflect upon the changed pattern of consumption in the digital era following the lowering of search costs and faster delivery of products (Rimmer and Kam, 2018: 1). This changed pattern has been accompanied by movements beyond the service economy and the coalescence of business with consumers and consumers with consumers. These disruptive business trends have heralded the shift from a company-centric approach to a consumer-centric economy replete with an array of channels and convenience options (Boothby, 2021). The switch has provided brands and original equipment manufacturers with abundant knowledge about their end users that was absent under the previous configuration.

Thus, the evolution of Consumerism 3.0 has been underpinned by the extension of the Internet across international borders. This gave rise to the emergence of Internet hubs based on the size of their international bandwidth. Their distribution belied the argument that the liberalization of telecommunications and Internet policy had led to the dominant role of the United States manifest in the success of Amazon, Apple, Facebook and Google. While these Internet giants had dominated popular services, Internet infrastructure had shifted towards Europe (Winseck, 2017). In 2010 14 of the highest capacity Internet hub cities were in Europe, six in North America, three in Asia and two in South America (Figure 3.7). Among the six leading hubs London, Frankfurt, Paris and Amsterdam were ahead of New York and Miami, with Tokyo, the highest ranked Asian-Pacific hub, in fourteenth position (Tranos, 2013). The shift in the Internet's centre of gravity to the Asian-Pacific region had to await the fourth phase of consumerism.

Note: International Internet bandwidth is measured in gigabits per second.
Source: Based on information derived from TeleGeography (2011) and Tranos (2011).

Figure 3.7   The top 25 Internet hubs, 2010

CONSUMERISM 4.0: REVOLUTION

Since the mid-2010s Consumerism 4.0 has emerged in the wake of the transition to Industry 4.0 to reflect the closing of the gap between producers and the everyday lives of consumers. In response, the production line has become a real-time respondent to shifts in consumer behaviour rather than an array of assembly line connections coordinated by computer programs at the behest of manufacturers (Welsh, 2020). Also, digital connectivity has provided an entrance into a newer customized world by enabling consumers to take advantage of, and be affected by, cutting-edge technologies, including wearables such as Apple watches and Fitbit trackers (IRMA, 2017). This consumerization process has been underpinned by the emergence of Supply Chain 4.0 comprising supply–demand networks which have been evolving within an ever shortening time span towards the ultimate goal of delivering a single item to meet a specific consumer's expectations (Christopher, 2021).

The Consumerism 4.0 revolution has been propelled by Industry 4.0 technologies, which have enabled the use of fewer resources to deliver greater consumer value through customized solutions that have been made to measure for specific individuals (Queiroz and Wamba, 2021). Additive manufacturing/3D printing has demonstrated how individual customization can be realized by designing, manufacturing, distributing and shipping a single unit.

Artificial intelligence and machine learning have allowed real-time changes to meet customer tastes, anticipate actual demand and predict distribution transit times (Miled et al., 2021). Augmented reality and virtual reality have helped consumers test out products, gain first-hand information and participate in co-creating the final product. Autonomous vehicles and robotics have raised the prospect of delivering smaller quantities in a shorter time. Big Data analytics, using information on and location of consumers, have enabled their needs to be understood better by business. Both cloud computing and the Internet of Things have hastened the realism of digital connectivity.

Digital connectivity has enabled consumers to link almost all touch points and places invisibly through an evolving Internet network, which has been the decisive factor in fully exploiting the opportunities of digitalization (Siemens, 2021). Due to digitization the needs, wants and expectations of consumers have become better known by business because they have much more data at their disposal about customers to enhance their marketing strategies.

Under Consumerism 4.0 the retail sector, in particular, has been distinguished by the popularization of the term omnichannel to characterize the seamless integration of all retailer–consumer touch points and the need to accommodate the resultant outcomes by transforming shops emptied by online commerce into showrooms (Hänninen et al., 2021). Social media influencers, combined with mobile technology, have revolutionized how retailers reach and comprehend the needs of their customers (Glucksman, 2017). This reach of social media has been extended by social shopping, which is an e-commerce method whereby the friends of shoppers become engaged in the shopping experience by using technology to imitate the social interactions found in malls and stores. In this process consumption on demand has been created by fast-moving technology companies to fulfil consumer demand through the immediate provisioning of goods and services (Figure 3.8). In this on-demand economy, supply is provided through 'a digital mesh layered on top of existing infrastructure networks' (Jaconi, 2014: 1).

Since 2015 China's Pinduoduo, founded by Colin Huang, has offered an important variant of the social shopping approach built upon mimicking offline behaviour online. The company has created a social e-commerce platform that has allowed an individual consumer to identify a product ranging from daily necessities to household appliances on WeChat, and then to club together with family and friends to make a team purchase within 24 hours and receive the product within 48 hours (Xiao, 2019; Hariharan and Dardenne, 2020). This interactive process has been driven by interactive games and rewards, feedback from families and friends and discounts from suppliers. The resultant concept of 'social commerce' has involved the combination of e-commerce channels with social media to build trust and loyalty between consumers and has been predicted as a likely future trend (Figure 3.9).

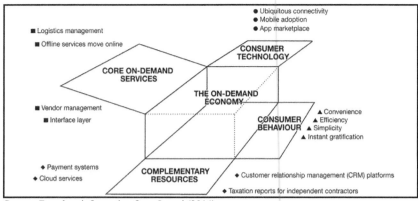

Source: Based on information from Jaconi (2014).

Figure 3.8   The on-demand economy

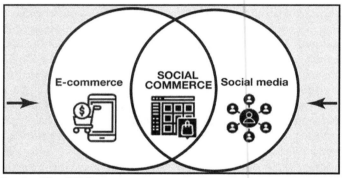

Source: Based on Xiao (2019).

Figure 3.9   Social commerce

By 2019, Pinduoduo, the social commerce newcomer, was issuing a challenge to the leading e-commerce giants in gross merchandise value – Alibaba and Amazon – at a time when e-retail sales worldwide surpassed US$3.5 trillion and involved 1.9 billion people purchasing goods (Statista, 2020a). Accounting for one-fifth of all sales, these retailing developments have had a profound effect upon the supply chain.

Supply Chain 4.0 is in the process of being streamlined to provide end-to-end visibility and greater agility in responding to unanticipated changes in supply and demand conditions (Christopher, 2021). This effort is designed to meet

Table 3.1   *Global parcel volume, 2019*

Country	Volume (million parcels)	Country	Volume (million parcels)
China	63,500	Canada	1,100
United Kingdom	16,100	Italy	990
United States	14,700	Australia	934
Japan	9,000	Brazil	850
Germany	3,700	Sweden	135
India	2,800	Norway	80
France	1,340	Total	115,229

Note: The Pitney Bowes Parcel Shipping Index measures mass for business-to-business, business-to-consumer, consumer-to-business and consumer-consigned shipments with weights up to 31.5 kg.
Source: Developed from information in Spadafora (2020).

the rising expectations of customers inherent in Consumerism 4.0 for delivery with an ever shorter time period. As everything cannot be accomplished in-house, the adoption of manufacturing as a service has allowed companies to manufacture their products without investing in massive infrastructure. Often, manufacturers outsource only a part of their production to such providers. Not only does this solution reduce the manufacturing lead time but also the cost of industrial parts.

Network-building by mobile apps has proceeded apace to extend the social networks of both business and brands in a digitally driven world to better connect with their customers and deliver better results. The number of mobile app downloads increased worldwide from 140.7 billion in 2016 to 218 billion in 2020 (Statista, 2021a). As noted by the Australian Competition and Consumer Commission (ACCC, 2021), most were on either Google's Android or Apple's iOS mobile platforms and were available through their respective stores.

Meanwhile progress towards the concept of consumption on demand arising from the commercialization of 3D printed products has moved at a slower pace. It is still in the process of progressing from bespoke medical devices and aircraft parts to the construction of bridges and houses, which will bring the elision of production and consumption into a single process, termed *productribution* in this study (see Chapter 6).

Supply Chain 4.0 has to accommodate unprecedented flows of goods and information driven by cross-border e-commerce (Van Asch et al., 2020). Indicative of the challenge posed by Consumerism 4.0, the total global parcel mass in 2019 has, according to the Pitney Bowes Parcel Shipping Index, exceeded 100 billion for the first time, bringing the criticality of last-mile fulfilment to the fore (Table 3.1). Also national figures highlight that China

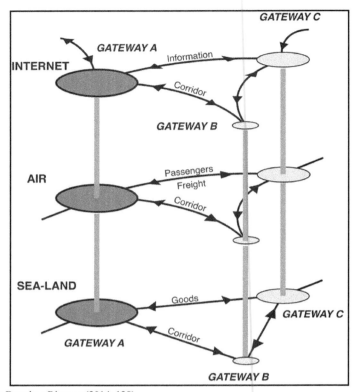

Source: Based on Rimmer (2014: 128).

Figure 3.10   Multilayered gateways

has emerged as a powerful air freight generator ahead of the United Kingdom and the United States, accounting for 60 per cent of parcels produced by the world's 13 major markets.

Access to supply chain and logistics infrastructure have become critical in the orchestration of the global economy. A coalescence of container ports, passenger airports and Internet hubs have resulted in the emergence of multi-layered global gateways and subgateways (Figure 3.10).

Global gateways are defined as having representation in the top 25 hubs across all three modes (shipping, air passenger transport and the Internet); subgateways two modes; and specialist hubs one mode (Rimmer and Dick, forthcoming). In 2019 the global gateways were represented by Bangkok, Hong Kong, Jakarta, Singapore, Los Angeles and New York followed by eight subgateways in Europe, five in Asia and the Middle East and one in North

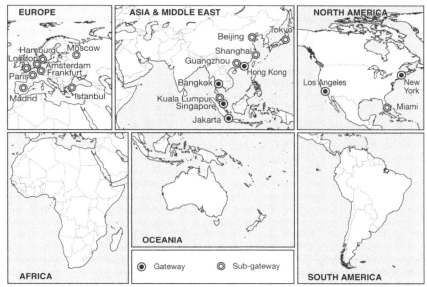

Source: LL (2020); IATA (2021); TeleGeography (2021).

Figure 3.11   Gateways and subgateways, 2019

America (Figure 3.11). Adding specialist container port, airport and Internet hubs to this list raises the prospect of defining wider regions with multiple facilities such as southern California and China's emerging Pearl River Delta, the Lower Yangtze and Beijing-Tianjin-Hebei (*Jing-Jin-Ji*) metropolitan regions. No weighting is applied to the transport and communications statistics, but the highest profits in these consumer hotspots were not in shipping or air transport but in telecommunications technologies.

By 2020 there had been 29 versions of the iPhone (Carey, 2021); new competitors had appeared through the advent of Google's Android mobile operating systems customized on Samsung devices; and texting and messaging had switched to wireless connections. According to the Pew Research Center (Silver, 2019), smart phones accounted for over 50 per cent of an estimated 5 billion cell phones. As four-fifths of consumer time using mobile devices had been spent accessing social media, businesses have been attracted to the space to interact with them and comprehend their needs, wants and expectations.

These businesses have included food delivery services provided by Deliveroo founded by Will Shu in London during 2013 as an intermediary courier service between consumer and restaurant. Since then the company has expanded to over 200 locations in Asia, Europe and Oceania to become one of the arche-

Table 3.2   *Deliveroo's revenue and usage statistics, 2015–20*

Year	Revenue (UK£million)	Loss (UK£million)	Users (million)	Restaurant (thousand)	Cities (number)	Valuation (UK£million)
2015	18	n.a.	n.a.	n.a.	n.a.	n.a.
2016	129	n.a.	n.a.	n.a.	n.a.	n.a.
2017	277	-199	3.1	5	50	315
2018	476	-232	3.9	10	100	1,000
2019	771	-317	6.0	80	500	2,000
2020	1,200	-223	7.1	140	800	10,500

Note: n.a.: not available.
Source: Iqbal (2022a).

types of the gig economy of the late 2010s, along with Just Eat and Rapps (Table 3.2). According to the *World Shopper Report 2021* produced by the global marketing communications agency Wunderman Thompson Commerce (WTC, 2021: 24), these companies exemplify the role of the 'aggregator' that collects 'data from other online sources on one place so consumers can assess the best items, services or deals to meet their needs'.

At the end of Consumerism 4.0's first decade, therefore, it was expected that these key trends would continue unchecked from the further adoption of Industry 4.0 technologies and digitization. During the early 2020s the emergence of artificial intelligence and distributed ledger block chain technology were anticipated to have a larger impact. By 2026 the global m-commerce market was expected to reach US$3,901 million compared with approximately US$492 million in 2019 (F&F, 2020). However, by early March 2020 these much anticipated developments were dramatically disrupted by the COVID-19 pandemic. This disruption accentuated trends in e-commerce and online consumer behaviour, which is discussed next under the rubric of Consumerism 4.1.

CONSUMERISM 4.1: ACCENTUATION

The COVID-19 pandemic has proved to be a 'tipping point of widespread proportions' (LaBerge et al., 2020). This is evident in the shocks occasioned by the virus on everyday life and in the global supply chains between suppliers and end consumers.

The immediate effects of the shocks have been evident in the marked shift in demand that has occurred as millions of people stayed home to control virus spread leading to the closure of cinemas, gymnasiums, restaurants, theatres and other venues. Not only has there been an exceptionally high demand and panic buying of everyday household items such as groceries, but also increased compensatory purchasing of clothing and retail technology items. Digital channels have become an alternative to in-person shopping in crowded stores. This public health emergence of international concern has led to the proliferation of e-learning in schools and universities, and the extension of telehealth in minimizing the risk of COVID-19 transmission between patient and health providers.

Global supply disruptions and demand shifts have been most marked in high-value goods such as mobile phones and communications equipment originating in Asia. Rather than back away from globalization and resort to local production, companies are advised that any void created will be filled by rival firms during the 'next normal' (Shih, 2020). This threat has prompted businesses to accelerate the digitization of their supply chain interactions and their internal operations by several years in seeking to match the expected changes in supply and demand (LaBerge et al., 2020).

The acceleration of digitization has been evident in the growth of Internet hubs between 2019 and 2020 at a time when the rankings of container ports and airports have been disrupted by the pandemic (Rimmer, 2020). For example, there was little change in the representation among the top 25 Internet hubs, with the top five – Frankfurt, London, Amsterdam, Paris and Singapore – maintaining their positions and Hanoi and Buenos Aires entering the top group at the expense of Warsaw and Bangkok (Table 3.3).

These likely long-lasting digital initiatives among Internet hubs have been most marked in the shift in media consumption from traditional to digital media during the pandemic. They have been manifested in the extension of telehealth. Also, they have been apparent in the cross-functional supply chain between supplier and the end consumer (Brady et al., 2020).

Matching supply and demand during the pandemic has proved to be a vast headache. Changes in consumption patterns have varied widely across the world due to the effects of COVID-19 on consumer sentiment and behaviour within national populations (Charm et al., 2021).

Such differences in adapting to configurational change have been manifested in the United States, where the easing of restrictions following the rapid vaccination roll-out has allowed restaurants and brick-and-mortar stores to return to full capacity in June 2021. While online retail sales may be slowing, shoppers are still spending (*Economist*, 2021a). Nevertheless, online activity has remained above historical levels and made streamlining a fast last-mile delivery an imperative for retailers and brands. As reported by Rachel Binder (2021), this has led to on-demand warehousing and the micro fulfilment of centres or storage being established close to the end consumer, the appearance of satellite kitchens ('cloud kitchens' or 'ghost kitchens') for storing, preparing, portioning or packaging food prior to on-demand delivery services and the creation of delivery management platforms for companies to access as and when required.

Table 3.3   *Changes in the capacity of the top 25 Internet hubs, 2019 and 2020*

Hub	2019 (Gbps)	2020 (Gbps)	Change	Hub	2019 (Gbps)	2020 (Gbps)	Change
Frankfurt	84,256	110,608	26,352	Tokyo	13,807	20,233	6,426
London	60,858	74,415	13,557	Istanbul	13,464	20,014	6,550
Amsterdam	54,036	71,188	17,152	Sofia	10,253	15,531	5,278
Paris	50,886	67,865	16,979	Jakarta	9,952	16,544	6,592
Singapore,	37,465	56,350	18,885	Madrid	9,708	14,112	4,404
Miami	25,012	30,674	5,662	Copenhagen	9,624	13,863	4,239
Hong Kong	24,295	33,829	9,534	Hamburg	9,441	12,233	2,792
Stockholm	22,411	32,037	9,626	Budapest	8,710	13,920	5,210
Marseille	21,303	28,899	7,596	São Paulo	8,056	10,745	2,689
New York	19,096	23,872	4,776	Warsaw	7,964	n.a.	-7,964
LA	18,061	24,706	6,645	Bangkok	7,785	n.a.	-7,785
Moscow	17,459	22,828	5,369	Hanoi	n.a.	11,439	11,439
Milan	16,743	21,121	4,378	Buenos Aires	n.a.	10,418	10,418
Vienna	15,755	23,935	8,180	Total	576,400	781,379	204,979

Note: Gbps – gigabits or gigabytes per second (i.e. 1 billion bits or bytes per second); this transfer rate is used as a measure of bandwidth on a digital data transmission medium such as optical fibres; LA = Los Angeles.
Source: TeleGeography (2021).

Also, during Consumerism 4.0 and its accentuation in Consumerism 4.1 'conscious consumers' have emerged in growing numbers within an age of social commerce (Woods Agency, 2017). What had been admired by others and driven self-esteem and social status from consuming and owning material goods has given way, in varying degrees, to the strengthening of a sharing or collaborative economy using connected devices and information sharing (Costello and Reczek, 2020; Sundararajan, 2019; Seddighi and Moradlou, 2021). According to Nikki Baird (2020), the conscious consumers are under-taking research before purchasing by examining websites for information on business and their manufacturing practices. Not only are they paying attention to public opinion on specific brands but also they are being affected by social influencers. Indeed, these consumers may be the harbinger of the shrinkage of consumerism by buying less and paying more and keeping goods longer. Retailers will have to respond in the 'next normal' by delivering experiences, being digital first, progressing to 'true' omnichannel retailing and rethinking how to organize the remodelling of their stores (Fiedler et al., 2020; Saran, 2020). As identified by the supply chain thinking of DHL, addressing these more complex consumption challenges without the benefit of using historical data for forecasting must become radically more collaborative and oriented towards resilient networks that accommodate change (Steins et al., 2021). Not only will this adaptation to configurational change in the 'next normal' hinge on the nature of online usage but also on determining shifts in purchasing habits, the effectiveness of vaccinations in curbing COVID-19 and the resilience of supply chains.

CONCLUSION

This chapter has identified, for the first time, the four waves in the development of post-war consumerism – transformation, progression, evolution and revolution – and the accentuation occasioned by the coronavirus pandemic. Particular attention has been paid to their drivers, their effects and their implications for supply chain management and logistics. These waves have been closely associated with the marketing trends identified by Sean Callahan (2020). The first wave was spurred by the invention of containerization that led to the globalization of trade and commerce, which overlapped during the 1980s with the peak of print advertising buoyed by computer and desktop publishing; the second wave in the 1990s coincided with the advent of the Internet and the World Wide Web; the third wave in the 2000s corresponded with the arrival of Facebook, LinkedIn, Twitter and other social networks; and the fourth wave was not only marked by Big Data and consumer empowerment but also by the maturation of social media and the rise of social shopping and social commerce. These parallels suggest that, as logistics and supply chain operations coalesce with technological advancement and consumption behaviour, it is time to take a closer look at how Supply Chain 4.0 is shaping up to meet those challenges at the interface. This will be the focus of Chapter 4.

4. Supply Chain 4.0: technology to the rescue

Supply chain operations under Industry 4.0 – involving integrated planning and execution, logistics visibility, manufacturing, procurement 4.0, smart warehousing, efficient spare parts management, autonomous and business-to-consumer logistics and prescriptive supply chain analytics – have been referred to as 'Supply Chain 4.0' (SC 4.0) or the 'digital supply chain' (WEF, 2017: 4). As shown in Figure 4.1, Supply Chain 4.0 is pivotal to the digital enterprise that also comprises the digital workplace, digital manufacturing and engineering, digital products, services and business models, and digital consumer and channel management.

This pivotal component of the digital enterprise assumes a radically different configuration from the now dated linear flow of products and information based upon the brick-and-mortar model of material distribution. The time is ripe for the dated linear model's reconfiguration following the advent of Industry 4.0's information-led technologies and the possibilities they bring to support supply chain management and logistics operations. Technological limitations are progressively less of a constraint in moving towards an integrated non-linear configuration in which information flows in an omnidirectional manner to the supply chain (Ferrantino and Koten, 2019). Indeed, businesses need to recognize the mutually reinforcing dynamics of technology production and technology consumption: consumers influence technological developments as much as technology affects consumption. An understanding of this mutual interaction is paramount in fuelling the development of a different configuration that reflects the vitality of Supply Chain 4.0. Yet there are no agreed guidelines as to how this desired end state can be achieved.

This situation gives rise to a series of issues. How can the vast array of Industry 4.0 technologies be deployed to reshape production systems and supply chain management and logistics operations? More particularly, how should Supply Chain 4.0's network be configured to optimize not only individual stages in the production process but also the entire value chain? How can this configuration be achieved to improve supply chain performance? Why have businesses failed to harness technologies in a holistic manner to meet this desired goal? And how can Supply Chain 4.0 be operationalized to overcome this dilemma?

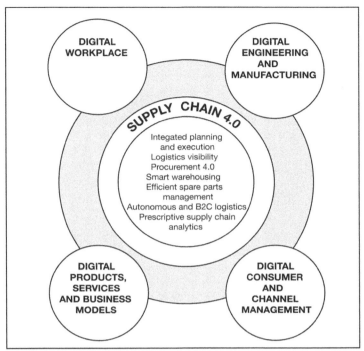

Note: The expanded framework has been used by McKinsey & Company and the World Economic Forum to identify advanced manufacturing's digital leaders or 'lighthouses' (see Chapter 5); B2C – business to consumer.
Source: Abstracted from WEF (2017: 4).

Figure 4.1   The digital enterprise

In addressing these issues an initial assessment is made of the array of Industry 4.0 technology possibilities to gauge their likely contribution to reshaping supply chain management and logistics operations. Once the possibilities of these intelligent technologies have been evaluated, a vision is given of the configuration that Supply Chain 4.0 needs to adopt to meet the functions required to respond to the end consumer's demands. The realities of this vision being achieved are questioned, given that experience has shown that, rather than occasioning a radical reconfiguration of technological innovations in supply chain and logistics operations, the outcome has typically resulted in suboptimal processes.

The challenge is to persuade businesses to abandon the practice of embracing new technologies merely to reinvigorate existing processes, operations and parameters built on the prowess of yesteryear's technologies. There are countless reasons for such a mindset, among them technology limitations being a key inhibitor. The lack of recognition of the dynamic interaction between consumers and technology (i.e. the socialization of technology) is also to blame. Finally, the suggested actions required of all stakeholders – carriers, financial services, gateway/infrastructure operators, governments, manufacturers, logistics service providers, suppliers and technology providers – are promulgated to realize the ideal vision of Supply Chain 4.0 outlined in this study.

POSSIBILITIES

Technology companies develop products to serve the needs of logistics companies. In turn, logistics companies create the demand for technologies that could enhance their operations and supply chain processes. An assessment needs to be made of how different Industry 4.0 technologies can contribute to shaping supply chain and logistics operations to enhance their responsiveness to consumer demand. A survey is undertaken of a range of supply chain and logistics possibilities afforded by an array of Industry 4.0's smart technologies that are radically altering production processes and business models across a range of industries (Table 4.1). Applications of supply chain management and logistics operations likely to be affected by these technologies are identified. Examples are given to illustrate the opportunities available to manufacturers, retailers and logistics service providers for overcoming delays in transportation, negligent cargo checking, mistakes by operators and failures from using outmoded information technology that were manifested in Supply Chain 3.0. The outpouring of academic literature reviews on the topic since the mid-2010s has not seen a ready source of examples. Generally, they concentrate on data sets derived from broad surveys of unidentified companies in specific sectors and rarely feature in-depth case studies of individual companies applying Industry 4.0 technologies to their supply chain and logistics operations. Therefore, recourse is made to an array of providers promoting supply chain software, warehouse systems, supply chain platforms, artificial intelligence, Big Data analytics and robotics. Exemplified by Dematic (warehouse systems), Honeywell (robotics), IBM (supply chain software) and Oracle (supply chain platforms), these providers have supplied stand-alone, cutting-edge solutions for smart factories, warehouses and logistics services. Collectively, these solutions drive successful fulfilment productivity to meet consumer demands arising from the proliferation of e-commerce and international competition.

A feature of this activity by 'solution providers' is the pioneering role being played by multinational corporations in high-income countries at the frontier of supply chain management, notably Amazon, General Electric, IKEA, Volvo, UPS and Walmart, with China's JD.com being an exception. As the

Table 4.1   *Examples of supply chain and logistics applications drawn from enabling Industry 4.0 technologies*

Industry 4.0 technologies	Supply chain and logistics applications	Examples in practice
Industrial Internet of Things	Sensors offer an effective way to track and authenticate products and shipments using Global Positioning System (GPS), and to monitor storage conditions of products.	Volvo uses an Internet of Things tracking solution in production and customization processes at its Blainville truck plant in France to advance visibility of the factory's supply chain operations (Actility, 2019).
Big Data analytics	Infuses supplier networks with greater data accuracy, clarity and insights, leading to more contextual intelligence shared across supply chains.	Walmart uses descriptive, predictive and prescriptive Big Data analytics to manage the steps of the supply chain from dock to store to optimize transport routes and keep costs down (Walmart Staff, 2017).
Cloud computing technologies	Focuses on cost reduction, greater elasticity, flexibility and maximum use of resources to increase competitiveness in managing information systems.	Amazon Web Services (formerly Kiva Systems) have launched on-demand cloud computing platforms and their Application Program Interfaces for use by individual companies and governments (AWS, 2021).
Augmented reality (mixed reality)	Scene capture, identification, processing and visualization.	IKEA helps customers visualize how their furniture will look in their house and how those pieces can be customized to fit the desired décor (Hamstra, 2015).
Advanced robotics	Act autonomously or partially, interact with people physically and react to sensor data.	Amazon uses robots in its fulfilment centres for order picking and packing (Weinberg, 2020).
Artificial intelligence	Self-learning system injects agility and precision into supply chain processes through algorithms automating demand forecasting, production planning and predictive maintenance.	UPS uses an artificial intelligence-powered GPS tool called Orion (On-Road Integrated Optimization and Navigation) to create the most efficient routes for its delivery fleets (Morgan, 2018).

Industry 4.0 technologies	Supply chain and logistics applications	Examples in practice
Blockchain	Provides transparency into the origin of consumer goods from source to end of consumption, accurate asset tracking and enhanced licensing of services, products and software.	Neumann Kaffee Gruppe, the world's leading green coffee group, uses a blockchain supply chain management system known as Trade Lens, developed by IBM for Maersk, to transform its container shipping and logistics (Boughner and McQueen, 2020).
3D printing/additive manufacturing	Combines manufacturing process, storage and distribution into one.	General Electric (GE, 2020) uses additive manufacturing to simplify supply chains in the aerospace industry by producing components at a range of locations to reduce transport costs.
Autonomous vehicle	Assists product delivery at the right time by truck or train between industry and warehouse to cut costs and better attend to customer needs.	Walmart has been working with Gartik, a self-driving startup, to test out an autonomous vehicle along a 3.2 km route between two stores in Bentonville, Arkansas (Myong, 2019).
Drones	Last-mile deliveries between warehouse and customer.	Jingdong.com uses drones to deliver parcels in remote rural areas of Jiangsu, Shaanxi and Sichuan provinces in China (JD.com, 2016).
Quantum computing	Theoretically can be used to tackle supply chain disruption occasioned by the pandemic.	World Economic Forum predicts that it will be commercially available in 2025 (Yoon, 2020).

supply chain is a critical element of their business model, they have been active in recruiting talent, running pilot studies and drawing upon or taking over startups involved in developing new technologies (IDB and WEF, 2019). Not only does this pattern of adoption suggest an unequal distribution of supply chain technologies, even within high-income countries, but also it implies that multinationals are, in turn, making demands upon their suppliers and logistics service provider to conform to their new practices. Amazon Prime, for instance, is putting a premium upon supply management and last-mile delivery by shrinking delivery windows to satisfy customers wanting delivery within a single day (Webster and Kumar, 2020). This pressure demonstrates the need to reengineer fulfilment networks so that inventories can be positioned closer to the end consumer and items picked faster in warehouses to meet this promise.

The list of individual technologies in Table 4.1 is useful in identifying their promising contributions to an ideal Supply Chain 4.0 dedicated to improving end-to-end visibility and data-driven decision-making. Rather than discuss the adaptability and strength of their individual contributions further, it is important to relate how these breakthrough technologies interconnect and combine with each other and converge in a step towards developing an idealized systems model. In this way business leaders can comprehend developments beyond their own sector and appreciate the transformation and disruption occurring across suppliers, consumers and markets arising from the adoption of individual or combined technologies. This task is assisted by drawing upon the technology segment of Deutsche Post DHL Group's Logistics Trend Radar (Heutger and Kückelhaus, 2020), which distinguishes those transformational technologies relevant within the next five years and those in the next five to ten years (Figure 4.2).

The three key enabling digital technologies connecting cyberspace and the physical world in Figure 4.2 are the inner circle of Big Data analytics, cloud computing and the Internet of Things that have important applications across the end-to-end supply chain (Factorachian and Kazemi, 2021). Already, the three technologies have transformed the traditional retail supply chain into a data-driven entity known as 'Retail 4.0' by sharing demand information to permit mass customization or personalization of products and services (Desai et al., 2013; Joshi, 2019). This has enabled online retailers to take the initiative and convey samples to customers based upon their past purchases and preferences. Nevertheless, the three technologies have made their own separate contributions.

Big Data analytics are used to describe annual sales and stock inventory, predict the future pattern of sales activities and prescribe the timing of product launches, shipment strategies and the type of offers to end users (Jeske et al., 2014; Nguyen et al., 2018). Cloud computing provides the opportunity for supply chain entities to share and exchange information to facilitate collaboration from order placement through to the end of the product's life cycle (Sundarakani et al., 2021). The Internet of Things exchanges information on a continuous basis and communicates through sensing devices using smart tags: barcode, near-field communication and Radio Frequency Identification. Their use is typified in Susan Biagi's (2020) account of those employed by Rogue Ale, Newport, Oregon to collect the temperature and humidity in the shipment of a tricky perishable product throughout its movement from the hop yard to the brewery within a 12-hour period and in the subsequent distribution of the final product (Figure 4.3).

The Internet of Things' open architecture put it ahead of 3D printing/ additive manufacturing as the pivotal logistics and supply chain technology because it can be bundled with other technologies (Ben-Daya et al., 2019;

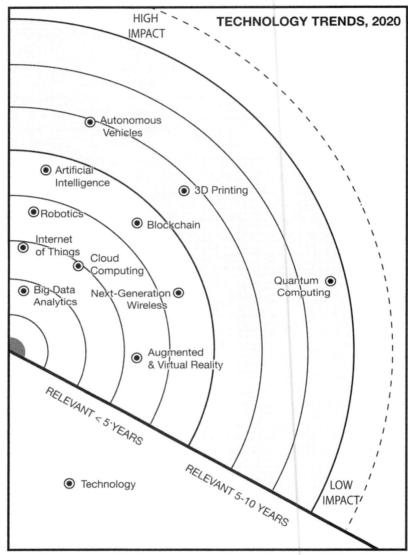

Note: The other segment of the figure covers social and business trends such as omnichannel logistics, the future of work and logistics marketplaces.
Source: Heutger and Kückelhaus (2020).

Figure 4.2 *The technology segment abstracted from Deutsche Post DHL Group's Logistics Trend Radar*

HOPS **CONSUMPTION**

Wet hops vulnerable to temperature and oxygen with short-shelf life, requiring rapid transpoort

Shipment of hops tracked through Intel's 'Connected Logistics Platform' to alert location every 10 minutes

Sensors track and trace hops by controlling temperature and humidity during transport

Manufacturer able to target use of hops with their arrival to reduce detrioration

Real-time data shared with business customers and consumers in 24 warehouses and 68 countries

Sensors reliant on satellites for positioning to update state of beer in transit even in ocean containers

Sensors used to monitor the positions, temperature and pressure of beer

Internet of Things technology is used to track beer when barrels and pallets are ready for shipment

BREWERY **DISTRIBUTION**

Source: Based on information from Biagi (2020), Hullum (2019), Intel (2018) and Violino et al. (2020).

Figure 4.3   *Stages in the production and distribution of craft beer from wet hops to consumption*

Tran-Dang et al., 2020). Not only has the Internet of Things links with Big Data and cloud computing made the supply chain smarter by optimizing performance, enabling preventative maintenance and avoiding disruptions from unexpected failure, but also it has combined with advanced robotics to enhance management practices. This has allowed the automation of repetitive tasks in large areas of manufacturing and warehousing, especially within the automotive and electronics industries. Deployment of autonomous mobile robots, coupled with the Internet of Things and artificial intelligence, also allows supply chain planning, execution and control to be highly automated to diminish human errors and product shortfalls.

Connecting the Internet of Things sensors to artificial intelligence technologies and their integration into supply chain management to generate solutions is still at an early stage of development. Nevertheless, once linked, support can be given to route optimization and improved reliability in logistics processes by supplying information that anticipates market demand and consumer requirements. Real-time assessments of the quality and safety of food and pharmaceutical products in the supply chain can be provided in this way to offer a competitive edge. Lineage Logistics, headquartered in Novi, Michigan, for instance, uses an artificial intelligence algorithm, which, according to Blake Morgan (2018), incorporates consumer and operations data to forecast when food orders will arrive and leave the warehouse.

Further, the interoperability of Internet of Things sensors with blockchain can be used beyond the association of distributed ledger technology with cryptocurrency to reduce risk in the data management of products and within the tracking system (Azzi et al., 2019; Wadhwa et al., 2020). Such transparent and accurate end-to-end tracking in supply chain practice and sustainability is illustrated in the study by Hyperledger CC-by 4.0 (2020) of seafood from ocean to table (Figure 4.4). While affixing the Internet of Things sensors to harvested fish allows the location of the shipment, temperature in transit and humidity to be gauged, blockchain improves visibility and product compliance with international standards because its open distributed ledger records transactions and enhances trust between producer and consumer by providing the necessary information without divulging trade secrets (Walker, 2021).

Combining the Internet of Things with handheld or head-mounted augmented reality devices or wearables enables their use in analysing data and acting upon it without human intervention; these can be deployed in vision picking in a warehouse and assisting customers with after-sales activities (Glockner et al., 2014). Also, the Internet of Things links with next-generation wireless networks can be employed in making products throughout the world. Nevertheless, this emphasis upon the transmission of data puts a premium on the cyber-security risk arising from the vulnerability of these links and networks, which can have a harmful effect upon the supply chain (Kench, 2021).

3D printing/additive manufacturing, which is located within the Deutsche Post DHL Trend Radar's five- to ten-year radius, is the other key disruptive technology with a comparable potential influence over the supply chain to that exerted by the Internet of Things. The technology is expected to have a marked effect upon supply chain operations by decentralizing production, driving product consumption, reducing complexity and time to market, improving resource efficiency and rationalizing inventory and logistics (Knowles, 2019). Already, 3D printing/additive manufacturing has shortened the time cycle across a range of industries by customizing or personalizing products online and manufacturing them locally. This process has led to the shortening of the

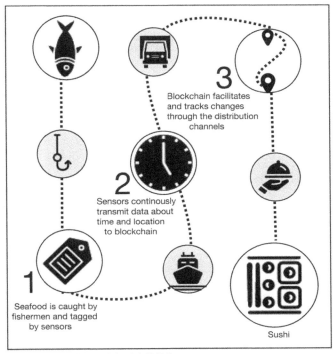

Figure 4.4   *Hyperledger Sawtooth's blockchain technology-driven solution*

supply chain by 'reshoring' production during the COVID-19 pandemic within high-income countries in sectors ranging from aerospace through the medical, automotive and construction industries to oil and gas (Roberts, 2021).

Autonomous vehicles are also within the five- to ten-year radius and high-light the scope for self-driving trucks in the supply chain between industry and warehouse (Perussi et al., 2019). Drones did not feature as a separate entity in Deutsche Post DHL's Logistics Trend Radar but could be regarded as part of the artificial 'Intelligence of Things' (Marr, 2019). Not only do drones have a role in scanning stock in an automated warehouse, but also in last-mile delivery.

Finally, quantum computing on the edge of the five- to ten-year radius is seen as an appropriate technology that, once developed using 'qubits' during this time frame, could, according to Speedel (2020), provide solutions to disruptions in the supply chain typified by the COVID-19 pandemic. Leaving quantum computing for inclusion in the future, the immediate task is to incorporate the other technologies into a vision of Supply Chain 4.0 (Insights Team, 2018). This will focus on leveraging the combination of the Internet of Things with other technologies in real-time automated sense-and-respond mechanisms.

VISION

Two issues need to be addressed in outlining a vision of Supply Chain 4.0. How can Supply Chain 4.0 be defined? And how, given the extensive array of possibilities afforded by Industry 4.0 technologies, can the ideal configuration of Supply Chain 4.0 be achieved? In response to these issues various definitions of supply chain digitization and transformation are discussed before key components of Supply Chain 4.0 are identified. Then our vision of Supply Chain 4.0 is presented, which discusses the form that maximizes competitive advantage.

DEFINITION

Supply Chain 4.0, as defined by Gemini (Rabb and Griffin-Cryan, 2017) and McKinsey (Gezgin et al., 2017), refers to the digital transformation of the supply chain brought forth by Industry 4.0. An analysis of the definition of Supply Chain 4.0 advanced by McKinsey (Alicke et al., 2016: 1), for instance, suggests that the process is about the application of digital technologies, which are designed to improve performance and increase consumer satisfaction:

> Supply Chain 4.0 – the application of the Internet of Things, the use of advanced robotics, and the application of advanced analytics of big data in supply chain management: place sensors in everything, create networks everywhere, automate anything, and analyze everything to significantly improve performance and customer satisfaction.

In response Rahul Asthana (2018) has observed that this definition, similar to that proposed by Gemini, stops short of explaining what is being 'transformed' in supply chain management. This has prompted him to clarify the transformation process by going back to first principles to suggest that the primary objective of altering the supply chain is to exactly match supply with real demand whenever they occur. This ultimate goal can be achieved by filling three information gaps in supply chains by: (1) removing uncertainties in consumer demand and the inability of businesses to accurately forecast what they want; (2) eliminating uncertainties in production that occasion changes in supply due either to the failure of yields to match forecasts or machinery breakdowns, or disparities between what is expected and what actually occurs; and (3) overcoming the lack of synchronization among upstream and downstream supply chain partners arising from the absence of relevant data sets as and when they are required.

According to Rahul Asthana (2018), resolution of demand uncertainty can be sought from new consumer data derived from social channels, weather inputs, economic performance and sensors and insights from artificial intelligence and machine learning algorithms that distil patterns from the new data (e.g. effect of temperature changes on demand). Production uncertainty can be overcome by using the Industrial Internet of Things to monitor machines on the shop floor, to track performance metrics and to use predictive analytics to pinpoint or prevent breakdowns. Synchronization can be resolved by employing new sources of data from blockchains to speed information flow through the supply chain. Thus the three information gaps will be closed by data and insights derived from the new technologies and, in the process, will enable supply to better match demand and transform supply chain management. This clarification of what is being transformed provides the necessary springboard for outlining an idealized configuration of Supply Chain Management 4.0 to accommodate emerging business phenomena.

AN IDEALIZED CONFIGURATION

Industry 4.0, with its extensive and ever expanding suite of intelligent technologies, offers endless opportunities for supply chains to assume, albeit predicated upon digitization, a new, more efficient, flexible and productive image. Before offering our ideal configuration of Supply Chain 4.0, it is important to summarize the central components of Industry 4.0 and their attributes derived from a survey by Birgit Vogel-Heuser and Dieter Hess (2016). Within the context of the multi-agent, cyber-physical ecosystem, outlined in Chapter 2, the key principles are: (1) service orientation; (2) decentralized decision-making; (3) interoperability between machines and humans and virtualization of resources; (4) flexible adaptation to address changing requirements; (5) real-time capability provided by Big Data analytics; (6) flexible automation to optimize processes; (7) data integration across disciplines and along the life cycle; and (8) data security stored in the cloud or distributed storage typified by the blockchain. Collectively, the adoption of these design principles should, according to Robert Recknagel (2020), lead to direct cost savings, enhanced speed, increased profitability, competitiveness in the global market and greater employee productivity.

Moving beyond these Industry 4.0 components in autonomously operated smart factories, the five key characteristics of an ideal Supply Chain 4.0 can be distilled from a compilation by Erik Hofmann and others (2019: 946).

Table 4.2   Elaboration of the five key characteristics of an ideal supply chain

Characteristic	Elaboration
Customer-centric	Design, produce and sell individualized products via omnichannel approach using innovative manufacturing technologies such as 3D printing/additive manufacturing.
Interconnected	Customers, suppliers and partners (e.g. logistics service providers) communicate and collaborate in real time based on shared and standardized data via platforms in a network of companies.
Automated	Increased efficiency based on flexible automation of physical processes via robotics.
Transparent	Global positioning system and cyber-physical system enable increased visibility into the diverse aspects of the supply chain such as bottlenecks and delays as well as traceability of products, notably the location of materials and proof of provenance.
Proactive	Decision-makers react anticipatorily to changing conditions and unexpected events based on real-time data analytics, machine learning and artificial intelligence.

Source: Hofmann et al. (2019: 946) drawn from Kearney (2015), Kersten et al. (2017) and Wu et al. (2016).

As elaborated in Table 4.2, the attributes are: (1) *customer-centricity* to provide consumers with an increasing variety of products and services; (2) *interconnectedness* between consumers, suppliers and partners in the supply chain to achieve interoperability; (3) *automation* of specific operational processes that are dangerous for workers; (4) *transparency* stemming from the greater availability of information to provide increased visibility of the supply chain and greater product traceability for better control, coordination and decision-making; and (5) *proactiveness* in anticipating changing customer preferences and resultant changes in demand, and reacting to unexpected events. Although all five attributes are pertinent to achieving better operational, managerial and transformational outcomes for companies, the emphasis on interconnectedness between consumers, suppliers and partners is critical given the spatial dispersion of design, production and distribution among a variety of firms and parties. Corralling these multiple stakeholders into an integrated supply chain, and sharing accurate real-time data between them, are vital ingredients in fostering interdependency and taking coordination, performance and end-to-end visibility to new levels.

Envisioning the digital and autonomous linkages within and between supply chain partners – suppliers, manufacturers, distributors and consumers – demands a new perspective. Over time, this strategic perspective will manifest itself in forms, functions and processes substantially different from those exhibited by existing supply chains. Indeed, Lifang Wu and others (2016: 396) view supply chain digitalization as a 'new interconnected business system which extends from isolated, local, and single-company applications to supply chain wide systematic smart implementations'.

A vertically integrated cyber-physical ecosystem is shown in Figure 4.5 by grafting the representation by Knut Alicke and others (2016) onto an earlier framework. The resultant integrated ecosystem merges the cyber (digital) and physical worlds to achieve a higher degree of interaction by allowing information to flow in all directions. This ecosystem reflects how opportunities, derived from digitalization of the industrial sector, are available throughout the supply chain process for stakeholders to monitor manufacturing and logistics operations in real time. These opportunities for full visibility across the entire supply chain are achieved by: (1) enabling full data management of both technology and people; (2) better forecasting of channel events, product, promotions, sales and weather from prescriptive and predictive analytics to mitigate the effects of adverse events on the supply chain ranging from labour unrest to typhoons (Forger, 2018); and (3) trusted end-to-end performance

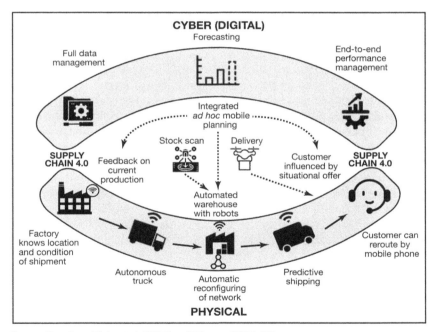

Source: Based on Alicke et al. (2016) and Rimmer (2014: 23).

Figure 4.5   *The integrated Supply Chain 4.0 ecosystem*

management to provide remote diagnosis and control of physical activities through integrated ad hoc mobile planning.

Control is exerted by the digital layer over this smart manufacturing supply chain moving goods from factory through autonomous truck, an automated warehousing system with drone scanning and robotic fulfilment within a wider automated network of connected distribution centres and predictive shipping to the consumer. Within this smart manufacturing and anticipatory shipping framework the consumer is afforded an array of options ranging from an ability to be influenced by situational offers, delivery by drone or truck and rerouting the delivery by mobile. Thus, the supply chain has progressed to a visionary ecosystem driven by the single-minded focus on creating consumer value.

REALITIES

Despite this Supply Chain 4.0 vision, current realities will hinder the platform's full implementation. How have supply chain management and logistics operations adopted technologies in the past? And how have these operations reacted when new technologies have offered a range of alternative possibilities? As discussed, existing supply chains have largely evolved from a linear flow configuration pegged upon brick-and-mortar retailing – a configuration that commences with the procurement of raw materials, through production, storage and distribution to retailing. The rise of e-commerce, multichannel and omnichannel retailing derived from advances of information and communication technologies, automation and robotics not only adds to efficiency but also increases productivity. Nevertheless, important lessons can be drawn from the limitations of adopting technologies in the past as instanced by Radio Frequency Identification, the Enterprise Resource Planning system and voice-picking technology.

The wireless communications technology Radio Frequency Identification has offered more benefits than the bar code in inventory control. It has been the right tool for identifying and tracking the location of objects remotely in real time without human intervention. This has created business value for companies with large inventories such as Amazon, Procter and Gamble and Walmart by enabling smart shelving and a reduction in checkout wait times (Matthews, 2020). Nevertheless, for other retail firms the tags have raised security problems because they have been easy to clone, posed issues when the tags could not be read with perfect accuracy and have been costly and difficult to integrate into regular supply chain operations (Furlong, 2017).

The Enterprise Resource Planning System software was a suite of customizable applications that centralized a company's data base, automated routine tasks and simplified business processes. This legacy system allowed businesses to integrate and manage their most important processes to boost productivity over the long term (Columbus, 2015; Hayes, 2022). Nevertheless, the system proved to be a bottleneck for manufacturers, whose business models were reliant on rapid life cycles and speed, because it was incapable of being scaled up to meet contemporary supply chain challenges. These shortcomings have prompted the evolution of a postmodern Enterprise Resource Planning System that incorporates an agile supply chain and integrates information technology both horizontally and vertically (Recknagel, 2020).

Voice-directed vision picking technology, often employing a headset and microphone to free up the worker's hands, has replaced the cost and time-consuming paper-based order picking in some warehouse management systems (Gialos and Zeimpekis, 2021). The technology has purported to offer a shorter training period, increased accuracy, greater productivity and safer warehousing (Glynn, 2018). Yet, as Insight Works (2018) has highlighted, use of voice-picking technology lacks supporting accuracy and could be counter-productive, with the cost of a mispick leading to mis-shipment, unnecessary cost of returns handling and the possibility of stock loss, hurting profitability considerably. In sum, this range of past technologies has not necessarily led to a radical change in operations because these technologies have been adopted more as a Band-Aid solution rather than a fundamental shift in the operations process.

Thus, while businesses may have been quick to embrace new technologies, the adoption process has been typically piecemeal, innovation has been ad hoc or disjointed and the efficiency or productivity gained has been characteristi-cally suboptimal. This adoption experience has been borne out by varying reac-tions of multinationals to three critical technologies expected to have a major effect upon Supply Chain 4.0: Big Data analysis, cloud computing and 3D printing/additive manufacturing (Makris et al., 2019). Big Data analysis was strongly preferred by multinationals. Cloud computing applications received only limited attention among them and 3D printing/additive manufacturing was even more constrained in its use due to uncertainty about its true added value among supply chain stakeholders. Even the vulnerabilities of the Internet of Things have been criticized as the 'Internet of Broken Things' due to the lack of concern about system dependability, privacy and security (Shackelford, 2016). Yet both the Internet of Things and 3D printing/additive manufacturing are regarded as the twin hallmarks of a true Supply Chain 4.0 operation.

Other technologies such as artificial intelligence, blockchain and industrial robotics have been widely discussed in the context of Supply Chain 4.0, but their integration has only just commenced within the industry and service sectors (Hahn, 2020). A survey of artificial intelligence in 2020 reported that companies overall had made progress in mitigating universal risks including cyber security, equity and fairness, but most still had a long way to go (Balakrishnan et al., 2020). The main barriers to the blockchain's implementation have been challenges in scalability (given the 1 mb size per block) (Barenji et al., 2020). Nevertheless, many critics and sceptics have also pinpointed market-based risks associated with its fluctuating value, high sustainability and poor economic behaviour after adoption (Biswas and Gupta, 2019). Amidst a 'robotics revolution' an estimated 80 per cent of distribution centres are still manually operated (RIA, 2020). More significantly, even among those that have embraced automation, like using robots in their picking and stowing operations, some have found scores of unanticipated challenges. Citing an investigation published in *The Atlantic* by the Center for Investigative Reporting's Reveal Group, Jason Del Rey (2019) reported that Amazon had invested in more than 200,000 robots across its warehouse network. However, the company had endured a higher rate of worker injuries at these robotic warehouses due to a procedural mismatch between robots and humans.

Such examples suggest that some businesses have embraced technologies merely to enhance or reinvigorate their supply chain and logistics operations to address perceived inefficiencies, notably the utilization of transport capacity or last-mile delivery. As demonstrated, this adoption procedure has led to the suboptimization of processes leading to the opportunities for organizations being outweighed by the threats. Indeed, concerns have been raised by Hartmut Hirsch-Kreinsen (2016, 2019) that the unequal diffusion of digital technologies in supply chain and logistics operations will overtax the resources of small and medium enterprises and lead to the potential 'dequalification' of workers and job losses.

These concerns are further compounded by issues stemming from the exaggerated growth prospects of digital capitalism, the increased economic power of big corporations arising from platform technologies and the growing autonomy of technological systems such as robots and self-driving cars at the expense of human control. Not surprisingly, these outcomes are prompting calls for government regulation of artificial intelligence and robotics in supply chain and logistics operations (Sanders, 2018). Above all, there are doubts as to whether there has been a sufficient technological jump from computer integrated management, which linked production and logistics over the entire value chain, to warrant the appellations of Industry 4.0 and Supply Chain 4.0. Other than massive disruptive economic, social and technological consequences, has anything more than an updating of work processes occurred? This issue of revolution versus evolution prompts an analysis of the challenges involving interrelationships between pre-Industry 4.0 technologies, supply chain operations and consumers.

CHALLENGES

These realities provoke a study of the issues experienced by supply chain operators in the way that they have embraced technologies during the pre-Industry 4.0 era. Under Supply Chain 2.0, paper-based, manual processes and limited data inputs characterized business decisions (Alicke et al., 2016). After the adoption of Supply Chain 3.0 the automation of single machines and processes occurred to incorporate digital components. Nevertheless, despite information technology being adopted and used to maximum advantage, digital capabilities were not developed beyond forecasting and planning algorithms due to the limited number of data scientists within organizations (De Haas et al., 2021).

This evidence of the lack of data maturity in supply chains suggests that the prime reason for the suboptimization of processes during the pre-Industry 4.0 era has stemmed from a failure to recognize the mutually reinforcing influence between consumer behaviour and technology development. On the one hand consumer behaviour democratizes technology, while on the other technology socializes consumer behaviour. This is not necessarily the whole story because part of the problem of supply chain suboptimization has been due to the limitations of existing pre-Industry 4.0 technologies such as Radio Frequency Identification, Enterprise Resource Planning and voice-picking technology.

The dynamics of the interplay between supply chain operators (businesses), technology and consumers during the pre-Industry 4.0 era, derived from these examples, are distilled in Figure 4.6. This distillation shows that supply chain entities have been *embracing* technologies to *enhance their operations*, which continue to create demand for new technologies to *invigorate extant processes*. In response, providers of pre-Industry 4.0 technologies have concentrated on developing technologies that meet demands aimed at invigorating extant processes. Technological adoption, as such, has enabled the supply chain entities to continuously increase the efficiency and responsiveness of their processes to meet their 'assumed' consumer expectations (i.e. based on historical data).

While new technologies have progressively been embedded into supply chains to enhance their processes, these insertions, ad hoc or planned, have done little to alter the pervasive linear flow configuration. What this cyclical process has ignored is the reciprocal influence that technological development and consumer (purchasing) behaviour have on each other: technology shapes consumer purchasing behaviour and the consumer also shapes technological trends. As a result, what we have witnessed is that technology has led to an invigoration, rather than a reconfiguration, of supply chain operations.

Such insertions of state-of-the-art technologies into supply chain operations have two notable fallouts. The first is a preoccupation among businesses to

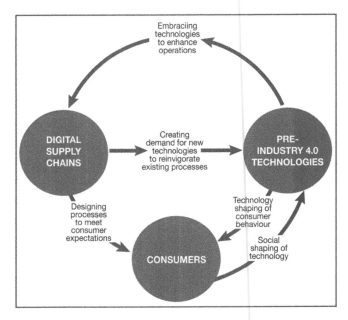

Figure 4.6   Supply chain operations pre-Industry 4.0

look towards technologies for solutions to increase operational efficiency at
the expense of process simplification, productivity and effectiveness. As noted
previously, Amazon's extensive investment in robots across its warehouse
network, despite enduring a higher rate of worker injuries, is a case in point
(Del Rey, 2019).

The second fallout is that such an approach constructs consumers as
'passive' technology users or simply captive customers. This staid view of
consumers ignores the notion that technological innovations may be influenced by the consumer socialization of technology. The two forces – technology innovation and technology socialization – mutually reinforce each other
through an innovation diffusion and social-shaping process, as demonstrated
by Pablo Boczkowski's (2004) account of the history of videotext newspapers
in the United States. He reveals how various stakeholder groups in the media
industry concurrently pursued interdependent technological and social transformations through an ongoing process. Partial outcomes in the technological
domain motivated subsequent social events and vice versa. Pablo Boczkowski
(2004: 262) characterizes this phenomenon as 'society became the technical
lab, and the resulting artifacts were embodiment of the compromises between
producers' preferences and adopters' behavior'.

These two fallouts are similar to those characterized by Jeff Berg and others (2020) as the first and third pitfalls of companies pursuing a service-to-solution approach during the COVID-19 pandemic, a point discussed in Chapter 5.

THE WAY AHEAD

The way ahead calls for a mindset change. It means supply chain entities should not interpret technology adoption as using Industry 4.0 technologies to *invigorate* extant processes. Rather, they should look towards harnessing the prowess of Industry 4.0 technologies to innovate by designing new operations processes to cater for changing consumption patterns and consumer purchasing behaviour. This would require supply chain entities to pay attention to the socialization between technology development and consumer purchasing behaviour, as depicted in Figure 4.7.

Extending the argument about the interaction dynamics between supply chain entities, technology and consumers, a customer-sensitive Supply Chain

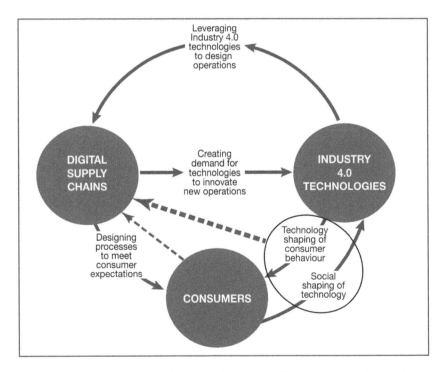

Figure 4.7   Digital supply chains leveraging Industry 4.0 technologies

4.0 will have to leverage upon Big Data analytics and the Internet of Things to analyse consumer behaviour at a granular level in real time. This will involve digital data-gathering and monitoring practices, such as mobile diaries, social media 'listening' and artificial intelligence-driven message boards to gain a deeper understanding of emerging consumer behaviour and contextual cues (Charm et al., 2020). Sensing preference shifts and succeeding changes in demand in this way will enable managers to respond to ever increasing consumer needs and complex requirements.

CONCLUSION

Supply chain and logistics operations have been affected by an ever increasing array of Industry 4.0 technologies, especially Big Data analytics, cloud computing and the Internet of Things, that have been embodied in software. The Internet of Things has also been actively involved with artificial intelligence, blockchain and robotics. Other technologies, notably autonomous vehicles, 3D printing/additive manufacturing and quantum computing, may not be fully realized for five to ten years. However, the unanticipated onset of COVID-19 has accelerated the rate of adoption of Industry 4.0 technologies to the extent that consideration now needs to be given to consumption on demand. The linking together of Industry 4.0 technologies, digital supply chains and consumers offers a way forward.

Also, supply chains have sought to match the numerous possibilities stemming from social commerce, which have been exploding on digital platforms to extend the seamless experiences promised by the adoption of omnichannel retailing. These opportunities have involved the increasing use of autonomous vehicles and drones, and the popularization of consumer logistics. Such prospects have underpinned consumption on demand and are discussed in Chapter 5.

5. Consumption on demand: race to meet changing consumption on demand

The COVID-19 pandemic has changed consumer behaviour both in the way people shop and the types of goods they purchase. Simultaneously, city lockdowns and international and state border closures have disrupted supplies. In response, business leaders have taken unprecedented action and adopted untested procedures to reorganize their supply chains to cope with the sudden swings in demand within the constraints of complying with the COVID-safe protocols mandated by authorities. As businesses introduce radical changes to their operations and people adjust their lifestyles under COVID rules, the 'digital future' has arrived far sooner than many futurists had anticipated.

The agile and, at times, radical adjustments businesses make in response to the pandemic's disruptions and physical restrictions provided us with a glimpse into a future where digital technology will dominate all things physical. This raises the following issues: How has demand shifted? How has supply been disrupted? How have businesses altered their supply chains in response? How has Technology 4.0 helped or hindered this process? And how do businesses manage their customers and employees affected by mandatory physical isolation and distancing and recurrent lockdowns during the pandemic?

In addressing these issues, we focus initially upon the consumption patterns arising from the shift in demand. Then we explore the unpredictability stemming from the disruption in supply before zooming into details on how businesses have reoriented their supply chains to meet consumption changes during the COVID-19 pandemic. Our aim is to understand the role of Technology 4.0 in shaping the configuration of the COVID supply chain. As such, we try to separate the hype from the reality. Given the psychological effects the lockdowns and restrictions have had on the public during the pandemic, we also explore how businesses have leveraged the prowess of Industry 4.0 to focus upon the safety of their employees and customers as part of their customer service. We conclude the chapter by presenting the accompanying concepts that have contributed to the making of the COVID supply chain, as a variant of the first-generation Supply Chain 4.0.

DEMAND SHIFT: THE CONSUMPTION THAT MATTERS

On 11 March 2020 the World Health Organization confirmed the global COVID-19 pandemic. Before and since that event there have been three visible shifts in consumption patterns not only in the goods demanded but also in the way purchasing has occurred. These shifts have aligned closely with consumer behaviour manifested in panic buying, herd mentality and consumer discretionary spending during previous historic crises or shock events, although COVID-19 represents a much broader healthcare crisis (Loxton et al., 2020).

The first noticeable shift in response to the pandemic that emerged globally has been the immediate demand for daily necessities and personal protective equipment. Once stay-at-home lockdowns were announced there was short-term panic buying of essential food and grocery items from supermarkets such as biscuits, eggs, flour, dried and canned food, minced meat, pasta, rice and vegetables. The panic buying was quickly extended to household necessities, notably baby nappies, hand-wash liquid and toilet paper. This was soon accompanied by an increase in the purchasing of personal protective equipment covering facial masks, gloves, goggles and sanitizer.

The second conspicuous shift stemmed from a set of stringent measures designed to curb the spread of the virus by enforcing physical distancing. These measures resulted in workplace and school closures, cancellation of sporting and theatrical events, curbs on public gatherings such as funerals, weddings and dancing and travel restrictions being imposed upon public transport. The resultant city-wide, statewide and nationwide 'lockdowns' occasioned working from home; online learning became the norm for tertiary students and schoolchildren; and mobility was limited in both time and space. These developments led to a sharp increase in the purchase of electronic goods, particularly cell phones, gaming consoles, notebooks and smart devices (IDC, 2021). Also, it arrested the decline in laptop and desktop sales caused by mobile phones, which redounded to the benefit of Taiwan's personal computer sector (HKTDC, 2021). Later, this surge, assisted by retailers adopting augmented reality, was extended to bicycles, gardening accessories, hair clippers, home gym equipment and household furnishings (Papagiannis, 2020). Finally, the upsurge has spread to the use of digital products on television typified by streaming services, notably Netflix and Stan.

The third shift in consumption patterns has been marked by the successful development of vaccines to counter COVID-19. In February 2021 no less than 73 vaccines were reported by Canada's McGill University to be under development, but attention here is concentrated upon the distributional attributes of seven vaccines that had been approved for public use in at least one country

Table 5.1   Seven vaccines approved for public use, 6 January 2021

Producer	Headquarters	Production	Doses (billion, 2021)	Storage	Distribution
Bharat Biotech International (Covaxin)	Hyderabad, India	Four facilities in India	0.7		India
Gamelaya (Sputnik V)	Moscow, Russia	China, India, Brazil, South Korea	1.2	Regular refrigerator	Argentina, Belarus, Guinea, Russia and seven other countries
Moderna	Cambridge, MA, United States	Cambridge, MA, United States	1	-20°C 6 months	Canada, European Union, Japan, South Korea, Switzerland, United Kingdom, United States
Oxford-AstraZeneca	Cambridge, United Kingdom	Belgium, Germany, India	3	Regular refrigerator	Argentina, European Union, India, Mexico, United Kingdom and 34 other countries
Pfizer/BioNTech	New York, United States/ Mainz, Germany	Brussels, Belgium, Marburg, Germany	1.3	-7°C	Saudi Arabia, United Kingdom, United States, 18 other countries
SinoPharm	Beijing, China	Wuhan, China	1		Bahrain, China, Hungary, Morocco, Pakistan, Serbia, United Arab Emirates
Sinovac	Beijing, China	Brussels, Belgium	0.3		Chile, Indonesia, Malaysia, Philippines, Singapore, Turkey

Source: Based on information in Pladson (2021).

(Table 5.1). Their approval has led to an ongoing scramble among national governments to first obtain vaccines from a limited number of producers and then roll them out (Shehadi, 2021). While the relative effectiveness and side effects of individual vaccines have been given much publicity, the real competition between them hinges on the capabilities of their respective supply chains in making the last-mile delivery to the consumer. As highlighted by Shahriar Tanvir Alam and others (2021: 12), the role of the vaccine supply chain 'is to deliver the right vaccine in the right quantity to be delivered to the right place at the right time'. We would add 'to service the right consumer' (Rimmer and Kam, 2018: vii).

VACCINE CONSUMPTION

On 3 May 2021, Our World in Data revealed that the countries that had performed well in controlling COVID-19 (Figure 5.1) – Australia, Japan, New Zealand, South Korea and Taiwan – still had slow vaccination rates on a par with some of the poorest countries in the world (Ritchie et al., 2021; Holder, 2021). Conversely, the countries that had performed poorly in managing COVID-19 by recording some of the world's highest numbers of infections and deaths – the United States and the United Kingdom – were recording higher vaccination rates on 6 May 2021 behind only Israel, United Arab Emirates, Chile and Bahrain. Our attention is, therefore, focused upon the first vaccines rolled out in these two countries – Pfizer, Moderna and Oxford AstraZeneca – and the logistics and supply chains for delivering them.

Of the three vaccines, Pfizer must be stored at -70 degrees Centigrade with a shelf life of five days in a regular refrigerator, whereas Moderna can use conventional frozen goods transport and Oxford AstraZeneca can be stored in a refrigerator. With the extra demands of the Pfizer vaccine, as it travels around both the United Kingdom (especially England) and the United States, our major focus is on the COVID-19 supply chain in these two countries.

Since its approval on 2 December 2020 the Pfizer vaccine destined for the United Kingdom has been drawn from the company's manufacturing plant in Puurs, near Brussels Airport in Belgium, to complement vaccine supplies from Oxford AstraZeneca in India and the Netherlands and an array of local plants, with Moderna in Spain and Switzerland playing a smaller role (Figure 5.2). As detailed by Richard Wilding (2020), the United Kingdom's approval of Pfizer has hinged on a series of logistical and supply chain constraints in moving the product from the continent via air or the Channel Tunnel; these have included the number of doses that can be stored in the bespoke vaccine boxes and the use of Global Positioning System trackers and thermal sensors to ensure that doses arrive safely at vaccination nodes.

On arrival in England the Pfizer vaccine has been distributed through the National Health Service (NHS, 2021) network comprising vaccination centres, hospital hubs, pharmacies and community services (Baraniuk, 2021). This network, which brought over 99.1 per cent of England's population (55.7 million) within 10 km of a vaccine source, also administered the Oxford AstraZeneca vaccine (Figure 5.3). Nevertheless, AstraZeneca experienced supply chain issues beyond England related to the availability of manufacturing ingredients from India's Serum Institute (Sharif et al., 2021). This reliance

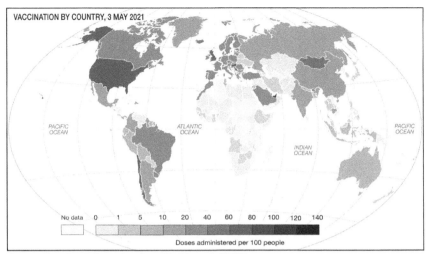

Source: Based on information from Ritchie et al. (2021).

Figure 5.1 Vaccination by country, 3 May 2021

upon specialist facilities abroad also occurred in the United States in sourcing the Pfizer vaccine.

Since 12 December 2020, when the United States Food and Drug Administration cleared the Pfizer vaccine for use, it has been flown in 'custom thermal shippers' designed to carry five packs of 975 doses at -98 degrees Centigrade from Puurs in Belgium to Chicago O'Hare Airport (Repko and Dunn, 2021). Then it has been taken by truck from the airport to supplement Pfizer plants producing and distributing the vaccine to the point of use (Figure 5.4).

Next, Pfizer's logistics partners, the freight integrators FedEx and UPS, have transported the doses with the requisite cold storage from Kalamazoo and Pleasant Prairie by air and road to the large health systems within the United States as part of the 'Operation Warp Speed' strategy adopted by federal, state and local governments (Figure 5.5). The doses handled by UPS for the eastern part of the country are afforded a gold priority label and embedded with trackers to gauge the location, temperature and condition of the vaccine on arrival at the company's 'Worldport' facility in Louisville, KY (United States Senate, 2020). Like FedEx's 'Priority Alert' system for the western half of the country operated from its Cold Center base in Memphis, TN, all packages are checked at the 24/7 command centre, faulty ones are intercepted and the remainder are expedited. Apart from these aberrations, the logistics movements of the Pfizer vaccine within a just-in-time system in the United States have appeared

Note: By 11 May 2021, the United Kingdom Government had drawn 100 million doses from Oxford AstraZeneca and Pfizer and 17 million from Moderna; an additional 280 million other doses are on order from five other companies, generating a total of 497 million doses.
Source: Based on information from BBC (2021) and DW (2021).

Figure 5.2   *Oxford AstraZeneca, Pfizer and Moderna COVID-19 vaccine production locations in Western Europe with Indian inset, July*

streamlined by being configured by consumption. Nevertheless, Simon Ellis (2020) has documented issues that still persist within the pharmaceutical industry that stem from the failure to configure the vaccine supply chain to align with consumption.

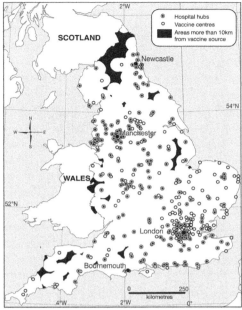

Note: Location of pharmacies and local vaccination services are not shown.
Source: Based on information from NHS (2021).

Figure 5.3   *England's major vaccination centres and hospital hubs, and areas beyond 10 km of a vaccine source, 28 July 2021*

This misalignment between the pharmaceutical supply chain and consumption has not only been exposed nationally within the United States but internationally by the surge in the highly transmissible Delta variant of COVID-19 around the world since late 2020. This variant has adversely affected countries in Asia that largely escaped the earlier wave, notably India, Indonesia, Thailand and Vietnam (Chang et al., 2021). As underscored by the subsequent highly transmissible Omicron variant, the tussle among countries to first secure the approved vaccines and rapid antigen tests before rolling them out to consumers has continued. Also, the struggle has pinpointed the failure to pursue an equitable global last-mile vaccine and rapid antigen test delivery plan, which has led to stark inequalities within and between national jurisdictions (WHO, 2021). As highlighted by the World Health Organization's Council on the Economics of Health for All (WHO Council, 2021), the need for vaccine supply chains to make the last-mile delivery to the consumer in many areas of the world, especially Africa, is still unmet. Not only will this shortcoming in the deployment of vaccines lead to an uneven recovery from the global pandemic, but also it

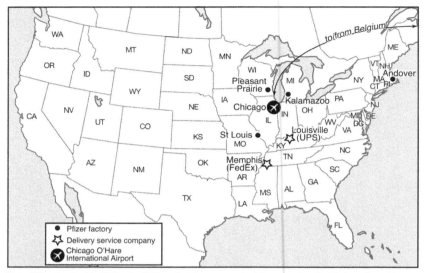

Note: Pfizer's plant in St Louis, MO undertakes raw material processing that is transferred to Andover, MA for manufacturing before being transferred to Kalamazoo, MI for formulation filling and packaging.
Source: Based on information from Neubert and Scheitz (2021).

Figure 5.4   *Production and distribution of Pfizer vaccine in the United States*

will have a flow-on effect due to the capacity of unvaccinated individuals to disrupt global supply chains.

SUPPLY CHAIN DISRUPTION: UNPREDICTABILITY

The marked shifts in demand occasioned by the pandemic have affected global supply chains resulting in the disruption of the flow of goods from manufacturer to consumer. Arguing that the pandemic is qualitatively different from typical disruptions in scale, scope and shifts, Craighead and others (2020: 838) have highlighted the need for supply chain management to foster '*transiliency* (i.e., the ability to simultaneously restore some processes and change – often radically – others)'.

Examples of the resultant unpredictability occasioned by the pandemic are illustrated initially by reference to China's car industry with Honda's joint venture, for instance, having two production facilities in Wuhan that were initially locked down on 20 January 2020. Then an attempt was made to gauge the overall effect of the disruption across the world during the early months

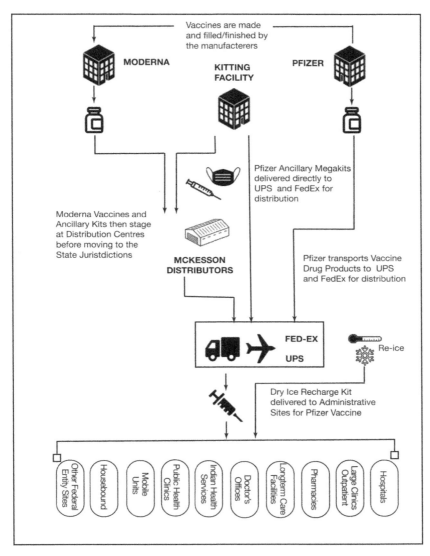

Note: McKesson is supporting the United States government as a centralized distributor for COVID-19 vaccines that are refrigerated (2–8°C) or frozen (-20°C).
Source: Based on USDHHS (2020).

Figure 5.5   *'Operation Warp Speed' vaccine distribution process in the United States*

of the pandemic. As this assessment was not repeated, attention is switched to focusing on the container industry – shipping lines, terminal operators and ports – to gauge the varying effects of the disruption on the global supply chain over a prolonged period.

During the early days of coronavirus supply chain disruption was manifested in China, the world's second largest economy, affecting an array of activities, including the disruption of the country's hog market (Wang et al., 2020). By 10 February 2020, millions had returned to work in the country after an extended Lunar New Year, but many factories remained closed in China to stem the spread of the virus (BBC, 2020a). Several large local automobile producers and parts manufacturers had continued their shutdown, including Dongfeng Motor Corporation at the epicentre of China's coronavirus epidemic in Wuhan, Hubei province (Figure 5.6).

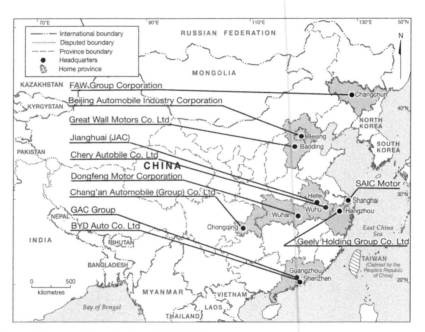

Source: Based on information from QIRI (2020).

Figure 5.6   *Main Chinese producers of automobiles during COVID-19, June 2020*

Progressively, these automobile plants reopened along with their foreign associates. On 12 February 2020, for instance, Valeo, the French car manufacturer, had restored operations in Wuhan. Then two days later Nissan and PSA, manufacturers of Peugeot and Citroen, respectively, had restarted operations followed four days later by BMW, Honda, Toyota and Volkswagen. Nevertheless, the shortage of spare parts from China led to Hyundai suspending operations in South Korea, Fiat Chrysler experiencing a similar predicament in Europe and Suzuki in Japan seeking parts from alternative sources to maintain production in India, its major market. Reportedly, many supply chain managers in these countries did not have a plan to address the vulnerability of their just-in-time operations with China. Meanwhile, the monthly production of automobiles in China had quickly recovered from the depths of the lockdown (Figure 5.7).

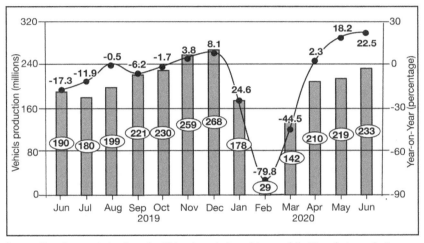

Source: Based on statistics from the China Association of Automobile Manufacturers in June 2020 (QIRI, 2020).

Figure 5.7   *Monthly production of automobiles in China between June 2019 and June 2020*

Manufacturing within China had recovered quickly, but other parts of the world had remained in lockdown. On 22 February 2020 94 per cent of the 'Fortune 1000' companies reported having supply chain disruptions (Sherman, 2020). By 11 March 2020 three-quarters of all companies stated that the coronavirus had disrupted their supply chains (Lambert, 2020). Consequently, on 17 March 2020, it was recounted that 55 per cent of companies planned or had already downgraded their growth outlook (Accenture, 2020). In September

2020, these figures were still being cited as a manifestation of the threat posed by the pandemic to industrial hubs and economic regions (Freeman, 2020). Recourse was therefore made to analyses of the container industry to focus on changes in the disruptive effects of the global lockdown over a longer period.

International border closures to reduce virus spread had strangulated the container trade in manufactured goods between Asia and Europe and the United States (Pooler and Hale, 2020). In April 2020 lockdowns had resulted in a marked drop in the transoceanic movement of seaborne containers carrying an array of commodities ranging from clothing through electronics and fresh fruit to scrap metal. By May 2020 almost 12 per cent of the shipping fleet was idle and, not surprisingly, purchases of new containers to add to the 150 million worldwide had stopped in an industry that had failed to earn the cost of capital for over a decade. Yet, by October 2020, the container industry was showing a marked resilience, underscored by a reduction in capacity of only 1 per cent (Notteboom et al., 2021). An upsurge in shorter voyages within regions, especially intra-Asia, using smaller, nimbler container vessels offered a faster transit to meet urgent consumer demand and countered the decline in airline freight capacity. This development was matched by the restoration of sailings on routes between China and both Europe and the United States and a sharp increase in freight rates. Nevertheless, issues remained.

These issues were largely port-specific and linked to the supply of containers (Goodman et al., 2021). In November 2020, for example, the container port of Felixstowe in the United Kingdom was congested due to imports of 11,000 containers of government-procured personal protection equipment that coincided with imports by retailers awaiting stock for Christmas in 2020 (Wood, 2020). By 2021 Felixstowe's large number of empty containers and stacks of long-stay containers were replicated at ports around the world, except in China, occasioning a marked increase in freight rates such as the fourfold increase between Asia and the United Kingdom (Ambrose, 2021). This condition has been generated by the recovery of China's economy with three full containers moving outbound for every full container arriving inbound.

The imbalance has prompted carriers to send containers back to China empty because the outbound rate to the United States, for example, has risen ten times the reverse leg. Also, container parks in Australian ports were at their capacity because containers were not released unless they were to be repositioned in China. This situation led to an assessment of Australia's supply chains, which reported only those handling imports of basic chemicals and some personal protective equipment, and exports of iron ore were particularly vulnerable (Australian Government, 2021). Nevertheless, the demand for agricultural produce from Australia to the rest of Asia was not being met and the shortage of containers also applied to exports of pulses from Canada, sugar from India and coffee and rice from Vietnam (Grain Brokers Australia, 2021).

Additionally, by June 2021, China's ports were congested with container ships waiting at anchor for an available berth to transport the country's marked increase in manufacturing output – a situation compounded by an outbreak of coronavirus among port workers first at the Port of Yantian in the Pearl River Delta and then at a container terminal at Ningbo-Zhoushan Port in the Yangtze Delta (Aljazeera, 2021; Paris and Xie, 2021). These lockdowns led to container ships being taken out of service and to a reduction in available container shipping capacity (Zlady, 2021). This situation is occurring at a time when changes in consumption patterns from services to goods in the United States are driving up demand for shipping and occasioning port congestion in Long Beach and Los Angeles (Remes and Saxon, 2021). The unpredictability of the global supply chain during the pandemic raises the issue of how businesses have reoriented their activities over time.

BUSINESS RESPONSE: REORIENTATION

The COVID-19 pandemic has seen a humanitarian crisis unfolding on a daily basis, as infections soar relentlessly like spot-fires ahead of a raging bush fire. With the recurrent imposition of snap lockdowns, mandatory physical distancing, reduction of non-essential operations and limited person-to-person contact, fundamental logistical and supply chain challenges have surfaced. How have businesses dependent on in-person interactions been able to reach customers and meet their expectations under these restrictions? How have businesses grappled with the challenge of reconfiguring their supply chains to cope with the simultaneous changes in consumer demand and uncertainties in supply in a physically constrained world?

Envisioning a new role for their operations considering these changes, many organizations have been directing their attention to gaining a deeper and real-time understanding of customer preferences. Others have responded both with speed and innovation, staging various near-term measures to safeguard lives, support work-from-home regimes and manage service expectations from both customers and business partners. Whether they have introduced radical changes to their operating procedures or executed specific surgical alterations to store formats and customer service protocols, these practical steps have formed the guiding principles for balancing near-term operational effectiveness and minimizing disruptions to customer experience.

Anecdotal evidence garnered from business responses show that the pandemic has given rise to three distinct responses. First, there were instances of the adoption of flexible manufacturing typified by Anheuser-Busch, the maker of Budweiser, and craft brewing distilleries switching from producing beer, gin, whisky and rum to meet the extraordinary demand for hand sanitizer (Levenson, 2020); the electronics giant Foxconn in Shenzhen, China, shifting part of its production from making the Apple iPhone products to manufacturing surgical masks (BBC, 2020b); and Ford, General Motors and Tesla Motors moving from producing automobiles to creating an array of medical personal protection equipment such as ventilators, respirators and face shields (Nerad, 2020). Second, there was a sustained launch of omnichannel initiatives by retailers during the pandemic that have involved: (1) maintaining sales through the strategy of 'buying-online and picking-up-in-store'; (2) meeting changing buying habits by seeking out fulfilment partners with multiple distribution points to reduce time in serving the consumer; and (3) providing multiple touch points to boost consumer loyalty (Seraphin, 2020). Third, logistics companies such as World Courier (2020) have instituted a host of contact-free procedures for pick-up and delivery in line with the seamless experience afforded by omnichannel retailing (Figure 5.8).

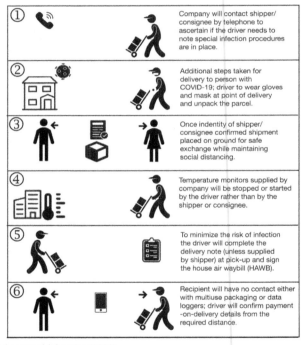

Source: Based on World Courier (2020).

Figure 5.8   *COVID-19: contact-free procedures for pick-up and deliveries*

In particular, the COVID-19 'black swan' event has created the perfect storm to test the efficacy of Big Data analytics in shedding insights on changes in consumption behaviour stemming from social distancing and quarantining. With the help of these analytics two major opportunities have arisen from the continuous collection of real-time data to gauge changes in consumption patterns and adapt marketing practices to meet the consumer's evolving needs (Sheng et al., 2020). First, the application of data mining and descriptive analytics has been used by Amazon to identify shifts in the market by distilling information on sales, inventories and market trends across retail categories and locations (Chaffey, 2021). Second, online channels have been used by brands such as IKEA, Knorr and Maggi during the pandemic to strengthen digital communications and interactions with consumers by employing social media to determine their emotional reactions (Hoekstra and Leeflang, 2020). This analytical process has been greatly enhanced through the application of artificial intelligence and machine learning to assess the effectiveness of advertising during the lockdown.

This deeper appreciation of consumption patterns has allowed companies to shift their focus from 'demand forecasting' to 'demand sensing', which has been promoted through YouTube (see, for example, SAP, 2019). Although the accuracy of calculating consumer requirements based on historical data has been improved by more advanced analytics, the resulting lagged monthly forecast falls short of detecting the 'true demand' of consumers for individualized and customized products (Kalaria, 2019). Given the availability of real-time point-of-sale data provided by Big Data analytics, including economic indicators, social sentiment and weather, it is possible to 'sense' true demand (Tany, 2018). Not only has the demand-sensing discovery process, derived from all e-commerce channels, helped companies such as Nestlé, the world's largest food manufacturer, to comprehend optimized daily forecasts of consumer needs and wants, but it has also shaped them by knowing what factors influence purchasing (SAS, 2019). The COVID-19 pandemic has shown that putting the consumer at the centre of the supply chain has helped companies to harvest the necessary data on buying habits, price points and product features to sharpen 'demand-driven planning' to help mitigate the volatile market conditions brought about by the uncertainties of border closures, lockdowns and other occasional regulations mandating physical restraints.

Demand sensing, in turn, has given rise to the exploration of new delivery methods within the consumer-centric supply chain that, in turn, can disrupt the logistics industry's cost structures, economic models and operating systems. Their number has included fully autonomous vehicles, which, despite gaining ground in the United States to accommodate the increase in purchases from the home, are regarded as being at a nascent stage of development (Chottani et al., 2018). Nevertheless, they would have been helpful during the pandemic by being able to operate effectively 24/7 in overcoming the shortage of drivers and shortfall of commodities due to panic buying (Research and Markets, 2020). Greater attention has been paid during the pandemic to drones to provide contactless delivery of food, as typified by a study in South Korea, which identified a propensity among the sample population to pay more for the service rather than risk infection by eating out (Hwang et al., 2020). Also, there has been an attempt in hospitals in both Haifa, Israel and New Jersey, United States during the first few months of the pandemic to minimize the necessity of distributing personal protective equipment over great distances by resorting to 3D printing for these essential goods such as an Air-Shade system for healthcare workers (Sterman et al., 2020). While companies in Europe and North America sought new delivery methods at a time when their countries had closed borders, issued self-containment advisories and banned public gatherings, the British Broadcasting Corporation (BBC, 2020c) reported that China had lifted its near total lockdown, factories had restarted, offices had reopened and, albeit tentatively at first, consumers had ventured outdoors and returned to stores.

In April 2020, McKinsey & Company orchestrated a virtual roundtable discussion to distil lessons from the initiatives that leaders of China's consumer and retail companies had introduced during the early phase of uncertainty following the outbreak of COVID-19 (Huang et al., 2020). A select group of executives drawn from the Budweiser Brewing Company, the Erdos Group, Lawson (China) Holdings, LVMH Perfumes and Cosmetics, Starbucks China and Wumart & Dmall were asked to designate: (1) their chief difficulties experienced in recovering from the lockdown; (2) their most successful measures that mitigated human and economic effects caused by the virus; and (3) how their operational emphasis had shifted during the pandemic. The three key takeaways from this discussion were the need to accelerate digitization, adopt flexible working policies and espouse creative marketing strategies.

Through April 2020 COVID-19 had changed circumstances not only in China but across the world (Callaghan et al., 2020). Consumers had become accustomed to staying home for weeks at a time and buying a wider range of products online. Store visits had slowed to a trickle, moving from being the norm to becoming the exception. Physical distancing and stay-at-home mandates compelled retailers, large and small, to launch omnichannel initiatives. Even mom-and-pop stores developed their own websites and mobile apps for online orders and offered contactless kerbside pick-up.

By the end of April 2020 these developments highlighted that retailers could not expect a seamless return to pre-coronavirus store operation norms. This situation has led to reimagining how business could be reoriented under the 'next normal'. Three key tasks were recognized by Praveen Adhi and others (2020),

Table 5.2   *Tasks for the 'next normal toolbox'*

1. Redefine the role of the store
Offer omnichannel fulfilment basics
Build an omnichannel staff
Enable personalization of in-store touch points
2. Reset cost structure
Shift complexity upstream
Rapidly digitize and automate non-value-added work
Improve omnichannel touch points
Introduce contactless self-service features for omnichannel transactions
3. Prepare workforce for the 'next normal'
Retain pre-COVID-19 talent
Improve training and onboarding
When rebuilding store teams, rethink workforce composition
Improve workplace flexibility

Source: Adhi et al. (2020).

which identified and elaborated the need to redefine the role of stores, reset their cost structures and prepare the workforce for the next normal (Table 5.2).

According to Praveen Adhi and others (2020), this focus needs to be buttressed by accommodating and streamlining the rising consumer demand for contactless options such as 'buy online and pick up in-store', and 'kerbside pick-up'. Also, an omnichannel staff needs to be built to guide consumers through their product discovery and post-purchase system that rewards them for increased online sales. By accessing online and offline data on loyalty and purchasing behaviour across channels, this process should, in turn, enable the 'personalization' of in-store touch points to offer the consumer an individualized service experience.

The redefinition of stores needs to be supported by changes to the retailing cost structure to reflect reduced post-crisis sales and store traffic (Desai and Mani, 2020). Costs will have to be reallocated and operations simplified to deliver a 20 to 30 per cent improvement in productivity to compensate for the shift away from physical stores and increasing volume of in-store omnichannel activities (Adhi et al., 2020). These factors have been demonstrated in the demise of high street retailers such as Arcadia and Debenhams in the United Kingdom that had a combined total of 500 shops (Guardian, 2021). Besides resetting store replenishment frequency and minimum stock levels, Praveen Adhi and others (2020) detail that the strategy must be underpinned by overcoming a reduction in post-crisis staffing levels, including lessening the complexity of store operations upstream and moving tasks such as price tagging and labelling to distribution centres or, where possible, vendor locations. Non-value-added in- and out-of- store work such as scheduling labour, self- and mobile checkouts and contacting managers and remote field officers should be digitized and automated. All of these supply chain recommendations require them to be underpinned by improved omnichannel touch points to reduce the cost of end-to-end orders by redesigning 'buy online pick up in-store' and improving inventory management. The last cost-saving option is to consider extending contactless self-serve features for omnichannel transactions to online order pick-ups, price checks and digitizing the process of managing returns.

The third task has been to prepare the workforce for the next normal following the pandemic's disruption of the retail workforce. A survey of apparel and specialty retail executives in the United States by Praveen Adhi and others (2020) during April 2020 reported that three-quarters of their staff had been furloughed or laid off since the onset of the pandemic, suggesting that their future workforce not only has to support the store's evolving role but also to flexibly accommodate any recurring virus-related disruptions. The risk of losing their pre-COVID-19 talent under these circumstances has led these respondents to give furloughed staff priority in filling new omnichannel roles ahead of any reopening of their physical stores and keeping these staff abreast of plans through one-on-one check-ins and online publications. These responding executives also mentioned that, in the interim period, they had introduced digital learning tools covering sales effectiveness, visual merchandising and price and promotion initiatives to improve training, retention and onboarding (i.e. organizational socialization for newcomers). A lasting effect of the pandemic in rebuilding a store team and rethinking workforce composition has been that both digital fluency and an ability to fulfil a range of roles have become prized attributes to be derived from the upskilling process. As further virus-related disruptions are a real possibility, businesses have placed a premium upon improving workforce flexibility by considering employee mobility across stores and incorporating gig workers.

Elaboration of these three tasks suggests that executing a digital strategy necessitates lifting product or service quality above the minimum level to meet consumer expectations (Nicola, 2019). During COVID-19 omnichannel integration has joined digitization as their minimum offering for consumers. Any forward-looking plan on the reopening of retailing during and after the pandemic will have to be centred, according to Praveen Adhi and others (2020), upon optimizing store network based on an omnichannel perspective, especially for apparel and specialty goods. This strategy has shifted the focus from the traditional emphasis on the economics of the four-walled store to generating e-commerce sales in the retailer's revamped profit and loss statement. Although the outcome has accelerated closures for loss-making outlets, and intensified rent negotiations and rationalized the footprints of essential but underperforming stores, it has provided the opportunity to add stores and distribution centres to underserviced areas. This strategy will enable retailers and their workforce to thrive in the 'next normal' provided that the process is accompanied by supply chain stabilization.

At the outset of the pandemic supply chain management was concerned about maintaining inventory levels in areas experiencing community transmission (Mysore and Usher, 2020). Once companies restarted operations in China and the rest of the world, the supply chain's emphasis shifted to the importance of gaining priority status from suppliers, pre-booking logistics capacity in air, rail and sea transport and rationing supply (McKinsey & Company, 2020: 65). This agenda led to greater attention being paid in the supply chain to identifying new suppliers, optimizing the network and updating demand management.

In April 2020, some months into the pandemic, Manik Aryapadi and others (2020a) identified five sets of obligatory and discretionary actions to help retailers deal with operators at each stage of the supply chain during COVID-19: supply, merchandising, distribution, logistics and fulfilment (Figure 5.9). Their five sets of actions have placed emphasis on securing demand, redirecting inventory in merchandising operations, adding capacity safely to distribution activities, balancing agility and flexibility in logistics and delivering fulfilment reliably.

In pursuing these strategies at each stage of the supply chain, the need for a redesignated supply chain team was recognized by Mysore and Usher (2020), who proposed that the team be led by the head of procurement and supported by a procurement manager, a supply chain analyst, regional supply chain managers and a logistics manager. Their fourfold agenda was designed to: (1) ensure risk transparency across tier 1, 2 and 3 suppliers by supporting supplier restarts, managing orders and checking new supplier qualifications; (2) manage ports, pre-book logistics capacity and optimize routes; (3) identify and rationalize critical parts and optimize locations; and (4) develop scenario-based sales and planning for operations, production and sourcing. These desiderata, according to Mysore and Usher (2020), were designed to promote the continuation of supply chain resilience once the pandemic was over.

By July 2020 Knut Alicke and others (2020) had linked digitization to resilience as the twin concepts involved in resetting and transforming supply chains for the 'next normal'. After recognizing the previous observations on the pandemic's trajectory, they have identified five emerging post-COVID trends likely to transform supply chains in the 'next normal'. According to Knut Alicke and others (2020), these trends warrant that companies: (1) inject a more agile response to attract government resources for a centralized approach towards meeting critical requirements; (2) create management functions devoted to addressing unidentified supply chain risks or indifference to

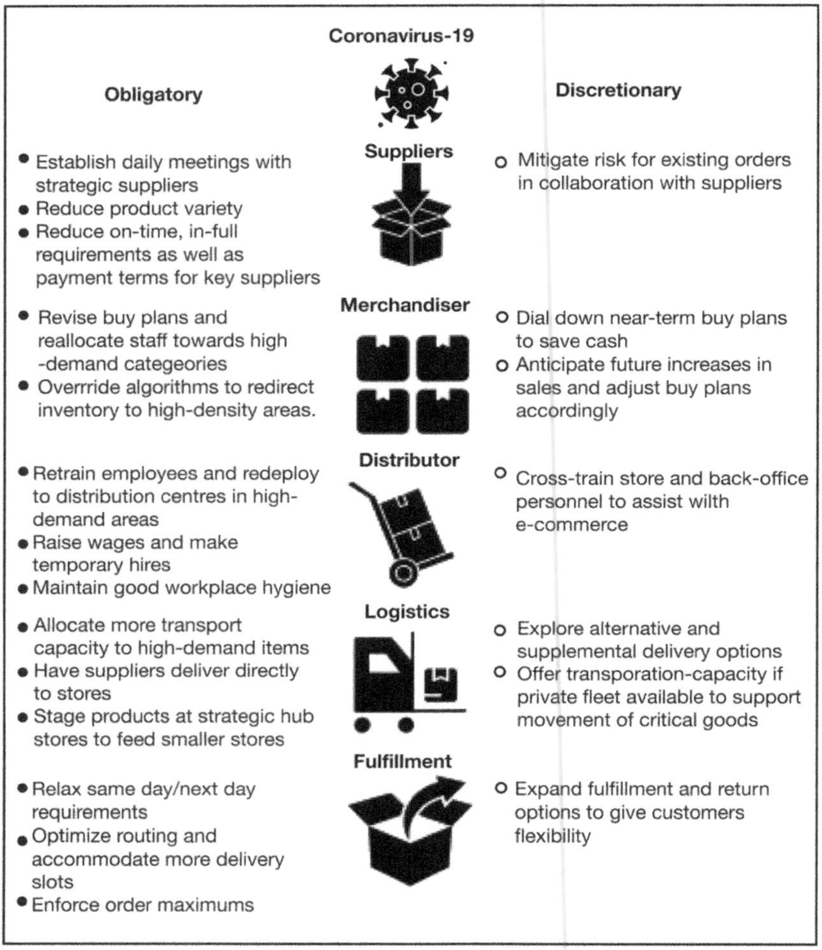

Coronavirus-19

Obligatory	Suppliers	Discretionary

Suppliers

Obligatory
- Establish daily meetings with strategic suppliers
- Reduce product variety
- Reduce on-time, in-full requirements as well as payment terms for key suppliers

Discretionary
- o Mitigate risk for existing orders in collaboration with suppliers

Merchandiser

- Revise buy plans and reallocate staff towards high-demand categeories
- Overrride algorithms to redirect inventory to high-density areas.

- o Dial down near-term buy plans to save cash
- o Anticipate future increases in sales and adjust buy plans accordingly

Distributor

- Retrain employees and redeploy to distribution centres in high-demand areas
- Raise wages and make temporary hires
- Maintain good workplace hygiene

- o Cross-train store and back-office personnel to assist wilth e-commerce

Logistics

- Allocate more transport capacity to high-demand items
- Have suppliers deliver directly to stores
- Stage products at strategic hub stores to feed smaller stores

- o Explore alternative and supplemental delivery options
- o Offer transporation-capacity if private fleet available to support movement of critical goods

Fulfillment

- Relax same day/next day requirements
- Optimize routing and accommodate more delivery slots
- Enforce order maximums

- o Expand fulfillment and return options to give customers flexibility

Source: Information from Aryapadi et al. (2020a).

Figure 5.9   Obligatory and discretionary options available to assist retailers in meeting customer demand during the COVID-19 pandemic

them; (3) shift the distribution network closer to the end consumer to counter supply chain disruptions and the unavailability of essential commodities; (4) focus on building capabilities to capitalize on the shift to online purchasing for essential commodities and remote working by adopting automation, end-to-end planning and a service centre network; and (5) fast-track sustainability to exploit the environmental benefits stemming from lower economic activity levels during lockdowns and accelerating the demise of dispensable contaminated activities. Such trends raise Richard Hogg's (2020) concern regarding the extent to which technology could offer a cure for future global supply chain disruption.

THE TECHNOLOGY FACTOR: THE HYPE AND THE REALITY

COVID-19 has prompted a reassessment of the technology factor elaborated in Chapter 4, especially the pre-pandemic hype versus reality assessments involving emerging technologies such as artificial intelligence, augmented reality, Big Data analytics, blockchain and the Internet of Things and the willingness of management to adopt them to transform their operations (Tran, 2018).

Some clues as to what could have materialized during a pandemic can be derived from revisiting the study done by Venkat Atluri and others (2018) prior to the pandemic. Their study of tech-enabled transformation drew upon the knowledge collaboration forged between McKinsey and the World Economic Forum in 2018, which established a global lighthouse network identifying a select group of companies that had adopted Industry 4.0 technologies (Leurent et al., 2018). Authors of the study argued that extracting full value from the application of digital and advanced analytic technologies such as collaborative robots, self-driving vehicles and virtual reality promised a trillion dollar opportunity for such companies within the aviation/defence, automotive groups, broader industrials and semi-conductors and other mobility industry segments (Atluri et al., 2020). Companies within these industry groups that had not gone beyond undertaking a series of digital pilots before the pandemic, due to concerns over cost and impact, had become trapped in what Sungeon Song (2019) has referred to as 'pilot purgatory'.

At the onset of the pandemic, Deloitte (2020), a global consultancy services company, assessed the degree to which individual industries were likely to be affected. Besides bringing multiple technologies into play the global manufacturing sites identified by McKinsey and the World Economic Forum had reportedly prospered by empowering their workforces and achieving environmental satisfaction without sacrificing cost (George and de Boer, 2020).

When the pandemic intensified Francisco Betti and others (2020) stated that the cutting-edge organizations in the McKinsey-World Economic Forum global lighthouse network had widened the gap with other companies in managing the unprecedented disruption. The 54 lighthouse firms had been split into two groups: (1) four-walled factories epitomized by Tata Steel in India

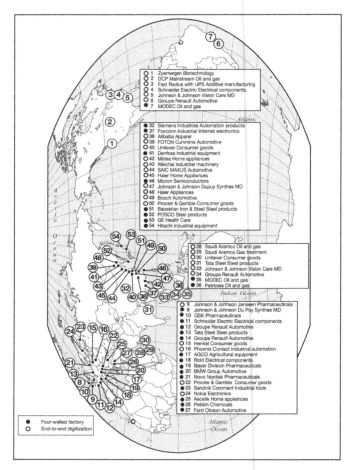

Note: MD – medical devices. Twenty sites were in Europe, 19 in East Asia, eight in the Middle East, Asia and Southeast Asia and seven in the Americas. The automotive category had eight sites followed by pharmaceuticals with seven and oil and gas six. Among individual firms Johnson & Johnson had five sites and Groupe Renault four.
Source: Information derived from Betti et al. (2020).

Figure 5.10   The global lighthouse network, 17 June 2020

and (2) end-to-end digitization across the value chain typified by the consumer goods producer Henkel located in Dusseldorf, Germany (Figure 5.10). Lessons distilled from these two groups of advanced manufacturing firms during the pandemic have identified the need for: (1) improving agility and customer

Table 5.3   *Key topics, tasks and Internet of Things tools for negotiating COVID-19*

Topic	Tasks	Tools provided by Industrial Internet of Things
Safeguarding operations	Ensuring employee safety and security, improving liquidity and lowering short-term costs	Plug-and-play sensors to ensure business continuity and minimize economic damage
Navigating the pandemic	Workforce tracing and monitoring to ensure employees and customers are safe distancing	Wearable trackers for staff to log contacts during shift
	Predictive maintenance with fewer people on the shop floor to fix things before they break	Advanced analytics to predict when machines will fail using past data to reduce cost and increase efficiency
Improving efficiency	Curbing waste	Use tools to monitor equipment and processes, and set thresholds and alarms remotely
	Working remotely	Data analysis and vision-based control systems to gauge state of assets in buildings and factories
	Cost structure	Shortage of workforce overcome by remote access and remote management with automation

Source: Information derived from Rosencrance (2021).

centricity across end-to-end manufacturing and supply chains; (2) increasing supply chain resilience by connecting and reconfiguring the multitiered digital ecosystem; (3) deriving greater speed and productivity from automation and workforce upskilling; and (4) boosting eco-efficiency to address increased regulatory complexity. These lessons prompted Aamer Baig and others (2020: 1) to reflect that during COVID-19 'we have vaulted five years forward in consumer and business digital adoption in a matter of around eight weeks'.

During the pandemic an array of technologies have been recommended as solutions to business reorganization or the supply chain reconfiguration process. Among them, Andreas Behrendt and others (2021) have singled out the Internet of Things for detailed attention rather than artificial intelligence and machine learning. This proposition has been taken a stage further by Stefan Fahrni and others (2020), who have outlined the roles the Industrial Internet of Things has played, along with Big Data analytics, in contributing to innovations by business during the early stages of the COVID-19 pandemic. These have ranged from the immediate issue of safeguarding operations, through short-term issues of connectivity and cyber security, to looking ahead to integration across the supply chain and in-line process optimization. As reflected in Table 5.3, these findings were incorporated in an overview by Linda Rosencrance (2021), which pinpointed the role played during COVID-19 by

Industrial Internet of Things tools in safeguarding operations, navigating the pandemic and improving efficiency.

HUMAN TOUCH: SAFETY AND CUSTOMER CARE

An abiding lesson to be drawn from navigating successfully through the COVID-19 disruptions has underlined the importance of 'customer engagement'. Integrating customers into innovation processes had been advanced prior to the pandemic to create user-related knowledge to better target future consumers (Höber and Schaarschmidt, 2017; Buesing et al., 2018). This activity had been coupled with the emergence of 'solution selling', as a means through which service firms provide solutions that fulfil the demands of a known customer. Before attempting to transition to this 'service-to-solutions' approach, drawbacks have had to be overcome in acclimatizing large numbers of consumers to virtual interaction. Also, there have been a series of imperatives for a customer care organization to address in analysing consumer sentiments. These imperatives have involved company leaders embracing new ways of working, particularly in advancing together with consumers – not to support purchases, but in connecting operations with savings prospects for both provider and consumer. Nevertheless, prior to the pandemic there was little interest in developing high-touch strategies to support the customer's journey.

Once the pandemic struck and forced consumers online, the concept of a 'service-to-solutions' approach was rapidly adopted to accommodate working from home. As reflected in a second contribution by Manik Aryapadi and others (2020b), companies switched from optimizing activities within a single channel to recognizing the importance of customer care channels in generating value from omnichannel engagement across all touch points. Exemplified by Apple's Genius Bars, same-day delivery and analytics-generated recommendations of products and services extending across physical and online channels, customers have come to expect personalized service from contact centres. Increasingly, customers are comfortable with service, technical and even financial advice being provided remotely. They expect the provider to offer more powerful online solutions on a 24/7 basis that are on a par with physical channels. In short, consumers expect a consultative approach that recognizes their needs and enables the tailoring of bespoke solutions to enhance their experiences. Companies adopting this consultative approach have moved their consumer care from a cost centre to a profit centre, because this approach has not only boosted customer lifetime value but also has increased consumption of both existing and new services.

Adoption of customer engagement, derived from investing in core customer segments and their needs, has enabled companies to steer their way through the

Table 5.4   *Five pitfalls hindering the achievement of effectiveness in*
                  pursuing a service-to-solution approach and six imperatives
                  for customer care organizations during the pandemic

Pitfalls
A focus upon efficiency at the expense of effectiveness
A one-size-fits-all mentality
A siloed view of the customer
Sales at all costs
Insufficient training for agents
Imperatives
Continue to shape customer expectations
Reinforce culture and connections with employees
Establish and maintain COVID-19 safe room
Scale an effective remote-working model
Aggressively expand the adoption of digital self-service approaches
Ramp up workforce flexibility

Source: Berg et al. (2020).

pandemic, as instanced by the dramatic shift to online shopping and ordering in Australia, China, Europe, the United States and many other countries (Mysore and Usher, 2020; WTC, 2021). This has given rise in many multinational corporations such as Hitachi (2021) to the inception of a customer engagement marketing team comprising the head of sales and marketing (team leader), a financial analyst and managers for customer communications, customer incentives and stock-keeping units. The team's designated task has been to communicate to business-to-business customers through a dedicated site and develop scenario-based risk communications (Briglia, 2020). Also, the team's responsibility has been to intervene, as required, across the customer journey, train customer-facing employees, monitor customer service execution, prevent leakage and to develop customer communications and reports about COVID-19 issues, practices and situations. Nevertheless, there are barriers to be overcome before such teams' effectiveness in customer engagement can be proven within a service-to-solutions approach.

Jeff Berg and others (2020) have highlighted five pitfalls for companies pursuing a service-to-solutions approach (Table 5.4). One pitfall has been the reluctance of companies to leave their past preoccupation with 'efficiency', embodied in average handling times, key performance indicators and service-level agreements, to focus upon 'effectiveness' derived from engaging with customers and growing by satisfying their needs. A second pitfall has been the continued adherence to a wholesale approach embodied in a one-size-fits-all mentality of pushing items regardless of their suitability of an individual consumer's particular needs. The third pitfall is to regard customer relationship management and service as separate items in a siloed approach rather than incorporating them in a complete view of the individual consumer's journey as the basis of customer care. A fourth pitfall has stemmed from ethical lapses in a sales-at-all-costs approach without any embodiment of a compliance standpoint and risk mitigation. The fifth, and final, pitfall is an underinvestment in training frontline staff, which has failed to attune them to the need to have meaningful conversations with consumers as the basis for accelerating company growth. The authors argue that addressing them could help organizations prepare for the new frontier in service to solutions.

As indicated by Jeff Berg and others (2020), when transitioning to a service-to-solutions approach three items are of paramount concern: frontline management skills, customers and technology offers. The managerial skills need to be focused on deriving solutions from orchestrating relations with consumers across the array of service channels through agents operating ethically and with integrity. Then a complementary emphasis on greater personalization in business-to-consumer sales is required to provide solutions that meet specific consumer needs, with feedback to ensure that the offers in the care channel not only meet expectations but also provide an opportunity for targeted marketing. Finally, attention must be paid to technologies that have enhanced frontline capabilities through harnessing consumer relations systems and tools typified by Cogito's (2020) consumer intelligence software. This provides agents with live sentiment analysis and clues on how to interact with customers in offering sales or new solutions. Thus, the adoption of a service-to-solutions approach has warranted a marked strategic shift.

Also, Jeff Berg and others (2020) have identified no less than six imperatives for customer care organizations to follow during the COVID-19 pandemic to ensure the safety of staff and social distancing arrangements (Table 5.4). First, there has been a need for leadership to use personal messages to provide information on pertinent issues such as finance and the availability of emergency payments as a means to continually shape consumer expectations. Second, more time has had to be spent on in-person activities to strengthen corporate culture through connections with employees using posters, team events and visits from senior management, adding flexibility to work schedules and incorporating a more empathetic approach to sick leave. Third, there has been a need to create and maintain a coordinated COVID-19 room within the customer care organization as an agile and responsive crisis nerve centre to support decision-making during the pandemic. Fourth, the evaporation of the on-site or local workforce has prompted the customer care organization to scale up a remote-working initiative that draws upon analytics and key performance indicators to gauge the effectiveness of working from home when one in five have reported poor Internet connectivity and disruptions from children and pets. Fifth, the pandemic has prompted the aggressive expansion of more user-friendly, digital self-service approaches that have advised customers of long wait times, call-back options and alternative do-it-yourself channels operated by upskilled workforces and supported by community forums on social media capable of resolving pressing issues. Finally, workforce flexibility has been increased to accommodate disruptions during the pandemic by adjusting the balance between full- and part-time workers, and between on-site and home workers to manage channels and phone calls; these adjustments have been difficult to accommodate in large business processing operations, especially those lacking infrastructures in remote locations offshore to ensure the supply chain can function.

According to Jeff Berg and others (2020), business continuity planning has had to become more frequent and rigorous to cope with any recurrent or seasonal COVID-19 outbreaks, shifts by consumers to digital channels, fewer but more complex calls and variations in technology and talent required to operate remote-working sites. Companies have had to adopt a true test-and-learn mentality during the pandemic to develop and effect changes quickly to accommodate the sense of urgency in customer needs and information by keeping channels open for dialogue. Investments have had to target people, processes and policy to provide better agent support, self-service, employee engagement and near-term automation of simple tasks using web forms, chatbots and interactive voice response updates, leaving complex process automation for the longer term. In particular, customer care organizations have had to invest in speech or text analytics to segment callers to handle the increased traffic occasioned by the pandemic and gauge the quality of the remote workforce.

By May 2020 Kevin Sneader and Shubham Singhal (2020) were ready to map out four key elements to make the 'next normal' work: (1) from just-in-time to a just-in-time and just-in-case supply chain; (2) from making trade-offs to embedding sustainability; (3) from online commerce to a contact-free economy; and (4) from simply 'returning' to 'returning and reimagining'.

The first transition will involve companies redesigning their vulnerable supply chains to add resilience and efficiency into their end-to-end value optimization and accelerating 'next shoring' by employing advanced technologies such as additive manufacturing and robotics to relocate activities closer to customers. The latter process has been reflected in Japanese auto makers and Korean electronics firms shifting the sourcing of parts from China to domestic locations. The second transition will involve companies reassessing their insurance premiums because not only did the pandemic shut down meat production in Australia and the United States, but also floods, sea-level changes and wildfires have put global supply chains at increased risk (Fink, 2020). The third transition from a personal to a remote, contact-free online relationship was accelerated during the pandemic in banking, construction, education, healthcare and manufacturing activities but, while there may be some reversals to the pre-pandemic situation, the 'digital transition' has become a reality underlining the future importance of the Internet of Things going forward. The fourth transition will require companies to go beyond their pre-pandemic activities by reimagining their businesses in the 'next normal' by adopting a speedy step-by-step recovery to hasten the adoption of digital solutions to accommodate remote work in offices and reconfigure production lines and processes in manufacturing. Collectively, the realization of these four transitions is expected to offer benefits to adopters in productivity, quality and end-to-end connectivity.

By February 2021 Starbucks was one of the companies that had addressed these four transitions in its global supply chain architecture, underpinned at each stage by a system of recording, reporting and analytics and collaboration. The company's supply chain was designed to cater for more than 100 million customers weekly in almost 33,000 stores offering coffee and tea, and food within over 83 markets around the world. Nevertheless, most attention was focused on 13 countries and the composite Latin American region contributing almost 90 per cent of 32,660 stores in September 2020 (Figure 5.11). The United States alone provided 47 per cent and China a further 14 per cent of these stores – the latter phenomenon being attributed to the company's finely attuned adaptation to Chinese culture (Lukashevich, 2020). However, at the beginning of the pandemic end-to-end connectivity in Starbucks' global supply chain network was marred by service alerts such as information asymmetry, delayed updates, unstructured data and decentralized information (Eberts et al., 2021).

In response to this situation attention was paid to Starbucks' deployment strategy and its tenets by adopting a change management strategy employing a data-driven approach to target user groups. When things have not gone according to plan an incident management platform has been developed to address these exceptions by seeking to unlock operational value through collaboration and insights into the causes of the value stream bottlenecks. Through this process Starbucks has reason to believe that the company has been able to streamline communications across the organization, break down functional silos, produce powerful insights and business intelligence and standardize process inputs and outputs to eliminate gaps (Eberts et al., 2021). The end-to-end journey has been marked by enterprise visibility, real-time updates, testable insights and a single source of truth, which ensures everyone within an organization bases a business decision upon the same data. Nevertheless, the incident management platform is still being tested because the easing of the COVID-19 situation in the United States has boosted Starbucks' sales and, as reported by Heather Haddon (2021), this has led to a shortage of key ingredients such as cups and syrup.

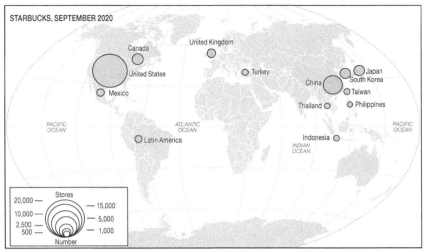

Note: No distinction is made between corporate and licensed stores.
Source: Based on information from Statista (2021b).

Figure 5.11   *Selected countries with the largest number of Starbucks stores worldwide, September 2020*

The Starbucks case study illustrates that companies have obtained an end-to-end customer view. They have drawn upon information from social media to empower employees during the pandemic and once it is over. These employees have been provided with training and support to use this wealth of information on both successes and failures to enable them to provide a higher level of customer care. This has involved paying attention to an array of home delivery options and contactless operations to accommodate the shift to working from home.

CONCLUSION

This chapter has compiled important findings about the race to meet changes in consumption on demand by drawing upon a series of core concepts from operational changes occurring since the unanticipated arrival of COVID-19 (Figure 5.12). The need to focus upon the entire end-to-end consumer journey has led to the incorporation of information on initial contact, purchases, touch points and pain points in responding to demand shifts occasioned by the COVID-19 pandemic. These shifts have disrupted the supply chain and highlighted the importance of 'transilience' in addressing unpredictability. The business response to this situation has focused upon the omnichannel environ-

Topic		Theme	Concepts
	**Demand shift**	The consumption that matters	Initial contact, purchases, touch points, pain points
	**Supply chain**	Unpredictability	Transilience
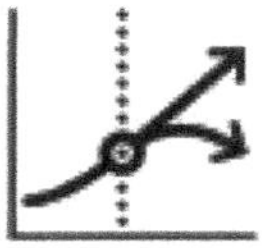	**Business response**	Reorientation	Omnichannel environment (drawing upon digitization)
	**Technology factor**	Hype and reality	Internet of Things Big Data Demand sensing
	**Human touch**	Customer safety and care	Customer engagement Service to solution approach

Figure 5.12   Summary of the findings of Chapter 5

ment, which has enabled companies to draw upon digitization to complement transilience by developing a detailed view of the consumer to inform seamless and consistent customer interactions. Tech-enabled advances – embodying more reality and less hype – have stressed the importance of the Internet of Things in enabling the better integration of managing customer relationships by drawing upon demand sensing. The importance of injecting a much needed human touch by responding to the need for safety and care embodied in both staff and consumer engagement will boost consumer satisfaction. Also, a service-to-solutions approach not only addresses these immediate concerns but, as outlined by Rachel Diebner and others (2020), provides a pathway to reimagining a post-COVID-19 future.

Already, Alibaba, Jingdong and many more e-commerce companies have developed a 'revolutionary' reimagining of the likely post-COVID retail landscape. Alibaba's high-tech grocery chain, Freshippo (2021), for instance, has provided new retail infrastructure to handle fresh produce, meats and seafood. The supermarket uses the Alibaba logistics system to draw products from around the world. Cherries from Washington state in the United States can be picked from the tree and delivered in-store within 48 hours. Shoppers can shop either in the traditional way or by using the Freshippo app. Also, the supermarket doubles as a fulfilment centre and offers delivery in 30 minutes within a 3 km radius. New formats for different customers include both Freshippo Mini for price-sensitive customers and a kiosk offering pick-and-go breakfasts for office workers. This changing retail landscape highlights the importance of customer connectivity discussed in Chapter 6.

6. Consumer connectivity: forging supply chain success in the digital ecosystem

The previous five chapters have demonstrated that supply chain configurations have been evolving in tune with changes in production technologies, competition and consumption patterns. COVID-19's unanticipated arrival has further accentuated the criticality of consumption, arm-twisting supply chain entities to adapt to real-time changes in consumption patterns. Supply chains, the gold standard of which used to be demand responsiveness, have had to shift gear to become demand sensitive in order to keep businesses afloat. Businesses, which have either embraced e-commerce prior to the pandemic or were quick to make the shift to trade online at the onset of COVID-19, appear to have negotiated the restrictions imposed almost unscathed, due primarily to their ability to connect digitally with consumers. Further, businesses capable of harnessing the prowess of Industry 4.0 technologies to transition from a service to a solution approach by working collaboratively with their customers also recorded both cost savings and market growth.

This chapter extends this observation by focusing upon a series of pertinent issues critical to supply chain success within a digital ecosystem. How can digital connectivity help supply chains gain competitive advantage? Why is consumer connectivity the lynchpin of supply chain success under the Industry 4.0 ecosystem? How are the digital ecosystems of Supply Chain 4.0 best poised to amass power? And why is Supply Chain 4.0 so different from the supply chains of previous eras?

These issues are addressed initially by identifying the pull factors transforming consumer connectivity into the new frontier of competitiveness. Then the hub of consumer connectivity is investigated because it has been at the core of supply chain operations during the COVID-19 pandemic. This leads to the contention that digital ecosystems of Supply Chain 4.0 powered by mobile apps are best poised to amass power. Finally, Supply Chain 4.0's critical differences from earlier manifestations are related through a study of network theory, which joins together production and consumption into the single entity of *productribution* made possible by Industry 4.0 technologies. This entity is relevant to both the nature of links between consumers and product suppliers, and the reconfiguration of knowledge, wealth and power discussed in a concluding comment.

TRANSFORMING CONSUMER CONNECTIVITY

Better connections with consumers and their external partners, according to Darl Kolb and others (2020: 1589), deliver higher value for companies. The full range of technologies and specific social effects involved in this process stem from the combined interactions of four waves of connectivity: globalization, socialization, personalization and datafication (Figure 6.1). Each wave does not precede the next precisely, but the waves rise and fall contemporaneously. Within this digital ecosystem connectivity with the consumer is seen as the next frontier of supply chain competitiveness through its focus on customer behaviour (Kaas et al., 2015; Kelly, 2020). Attention has been centred,

Waves	1. Globalization	2. Socialization	3. Personalization	4. Datafication
	1960s—	Early 2000s—	Late 2000s—	Early 2010s—
Technology	• Personal computer • Mobile phones • Internet • World Wide Web	• Rise of social media platforms, (e.g. Facebook, Myspace, WeChat). • Users become co-creators (e.g. Instagram, TikTok, YouTube). • Social media (e.g. Face Time, Skype, Teams, Zoom).	• Smart phone • Mobile 'apps'.	• Artificial intelligence • Robotics
Social effects	• Condensed geography but still constrained by time zone differences. • Reduced challenge of staying connected with customers and employees • Inclusion in global sphere may marginalize workers (e.g. women)	• Digital tools have enhanced socialization • Enacted agency of actors to unlock capabilities and, power within digital environments to create spaces for individuals and communities.	• Intensely personal but brings with it involvement in professional life. • Enable data to be transmitted from individuals to connections, GPS, networks and organizations to create a double of the individual.	• Enables gathering, storage and analysis of data on customers and employees. • Sharing and selling data. • Application of business analytics and algorithms.

Note: 'Datafication refers to the process by which subjects, objects, and practices are transformed into digital data' (Somerton, 2020: 1).
Source: Based on information in Kolb et al. (2020).

Figure 6.1   *The four waves of connectivity*

therefore, upon the benefits to be derived from competing for the connected customer.

Already, an extensive survey of car consumers across Asia, Europe and North America by Dominik Wee and others (2015) has shown that the proportion of car consumers willing to switch from a car manufacturer offering no apps, data and media to another that could provide them had increased from 20 per cent in 2014 to 37 per cent in 2015. Over the same period the share of consumers willing to use a subscription model to pay for car-connected services had increased less markedly from 21 per cent to 32 per cent. These results have led to the development of new business models.

Since these earlier findings on 'connected customers' interest has been centred upon technologies that are striding forward to advance connectivity. As illustrated by the retail sector, companies embracing consumer connectivity as their strategy for growth will accrue economic value. The most promising opportunities to reap these rewards lie in capturing relevant data with a high degree of reliability and security and analysing them in real time (Ota et al., 2017). Such advances are key to an industry that needs to provide the kind of convenience and personalized shopping experience e-commerce customers have come to expect.

A study by Claus Gerckens and others (2020), on behalf of the McKinsey Global Institute and the McKinsey Center for Advanced Connectivity, has suggested that the large-scale implementation of advanced connectivity in retail will realize between US$420 billion and US$700 billion in new gross domestic product value by 2030. Also, the authors explored three main contributors to this total – end-to-end product visibility, frictionless in-store experience and enhanced personalization – to gauge the potential values at stake within each arena.

End-to-end product visibility will contribute between US$100 billion and US$160 billion in cost savings and additional revenues between US$60 billion and US$100 billion (Gerckens et al., 2020). These values, stemming from better visibility across the supply chain, will be derived from computer vision, use of trackers, active radio frequency identification, weight sensors and other technologies, which will help retailers manage their inventories more successfully at a product level. This should improve warehouse operations, reduce stock-outs and generate valuable customer data.

Frictionless in-store experience will reduce costs by a further US$150 billion to US$250 billion (Gerckens et al., 2020). These reduced costs will stem from the deployment of artificial intelligence and geofencing (i.e. location-based targeting), which will direct shoppers within a certain vicinity to desired products by remembering their preferences. Augmented reality will help shoppers see exactly how a product performs. Also, checkout will be eliminated using artificial intelligence, machine learning, payment beacons, radio frequency identification scanners and trackers by allowing consumers to pay for merchandise in-store as easily as they do online.

Enhanced personalization will add between US$230 billion to US$400 billion in revenue (Gerckens et al., 2020). Although fewer than 10 per cent of retailers were reported to be using digital strategies to personalize their customers' shopping experience, those that do increase sales by 15 to 20 per cent. Not only can algorithms use data collected across channels to deliver personalized promotions in real time, but also artificial intelligence can give sales associates customer insights to make highly targeted product recommendations.

Nevertheless, not all retail players are positioned to benefit equally from these developments. This has led Claus Gerckens and others (2020) to stratify retailers into three groups: (1) the online players able to incorporate cutting-edge technologies, segment their customer base and expand into new channels and geographies; (2) traditional players able to make use of data capture and application services such as performance monitoring to support their business capabilities; and (3) smaller players unable to benefit from investment in superior technology without the necessary capital and scale. If traditional players added analytics, they may be able to keep pace with e-commerce giants. However, the gap between smaller players and both the online and traditional players will widen.

Moving beyond the deployment of connectivity in retailing to also include its implementation in healthcare, intelligent mobility and manufacturing systems could boost global gross domestic product. By 2030 the total, according to Ferry Grijpink and others (2020: 1), will range between US$1.2 trillion and US$2 trillion depending upon the availability of: (1) 'advanced connectivity' comprising existing technologies (e.g. low power and low maintenance such as narrow-band Internet of Things and short-range devices such as radio frequency identification/Bluetooth); and (2) 'frontier connectivity' covering more radical and capital-intensive technologies with a limited geographical footprint such as high-band 5G and low earth orbit constellations. As much of the anticipated growth will be in making more use of advanced connectivity reliant upon mobile networks with low-to-mid-5G coverage, it is important to discuss its hub.

THE HUB OF CONSUMER CONNECTIVITY

Digital technologies have transformed consumption from purchasing to a prolonged act of experience, which involves sharing, commenting upon and providing feedback on online platforms and apps that extend beyond post-consumption (Thrift, 2006). Online platforms have the capability of engaging consumers in a more intense way. They reflect a new business model through which companies extract value not only from selling products to consumers, but also from harvesting their data. These data record the frequency of site visits, product purchases and services searched, which can be sold to other companies. Likewise, customers can benefit from feedback on products disclosed by other consumers on the platform.

These digital platforms are attractive to product suppliers and retailers because of their ability to increase consumer engagement compared with other forms of connectivity mechanisms. In general, the more features and interfaces the platform has with other tools, the higher the likelihood that the platform will become the preferred touch point of consumers in their routine online shopping adventures. Most existing platforms have grown from a core foot-hold in a given customer segment, such as Uber in the ride-sharing business and Amazon and eBay in e-tailing.

To gauge their relative effectiveness in providing customer care, we have reviewed a number of major e-commerce platforms – television, Internet and social media – and assessed them in terms of their approach to connecting with customers and also in facilitating interactions between customers. The consumer connectivity power of television, the Internet, YouTube and social media is compared and contrasted based upon their respective cognitive links, degree of consumer participation and product knowledge and service information (Table 6.1). Cognitive links for television, the Internet and YouTube advertising all have specific requirements – a compelling message, a verifiable written message and an audio-visual image – to leave either a lasting impression or to demonstrate value. In contrast, social media relies upon the flow of social discourse to constantly add value and produce a lasting effect. Consumer participation involved in television, the Internet and YouTube advertising is rated as passive, whereas the consumer is cast as co-creator of product data through immersive participation in social media advertising. Product knowledge and service information for television, Internet and YouTube advertising are all reliant on one-sided, fixed information, while in social media vendor information is absorbed progressively by the consumer and augmented by feedback, which constitutes data in the making. On all of these counts social media exhibits greater consumer connectivity power than the other advertising variants. This has had three distinctive effects.

First, under the digital ecosystem, product knowledge has no longer become the exclusive domain of manufacturers or suppliers. With the growing hegemony of social media, product knowledge has been increasingly produced by consumers and service information and product user friendliness have become common talking points. Digital advertising via social media apps has encouraged consumers to continuously engage with digital products and services to foment 'flow', a psychological state of enjoyable immersion being pursued at great cost for the sake of doing it (Csikszentmihalyi, 1990).

Table 6.1   *Key characteristics of advertising by television, the Internet,*
                YouTube and social media

	Television advertising	Internet advertising	YouTube advertising	Social media advertising
Cognitive link	Requires a compelling message to convince and to leave a lasting impression	Requires a verifiable written message to convince and to demonstrate value	Requires authentic-looking audio-visual images to convince and to demonstrate value	Relies on social discourse (flow) to continuously add value and generate impact
Consumer participation	Passive observer: watching, appreciating and absorbing (mind-numbing participation)	Passive reader: reading, appreciating and absorbing (mind-numbing participation)	Passive observer: watching, appreciating and absorbing (mind-numbing participation)	Co-creator of product data (immersive participation)
Product knowledge and service information	One-sided, fixed information provided by vendor	One-sided, fixed information provided by vendor	One-sided, fixed information provided by vendor	Vendor information progressively augmented by consumer feedback usage data 'in the making'

Second, underpinned by a contradictory ethos of participatory commodification, social media and mobile apps place consumers as 'co-creators' of product knowledge, data and services together with companies and other consumers (Prahalad and Ramaswamy, 2004a). This is very different from advertising on television, the Internet and even on YouTube because the interaction between the firm and the consumer has become the place for value creation and value extraction (Prahalad and Ramaswamy, 2004b).

Third, social media configures product knowledge as data on what is experienced or recommended. This information is frequently configured as being tentative and open for reinterpretation or challenged by other users or 'netizens' (Prainsack, 2014). The tentative and co-created nature of product knowledge carries considerable social, economic and technological ramifications for both the manufacturer and supplier.

These three outcomes of advertising have 'e-scaped' from producers of goods and suppliers with the increasing prominence of social media. The patron of product knowledge no longer sits solely with the manufacturer, supplier or vendor. Increasingly, the consumers and consumer communities are the content builders.

Consumer participation in co-creating contents in the digital era is not only motivated by a desire to share and contribute but has also been the result of a new phenomenon referred to by Peter Vorderer and others (2016) as 'permanently online', a situation where the smart device is permanently switched on and the user stays online perpetually. This phenomenon has dissolved the boundary between 'media use' and 'media non-use', especially among Generations Y and Z, the netizens, who find it exceedingly easy to navigate digital ecosystems via their mobile devices (Zhou, 2019). The netizens want to remain online, not necessarily to fulfil a specific need, such as to receive messages or to find information, but simply because they are concerned with the fear of missing out and enjoy the feeling of acceleration (Vorderer and Kohring, 2013; Zhou, 2019).

Characterized by an uneasy and, at times, all-consuming feeling, the fear of missing out has become ever more pronounced in the age of social media. The unprecedented awareness of what food others are eating, what movies peers are watching and how friends and colleagues are spending their vacations is increasingly predisposing more people to the fear of missing out. This fear does not necessarily lead to terrifying anxiety all the time; it could also induce occasional energizing flashes. Such intensified moments may drive reactive behaviours on social media sites, heighten self-perceptions and transpose into real-world consumer actions.

Drawing upon various participatory paradigms in the digital economy and culture defined in Table 6.2 – co-creation, prosumption, Big Data and citizen science – digital connectivity gives a new twist to user interaction with a product and its socially constructed knowledge. Consumers have been configured as co-creating and analysing product data, such as user-friendly features, through digital devices and platforms together with companies and other consumers.

The idea of the consumer as the co-creator of product knowledge and data has had the usual problems associated with user-generated knowledge in digital environments. Typically, only a small minority of users during the first decade of the new millennium was engaged in such creative activities (Van Dijck, 2009: 44). Since then digital platforms and devices have both guided and constrained creative possibilities for user-generated content. Often the data generated by users have been harvested for corporate gain, such as discovering consumer preferences, which has weakened the power of legislators within an emerging global ecosystem consisting of autonomously operating online platforms (Harris et al., 2016; Van Dijck and Poell, 2013, 2016). Besides harvesting data on consumers, business attention has extended to launching mobile apps on every conceivable product and service in a bid to connect consumers to their operations.

Table 6.2   *Key participatory paradigms in the digital economy and culture*

Paradigm	Definitions
Co-creation	'… *co-creation* fundamentally challenges the traditional roles of the firm and the consumer. The tension manifests itself at points of interaction between the consumer and the company – where the co-creation experience occurs, where individuals exercise choice, and where value is co-created. Points of interaction provide opportunities for collaboration and negotiation, explicit or implicit, between the consumer and the company – as well as opportunities for those processes to break down' (Prahalad and Ramaswamy, 2004a: 9).
Prosumption	'*Prosumption* involves both production and consumption rather than focusing on either one (production) or the other (consumption). It is maintained that earlier forms of capitalism (producer and consumer capitalism) were themselves characterized by prosumption' (Ritzer and Jurgenson, 2010: 13).
Big Data	'*Big Data* is characterized by being generated continuously, seeking to be exhaustive and fine-grained in scope, and flexible and scalable in its production. Examples of the production of such data include: digital CCTV; the recording of retail purchases; digital devices that record and communicate the history of their own use (e.g. mobile phones); the logging of transactions and interactions across digital networks (e.g. email or online banking); clickstream data that record navigation through a website or app; measurements from sensors embedded into objects or environments; the scanning of machine-readable objects such as travel passes or barcodes; and social media postings' (Kitchin, 2014: 2).
Citizen science	'*CS [citizen science]* represents a significant change in how we assess and enact relevant expertise and authority when we create scientific knowledge, and how it does or should affect the ways in which we discuss and support participation' (Prainsack, 2014: 19).

Note: Italics added.

THE POWER OF MOBILE APPS

The explosive popularity of mobile apps is underscored by the exponential rise in app downloads (100 million) within three days of the launch of Apple's App Store in July 2008 when it went live with 500 apps (Shah, 2016). Since then, the number and downloads of mobile apps have both grown exponentially. During the first quarter of 2021 Statista (2021c) reported that Google Play had 3.48 million apps, with another 2.23 million on Apple App Store, 0.67 million on Windows Store and another 0.46 million on Amazon App Store. Also, the number of mobile app downloads increased from 140.7 billion in 2016 to 218 billion in 2020 (Statista, 2021d).

Because of the fear of missing out, social media apps are among the most popular. According to David Curry (2021a), TikTok (850 million), WhatsApp (600 million), Facebook (540 million) and Instagram (503 million) had the most downloads globally in 2020. In January 2021, active users of WhatsApp

Table 6.3   *Most popular global mobile messaging apps, January 2021*

App (name)	Date (year)	Headquarters (location)	Active users (million)
WhatsApp[a]	2009	Menlo Park, USA	2,000
Messenger	2011	Menlo Park, USA	1,300
Wēixìn/WeChat (微信)	2011	Guangzhou, China	1,213
Tencent QQ (腾讯QQ)	1999	Guangzhou, China	617
Telegram	2013	Dubai, United Arab Emirates	500
Snapchat	2011	Santa Monica, CA, USA	498

Note: [a] Acquired by Facebook in 2014.
Source: Information on active users derived from Tankovska (2021a).

and Messenger, owned by Facebook, dominated the most popular mobile messenger apps with strong challenges coming from WeChat and QQ messenger
services owned by China-based Tencent Holdings (Table 6.3). As a cheaper
alternative to operator text messaging using a short message service, these
social messaging apps, incorporating pictures and videos, have offered an
array of beneficial options for businesses.

Outside social media, mobile apps have found their way into every conceivable area, typified by banking, car buying, fitness, gaming, healthcare and
translation. The reasons for businesses embracing mobile apps are numerous.
They include being visible to the customer at all times, the creation of a direct
marketing channel, delivering value to the customer, building brand recognition, improving customer engagement and standing out from the competition
as well as the cultivation of consumer loyalty (Haselmayr, 2021).

In e-commerce, mobile apps have been harnessed to build a closer partnership between suppliers and consumers of both products and services.
Nike, for instance, uses a combination of apps to grow sales through customer engagement. Apart from its main Nike (shopping) app, the company
boasts a total of 47 apps – 31 Apple iOS apps and 16 Google Android apps
(SensorTower, 2021). Among the more popular apps in the company's range
are: Nike SNKRS, providing insider access to sneaker release and also serving
as the hub of sneaker culture; Nike Run Club, supplying a holistic running
experience together with customized coaching plans and non-stop motivation
from friends; Nike Training Club, offering guided workouts; Nike Adapt,
empowering users to fine-tune each shoe to get the perfect fit from the phone;
and Nike SB, contributing a specifically designed skate-boarding line of shoes,
clothing and equipment. Through its myriad customer-segmented apps, Nike
harvests an extensive array of data about each of its customers that range from
purchasing habits and preferences to walking routes and workout routines in
addition to personal information. In an interview with Heidi O'Neill, head

of the Nike Direct retail and e-commerce business, Khadeeja Safdar (2019) reported that Nike's app ecosystem is providing content, community, activity and connection for consumers beyond transaction. The data collected enables Nike to not only personalize what each customer sees on their apps to offer them a unique interactive experience but also plan which designs to produce, what items to stock in which stores and how to use their network of stores to provide service hubs to support their members.

Designed to enable users to perform specific tasks based on needs, apps run within a software framework embedded in a digital platform, which Geoffrey Parker and others (2016) argue as having fundamentally changed how businesses operate in the digital economy. Contrasting platform business models with the traditional linear pipe flow mode of operations (supply chain is a typical example), the authors explain that platform business models create a central infrastructure that allows external producers and consumers to connect and exchange value with each other.

This is how iPhone differentiated itself from earlier generations of smart phones, such as IBM's Simon, launched in 1994 and widely regarded as the world's first smart phone, or BlackBerry 5810, a popular handheld device in the early 2000s noted for its 'qwerty' keypad and its innovative wireless email (Shah, 2016). These earlier generations of smart phones did come with some preloaded features (not called apps at that stage) such as Address Book, Alarm Clock, Calculator, Calendar, Mail, Note Pad, Java games and Sketch Pad. However, once built, these phones could not have new features added.

The iPhone changed that. It introduced the App Store, allowing third-party app developers to reach all iPhone users. The availability of the App Store, according to Lisa Eadicicco (2017), is the very reason 'we can summon taxis without speaking a word, dispatch magically disappearing photos and transfer digital payments with the press of a button'. Users can augment the functionality of their iPhones by picking and choosing the apps of use or interest to them, bringing about the 'personalization wave of connectivity' (Kolb et al., 2020: 1591). Through the app, platform businesses offer an intelligent governance mechanism in which producers and consumers can interact in multiple ways beyond simple transactions, including rating their experience with each other, thus producing a feedback loop and generating a network effect in the process (Parker et al., 2016). To distinguish these platform businesses from asset builders, service providers and technology creators exemplified by Walmart, Accenture and Microsoft, respectively, Barry Libert and others (2014) have dubbed representatives such as Airbnb, Alibaba and Uber 'network orchestrators'.

A NETWORK THEORY OF 'PRODUCTRIBUTION'

In the digital era, Parker and others (2016) contend that the relentless interactions of producers (or suppliers) and consumers have created demand-side
economies of scale, which give large companies in a platform market
a network effect advantage difficult for competitors to match. In the domain
of goods production and distribution, a similar phenomenon has also emerged.
Companies that could link producers (or suppliers) to consumers via their
digital platforms with physical logistics resources to align with the consumer
purchasing journey have also created a network effect that is hard for competitors to emulate.

Harnessing the prowess of Industry 4.0 technologies, such as 3D printing,
cloud computing, machine learning and Internet of Things, these companies
have found ways to amalgamate production with distribution into a single
(almost) seamless operation, creating what we term productribution (Figure
6.2). Within the resultant productribution retailing environment, supplier–
consumer interactions have taken centre stage. These interactions grow the
network effects through the way producers and suppliers reach out to consumers to meet their consumption needs and to promote further consumption by
promulgating social shopping. Also, the frequency and intensity of consumer
responses when sharing experiences in social media further enhance the
network effects, forming the foundation of digital supply chain operations.
Under the digital ecosystems of Industry 4.0, the competitive strength of

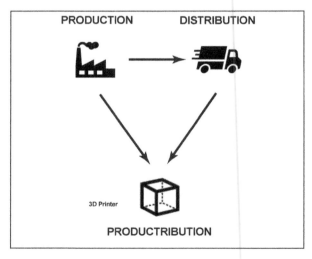

Figure 6.2   Formation of productribution

supply chains has been derived from their productribution network capabilities to dynamically fulfil various forms of consumption demands. In response to these demands, the shape of productribution networks has also been designed to reflect their dependence upon the specific interactions between product suppliers and individual consumers.

Viewed from the perspective of a value network, the productribution eco-system is an extension of the omnichannel retailing landscape by propagating the seamless experience of the online–offline consumer purchasing journey with commodities produced and delivered on demand such as 3D printed medical devices, car spare parts, cooked meals and farm produce. Major product manufacturers, suppliers and retailers operating through a digital platform, reinforced by a physical productribution network, have assumed an array of different forms. Competition between businesses has been dictated by the varied and dynamic capabilities and capacity of the productribution networks, over which they have control, ready access to or in which they have been embedded.

Under Consumerism 4.0 the operational dynamics of the productribution ecosystem have been shaped by one, or a combination, of six different forms of network-driven capabilities (Figure 6.3). These range from network-spreading through network-tiering, network-bonding, network-building, network-forming to network-scoping.

Table 6.4 shows the nodes, last-mile delivery options, operations characteristics and examples of the six productribution networks. A series of case studies has been chosen from the list of examples to highlight their chequered history during the pandemic. A recurrent feature of this analysis has been the growing role afforded to 3D printing.

Network-Spreading Productribution Capability

Network-spreading businesses have been capable of expanding their production and distribution functions in different regions of the world. Their economic power to invest in productribution facilities at strategic locations has enabled them to enlarge their global presence. This dominance has allowed them to connect multiple smaller, geographically distributed third-party logistics networks to augment their coverage. Also, they have been able to engage in supplying the widest range of products, from items as small as a ring to bulky furniture and from farm produce to cooked food.

These businesses are exemplified by the Amazon and Alibaba market-places, which operate through an online presence alone (Table 6.5). Often perceived as rivals, their business models differ, making comparisons difficult (Investopedia Team, 2021). Amazon acts both as a retailer of new goods and as a platform for other retailers to sell goods to buyers, taking a commission

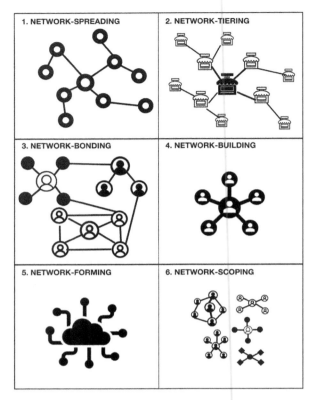

Figure 6.3   The six different forms of productribution networks

on the sales price, whereas Alibaba operates as a broker between buyers and sellers online through an extensive set of websites. When Amazon undertakes fulfilment, products are stored in its warehouses, packed, shipped and delivered speedily by its own land and air fleet or service partner and, if its Prime service is used, the product is received within two hours, the same day or in two days. Conversely, Alibaba coordinates track-and-trace logistics and provides information for delivery (i.e. like Amazon's fulfilment by merchants engaged in warehousing, shipping and delivering their own products to customers). Also, Alibaba's largest site Tabao offers a fee-free marketplace with sellers paying a fee to rank higher on the internal search engine while its Tmall website generates income from well-known brands such as Gap and Nike.

As seeking to gauge the respective global reach of Amazon and Alibaba does not go beyond the listing of 100 plus countries and the former's focus on North America and the latter's upon Asia, attention is centred upon the one real

Table 6.4   *Nodes, last-mile delivery, characteristics and examples of the network-driven capabilities comprising the productribution ecosystem*

Productribution capability	Nodes	Last-mile delivery	Key operational characteristics	Examples
Network-spreading	Warehouse distribution centres	Direct delivery to consumers using robots, drones and autonomous vehicles	Global image Possibility of on-site production	Alibaba* Amazon* CEVA Logistics DHL Mercado Libre US Postal Service
Network-tiering	Logistics stores	Deliveries and consumer pick-up	Penetration of distribution networks	Post Office shops UPS Stores*
Network-bonding	Franchised stores	No consumer pick-up	Homogeneity in product ranges Comparable services on all nodes No last-mile delivery	7-Eleven* Automotive suppliers Office Works Repco Starbucks
Network-building	Apps Virtual space	App-coordinated personalized delivery	Small businesses or individual customers at home linked to store	Deliveroo Delivery Hero Just Eat Uber Eats* Zomato
Network-forming	Virtual space	Consumer pick-up	Businesses and consumers form their own networks using the platform Specialized services linking people or businesses of similar interests together	Facebook* Twitter TikTok/Douyin*
Network-scoping	Embedded network sites	Consumer scheduled arrangement	Essentially referral services	Airbnb Shopify Trivago*

Note: * Case studies.

comparison that can be made. This involves comparing their cloud infrastructure and platform services (CIPS) – the Seattle-based Amazon Web Services (AWS) and Alibaba Cloud (阿里云 *Ālǐyún*) headquartered in Singapore – to evaluate their global reach. These cloud and infrastructure services are defined by Gartner, a global research and advisory firm, 'as standardized, highly automated offerings, in which infrastructure resources (e.g., compute, networking

Table 6.5   *Amazon and Alibaba, 2020*

Amazon	
Revenue	US$386 billion[a]
Employees	1,298,000[b]
Business model	Business to consumer and consumer to consumer
Global reach	100+ countries, primarily North America
Warehouses	175 fulfilment centres globally (pick and pack for customers)
Warehouse space	411 million square feet (299 North America; 102 international; 11 AWS[3])
Stock-keeping units	Warehouse management system using barcode to locate item on shelf
Last-mile delivery	Sortation centres (sorting packages by zip code)
Alibaba 阿里巴巴集团控股有限公司	
Revenue	US$72 billion
Employees	117,600
Business model	Business to business (Alibaba) plus business to consumer (Taobao) and
Global reach	consumer to consumer (Tmall)
	100+ countries primarily Asia

Note: [a] 31 March 2020; [b] 31 December 2020; [c] AWS – Amazon Web Services.
Source: Bowles (2021); Schwarztman (2020); USSEC (2021a, 2021b).

and storage) are complemented by integrated platform services' (Bala et al., 2020).

This attempt to provide a better assessment of their respective global reach for these services is based on contrasting the coverage of AWS's 25 regions (Figure 6.4) and Alibaba Cloud's 23 regions (Figure 6.5), which house one or multiple activity zones comprising a set of data centres that are physically separate. These regions, according to Kevin Xu (2020), offer a good indicator of past, current and future investment priorities of the two public cloud vendors. AWS has not only made investments inside China, but also it is the only one of the two with representation in both Africa and Latin America. Conversely, Alibaba Cloud's investment has been heavily focused on China and its overall worldwide footprint has lagged behind AWS's distribution. Also, AWS has a declared intention to add an additional five regions but there are no clues as to where Alibaba Cloud will go next. In 2020 these differing patterns prompted Laura Sheff (2020) to report that Gartner had declared AWS as the outright leader in cloud global infrastructure and platform services ahead of Microsoft and Google, and Alibaba as the leading niche player with its domestic counterpart Tencent Cloud entering the list for the first time.

The effect of COVID-19 on the seemingly impregnable online position of Amazon and Alibaba's network-spreading productribution capabilities by their respective challengers – Walmart and Pinduoduo – is worth noting (*The Economist*, 2021b). During 2020 Amazon was ranked ahead of Walmart –

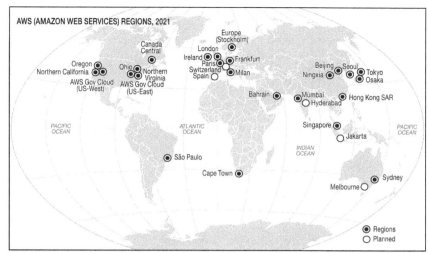

Source: AWS (2021).

Figure 6.4   Amazon Web Services' 25 existing regions and five planned regions

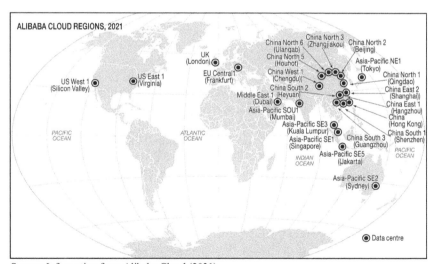

Source: Information from Alibaba Cloud (2021).

Figure 6.5   Alibaba's 23 regions

the world's largest physical retailer – in profits, assets and market value in Forbes' *Global 2000* but not in sales (Dobosz, 2021). Walmart responded by adding online activities to its physical presence to be more like its rival in garnering booming profits during the pandemic (Grothaus, 2020; Kinder and Stateler, 2020). Competitive threats to these e-commerce activities, especially in Europe and North America, may come from smart phones replacing personal computers and lead to the attractiveness of social commerce. Should commerce through smart phone and short-form video arise, the clash will involve supply chain and logistics operations, particularly as both Amazon and Walmart are already engaged in direct-to-consumer deliveries, and threaten to compete against UPS and FedEx (Baertlein, 2021). Meanwhile, by the end of 2020 the fast-growing Pinduoduo's team-buying model had exceeded Alibaba in terms of users in China, but, according to *The Economist* (2021c), still fell short of contesting the latter's control of one-fifth of the country's retail sales.

Network-Tiering Productribution Capability

Businesses such as the locally owned, neighbourhood UPS Stores in the United States have the capability to offer customers a hierarchically organized, on-demand productribution network. This feature has stemmed from UPS's well-established and extensive geographically distributed logistical networks within a company originally founded as a private messenger service in Seattle in 1907. The company had gone national by 1975; become global from 1989 to eventually operate in 220 countries; entered retailing in 2001 to offer mail boxing, packing, printing and shipping services; and extended to weekend operations in 2018 (UPS, 2021). The key attribute of these networks, like those of franchised postal services, has been their swift last-mile delivery capability, reflecting that speed and ease of shipment matched the importance of production. In 2021 UPS Stores operated 3D printing at 20 locations located relatively close to consumers with activities concentrated around Chicago, San Francisco and, to a lesser extent, Orlando (Figure 6.6). Franchisers under this network configuration possessed the logistical means and capacity to deliver 3D printed products on demand and compete favourably against companies with network-spreading capability.

Where industrial-scale volume of additive manufacturing is required, and computer numerical control machining processes, injection moulding and urethane casting and other additive technologies are involved, UPS has invested in a Fast Radius industrial-grade 3D micro factory located at its distribution facility in the airport at Louisville, Kentucky, United States (Figure 6.7). This 'end-of-the-runway' presence allows the Fast Radius facility to make and deliver parts extremely quickly. Besides its facility offering a 3D printing package at Louisville, Fast Radius provides a similar array of additive tech-

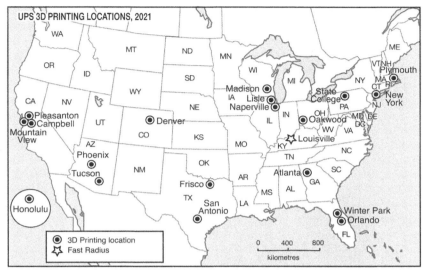

Source: Information from UPS Store (2021).

Figure 6.6   UPS Store locations with 3D printing services, 2021

nologies providing on-demand digital manufacturing, warehouse and next-day delivery at other micro factories providing parts for the production of robot pickers and advanced motorcycles. By September 2018 the array of micro factories operated by Fast Radius (2018), with its headquarters in Chicago, had led to the company being named by the World Economic Forum as one of the world's nine best companies in implementing Industry 4.0 technologies in a list including Bosch, Haier, Procter & Gamble, Schneider Electric, Siemens and Johnson & Johnson.

Network-Bonding Productribution Capability

The capability of businesses to leverage peer entities in their franchised network to collaborate in meeting on-demand productribution needs of customers are characterized by 7-Eleven. This largest multinational chain of retail convenience stores operating seven days per week between 7 am and 11 pm originated in 1927 in Dallas, Texas as Tote'm Stores, which became 7-Eleven in 1946 (USSEC, 2021c). The company has remained headquartered in Dallas, despite 70 per cent being acquired by the Japanese company Ito-Yokodo in 1991, reorganized as a wholly owned subsidiary of Seven-Eleven Japan Co. Ltd in 2005 and now held by Chiyoda, Seven and I Holdings Co. Ltd based in

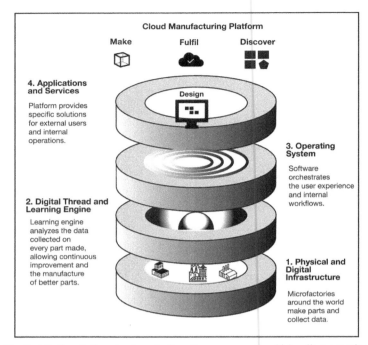

Cloud Manufacturing Platform

Make   Fulfil   Discover

4. Applications and Services

Platform provides specific solutions for external users and internal operations.

Design

3. Operating System

Software orchestrates the user experience and internal workflows.

2. Digital Thread and Learning Engine

Learning engine analyzes the data collected on every part made, allowing continuous improvement and the manufacture of better parts.

1. Physical and Digital Infrastructure

Microfactories around the world make parts and collect data.

Note: The Fast Radius platform has been built on four components, which collect, organize and analyse data during every step of the product life cycle. Besides its facility at Louisville, the company provides computer numerical control machining, injection moulding, urethane casting and additive technologies at other micro factories.
Source: Based on an original Fast Radius (2021) photograph in colour.

Figure 6.7   The Fast Radius cloud manufacturing platform

Tokyo. By January 2020 7-Eleven, according to Statista (2020b), operated in 17 countries around the world (Figure 6.8).

In January 2020 the global distribution of 70,207 7-Eleven stores displayed a distinct Asian bias accounting for over four-fifths of all stores. Almost 30 per cent of the stores were in Japan followed by over 16 per cent in Thailand and 14 per cent in South Korea (Table 6.6). By August 2020 10,000 stores in the United States and Canada had been augmented by 7-Eleven's takeover of 3,900 Speedway Stores for US$21 billion. In Australia there has been an emphasis on 'My 7-Eleven App', offering app-exclusive deals, rewards and a fuel price lock (7-Eleven, 2021). Nevertheless, it is in Japan that 7-Eleven demonstrates its network power where individual franchisees have a specific set of collaborative activities to benefit its customers with some freedom to adjust during the pandemic (Ikeshita and Miyajima, 2020). Besides offer-

Source: Based on information in Statista (2020b).

Figure 6.8   *Distribution of economies with 7-Eleven stores and those from where it has been withdrawn*

ing a wide variety of cosmetics, drinks, food and goods, the locations have a Money Exchange Machine for foreign currency, a Seven Bank Automatic Teller Machine, a tax-free service for items of personal use outside Japan plus a free Wi-Fi service.

Network-Building Productribution Capability

The ability of aggregators to develop function-specific apps, instanced by Uber Eats, has enabled them to create networks of businesses and enterprising consumers to collaborate in organizing on-demand productribution services to customers. In 2009 Uber Technologies, the forerunner of Uber Eats, co-founded by Garrett Camp and Travis Kalanik, established a ride-sharing service built on smart phones, heralding the advent of apps and on-demand work in San Francisco (USSEC, 2020). After Uber ride sharing had spread around the world to 63 countries, the partners sought to expand its reach into other areas beyond its personal mobility platform by adding the Uber Freight platform (Iqbal, 2022b). In 2014, as part of this process of 'Uberization', the partners experimented with an online food-ordering and delivery platform in Santa Monica, California, to rationalize its platform synergies. Users were able to read fixed-price menus and reviews, order food from local participating restaurants, pay with a card and have the meal delivered reliably and quickly

Table 6.6   List of 7-Eleven stores by date and country, January 2020

Country	First store	Stores (2020)	Country	First store	Stores (2020)
Asia			*Europe*		
China	1992	3,156	Denmark	1993	172
Hong Kong	1981	n.a.	Norway	1986	154
India[b]	2021	0	Sweden	1984	83
Indonesia[a]	2009–17	0	Spain[a]	2000	0
Japan	1927	20,988	United Kingdom[a]	1985-97	0
Laos[b]	2020	0	*North America*		
Macau	2005	n.a.	Canada	1969	636
Malaysia	1984	2,411	Mexico	1976	1,829
Philippines	1984	2,864	United States	1953	9,364
Singapore	1983	411	*Oceania*		
South Korea	1989	10,016	Australia	1977	708
Taiwan	1979	5,647	*Middle East*		
Thailand	1989	11,712	Israel[b]	2021	0
Turkey[a]		0	United Arab Emirates	2015	12
Vietnam	2017	44	Subtotal		12,958
Subtotal		57,249	Grand total		70,207

Note: [a] Former location; [b] planned location; n.a. not available.
Source: Based on information in Statista (2020b).

by courier through accessing a dedicated app or web browser under what has become the Uber Eats platform. Since then the model has become operational in 30 economies but has exited Egypt, India, Saudi Arabia and South Korea (Figure 6.9).

Uber Eats' performance between 2016 and 2020 shows a sharp increase in revenue, gross bookings, available cities and supported restaurants (Table 6.7). This was particularly marked in 2020 during the ongoing COVID-19 pandemic when people reduced ride sharing and shopping with strangers, ordered food delivery to their homes and heightened their fulfilment expectations. The rapid growth in business has not generated a profit for Uber Eats because the reported cumulative delivery fees on all orders of between 20 and 30 per cent charged to customers are less than the cumulative payments to the drivers (Barre, 2020). This apparent irrational behaviour has been driven by a bid to generate market share in a highly competitive business activity. In the United States, for instance, Uber Eats has been in competition with DoorDash, which in 2019 had become the country's most popular local delivery company. In 2020 Uber Eats responded by acquiring Postmates to boost its share of fast

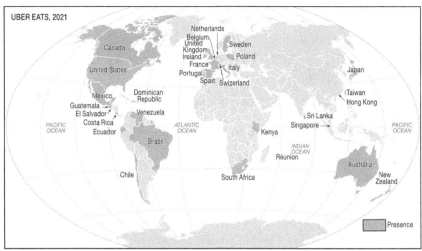

Note: Not shown are minority operations with Yandex Taxi in Russia and Grab in Southeast Asia; and departures from India and South Korea in 2019 and Czech Republic, Egypt, Honduras, Romania, Saudi Arabia, Uruguay and Ukraine in 2020.
Source: Based on information from Chapman (2020), Curry (2021b) and WP (2021).

Figure 6.9   *Economies in which Uber Eats operates*

Table 6.7   *Uber Eats revenue, gross bookings, users, cities available, supported restaurants and annual average spend, 2016–20*

Date	Revenue (US$ billion)	Gross bookings (US$ billion)	Users (million)	Cities available (number)	Supported restaurants (number)	Annual average user spend ($)
2016	n.a.	n.a.	5	120	n.a.	n.a.
2017	0.6	3.1	9	200	80,000	141
2018	1.5	7.9	15	500	100,000	220
2019	1.9	14.5	21	1,000	220,000	n.a.
2020	4.8	30.2	60	6,000	600.000	n.a.

Source: Information derived from Curry (2021b).

delivery in the United States from 19 per cent in 2019 to 30 per cent (Curry, 2021b). During COVID-19 Uber Eats became central to Uber's operations because it was able to take advantage of the closure of restaurants during lockdowns and border closures. In 2020 delivery produced more revenue than the company's mobility sector, which generated 50 per cent less income than in 2019 (USSEC, 2021d). The popularity and expansion of Uber Eats has underscored the network-building productribution capability of function-specific apps, which have enabled companies to thrive and strengthen their grip over the takeaway market.

Network-Forming Productribution Capability

The ability of businesses, such as Facebook (now Meta), to create a social networking platform to entice users to form their private (exclusive) networks has allowed them to collaborate in organizing on-demand productribution for network members. Originally created by Mark Zuckerberg and fellow college students, Eduardo Saverin, Andrew McCollum, Dustin Moskovitz and Chris Hughes, as a tool for Harvard students in Cambridge, Massachusetts in 2004, the tool spread rapidly to other universities in the United States before going public in 2006. Ten years later the Facebook app had 3 million followers of whom 70 per cent were located outside the United States and instrumental in influencing purchases (WPR, 2021).

By 2019 Facebook had become the leading worldwide social commerce channel with 2.8 billion global monthly annual users. Facebook's global reach had extended to 228 economies. A division of these economies into quartiles resulted in the first quartile encompassing 57 economies ranging from 251 million in India to 5.8 million in Portugal (Figure 6.10). Central America, large parts of Africa, Central and Eastern Europe and East Asia (including China) are absent from the first quartile. Nevertheless, Facebook's overall reach has led to it being considered one of the 'Big Five' technology companies in the world together with Apple, Amazon, Google and Microsoft.

In January 2020 Facebook's global penetration rate was 28.5 per cent; this ranged from 68.6 per cent in North America, through 54 per cent in Latin America and the Caribbean, 47.4 per cent in Europe, 35.7 per cent in the Middle East, 19.4 per cent in Asia to 15.9 per cent in Africa (Tankovska, 2021b). By January 2021 penetration rates in economies with the largest number of Facebook users expressed as a proportion of their populations show a different pattern (Table 6.8). Economies in Southeast Asia (Philippines, Thailand and Vietnam) and Latin America (Mexico, Colombia, Argentina and Brazil) recorded the highest percentages and those in South Asia (Pakistan, India and Bangladesh) the lowest. Also, in January 2021 Josh Makarian (2021) reported that Facebook ranked first among the top 10 social media sites with 2.8 million monthly annual users, but this understates the company's overall strength because it does not include Facebook Messenger or the company's acquisitions of Instagram in 2012 and WhatsApp in 2014, which add another 4.3 billion users.

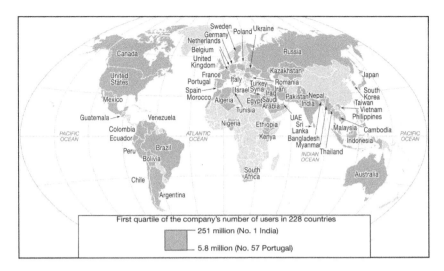

Source: Based on information in Facebook (2021) and WPR (2021).

Figure 6.10   The 57 economies with the largest number of Facebook app users, 2019

Table 6.8   Penetration rates in economies with the largest number of Facebook users, 2021

Economy	Users (million)	Population (million)	Ratio (per cent)	Economy	Users (million)	Population (million)	Ratio (per cent)
India	320	1,393	23.0	Bangladesh	41	166	24.6
United States	190	333	57.1	Pakistan	40	225	17.7
Indonesia	140	276	50.7	United Kingdom	38	68	55.9
Brazil	130	214	60.7	Turkey	38	85	44.7
Mexico	93	130	71.5	Colombia	36	51	70.5
Philippines	83	111	74.7	France	33	65	50.8
Vietnam	68	98	69.3	Argentina	31	46	67.4
Thailand	51	70	72.8	Italy	31	60	51.6
Egypt	45	104	43.2	Germany	29	84	34.5

Source: Data from WPR (2021) and Tankovska (2021c).

Within this broad business model by 2019 Facebook had developed local-ized marketplaces for users in specific localities within 70 countries to buy and sell everything from cars, clothes and televisions (Pahwa, 2021). In Australia's state of Victoria, for example, there are Facebook Marketplace Melbourne and Facebook Marketplace Geelong. Also, product-specific marketplaces have been created for trading in cars and furniture. Despite these regional and product-based initiatives, Facebook's penetration in China has been rel-atively low because the country has its own platforms totalling 960 million social network users in 2020: Sina Weibo, Tencent QQ and QZone, WeChat, Douban, Tencent Video, Douyin and Xiaohongshu ('Little Red Book') (C2VA, 2020). Since 2016 the Beijing-based Douyin launched by the Chinese tech firm ByteDance has aggressively moved into social commerce overseas and, according to Hannah Murphy (2021), aims to compete with Facebook in the United States through TikTok, its sister app.

In 2019 TikTok's popular short video platform sound-tracked by musical clips with tagged adverts promoted by social media influencers was banned in India, its leading foreign market at that time. Nevertheless, by August 2020, TikTok had performed well in illustrating the power of its network-forming productribution capability by accruing 689 million foreign active users com-pared with 600 million users in China (Figure 6.11). The subsequent acceler-

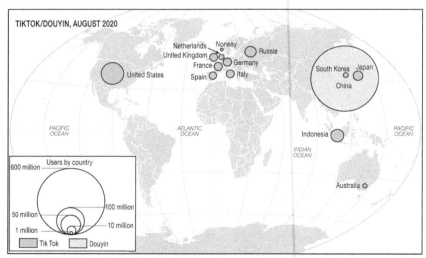

Note: TikTok has been banned in India and in Pakistan.
Source: Based on information from Iqbal (2021) and Williamson (2020).

Figure 6.11   Economies with over 1 million TikTok/Douyin users, August 2020

ation of its e-commerce thrust is illustrated in Indonesia where TikTok seeks employees to establish logistics operations and to educate eligible merchants on how to sell on their own or through an affiliate using short creative video content for a commission of 2 per cent for the platform in return for paid delivery and payment services (Ren, 2021; TikTok, 2021).

Beyond these activities in Southeast Asia large clusters of users of the video-sharing app are located in East Asia, Europe and the United States through its social commerce relationship with Shopify, a Canadian-based e-commerce platform for online stores and retail point-of-sale systems.

Lawmakers in the United States, its largest foreign market, are concerned that TikTok's users, mostly under 25 years of age (Gen Z and Alpha), will reveal personal data not only to improve ByteDance's artificial intelligence algorithms but also to assist the Chinese Government. In August 2020 this prompted ex-President Trump to issue an executive order to ban TikTok (BBC, 2020d). While President Biden has revoked this ban, he has tasked the United States Commerce Secretary to investigate foreign apps that target American privacy or security (Kelly, 2021). At least in the short term, this has led to advertisers being more relaxed about the TikTok app. New developments include a tool for popular creators of videos to derive a commission from the sale of products and to incorporate livestream shopping from Douyin to allow users to buy using a few taps. As 40 per cent of TikTok users do not have a Facebook account, the response has been to establish Facebook Shops and for Instagram to add a TikTok clone known as Reels (Murphy, 2021).

Network-Scoping Productribution Capability

The capability of businesses based on scoping and connecting a vast range of available networks to enable businesses and consumers to secure timely on-demand production and delivery services to customers is exemplified by Trivago. In 2005, 'trivago' was conceived by a group of graduate friends, Rolf Schrömgens, Peter Vinnemeier and Stephan Stubner (later replaced by another graduate Malte Siewert), in a garage in Düsseldorf in western Germany. By 2016 Trivago N.V. had been incorporated as a private company with limited liability in the Netherlands and developed into a global hotel and accommodation search platform managed in three segments: the Americas, developed Europe and the rest of the world (Figure 6.12).

By 31 December 2020 Trivago's (2021: 37) searchable data base comprised 5 million hotels and 3.3 million alternative types of accommodation. These were accessible anytime and anywhere, online and on mobile devices using websites and apps. As Trivago provided a search site, users did not book directly on its platform. Once a user has clicked on accommodation at a given price, the user is referred to one of the relatively small number of advertisers'

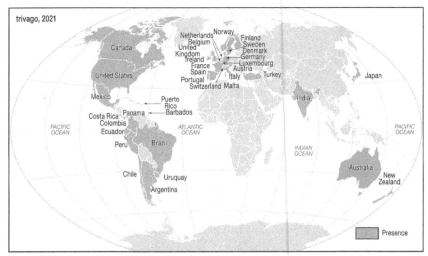

Source: Based upon information in Trivago (2021).

Figure 6.12   *Economies in Trivago N.V.'s three segments: the Americas,*
developed Europe and rest of the world (main countries only)

websites to complete the booking. Since 2018 the company's business model has been subject to litigation in Australia relating to the way certain advertisements displayed on Trivago's website were in breach of Australian consumer law (Trivago, 2021: 95). As Trivago's revenue was reliant upon a small number of advertisers and was affected adversely like the travel industry in general by COVID-19, the company has had to concentrate on local rather than international locations (USSEC, 2021e).

REVIEW OF THE SIX NETWORKS

The productribution capability exhibited by these six networks can be distilled into three integrated objectives: data collection, individualized solutions and consumption satisfaction. Data collection feeds consumer purchasing patterns to build analytics that help design individualized one-to-one commerce solutions such as smart assistants like Google Home and voice commerce to further promote consumption (WTC, 2021). Data from satisfied consumption feedback into the productribution network will result in the building of more refined algorithms to meet individual needs in space and time, fuelling a greater level of consumption and, by extension, a higher level of consumption satisfaction.

Social media, therefore, has become a potent force in the shadow of Consumerism 4.0 by intensifying the scramble to grow supply chain productribution capabilities. The growing popularity of m-commerce, fuelled by the fear of missing out, has accentuated the habit of impulse shopping. Social shopping has become the new norm. Indeed, shopping is no longer based on needs. Nor is it driven by marketing, promotion and sales campaigns. The consumption journey is now based on new data-infused ways of experiencing shopping, purchasing and delivery. Competition between firms will be fought between networks based on the strength of their consumer connectivity.

When the network orchestrators first commenced operations observers such as Tom Goodwin (2015) marvelled that Airbnb, the world's largest accommodation chain, owned no real estate; Facebook, the world's most popular social media company, created no content; and Uber, the world's largest taxi company, owned no fleet. Since then observations of these companies that superimposed thin horizontal layers over the top of supply systems of businesses with fixed assets and interfaced with a large number of people have been revised. Now there is a realization that Airbnb increasingly owns real estate, Facebook is commissioning content and Uber buys motor vehicles (Temperton, 2018). This comprehension, as recognized by Tom Goodwin (2018), underlines that the battle for consumers, as these companies have matured, has become physical instead of purely virtual.

Given that the most successful incumbent platforms are owned by some of the industry's largest and most well-capitalized technology firms, the continued growth of multiple, interconnected platforms will form a cluster of interconnected hubs where consumer connectivity will blossom. These will be the productribution networks of knowledge, wealth and power. This outcome has raised the need, as highlighted by Barbara Prainsack (2020: 444), for 'radical solutions to ensure that digital data is not used to merely increase power and profits for the privileged'. As recognized in discussing some productribution case studies, they are being subjected to regulations, institutions and research activity designed to ensure that the digital data's political economy contributes to the well-being of society.

CONCLUSION

This chapter has highlighted that human beings are social animals and desire connectivity with each other, business and organizations. Digitization has permitted business to connect with their customers in unprecedented ways. This enhanced consumer connectivity under the digital ecosystem has given rise to various productribution networks that have empowered product suppliers, retailers and service providers. Digital connectivity has allowed them to influence consumer shopping behaviour through the creation of touch points and the offer of delivery options.

Supply chain success in this digital ecosystem has hinged upon consumer connectivity being achieved through digital means. This proposition has been supported by abundant evidence drawn from the attainments of Amazon, Alibaba, UPS Stores and 7-Eleven in building digital consumer activity from the development of their digital platform-mediated business networks. The proposition is reinforced by platforms of connectivity associated with the creation of a network of consumers. As discussed, Facebook and TikTok have built digital consumer activity from a digital platform-mediated social network. This strategy has accorded other businesses, such as Uber Eats and Trivago, who, with few assets, have developed almost limitless 'power' from owning their social networks to create the new fuel of supply chain operations – consumer consumption data.

Mobile apps have been the prime vehicle for these global corporations to secure consumer connectivity, which, due to their ubiquity, have become the seat of enormous power. These mobile apps have created a 24/7 social presence that has connected consumers to suppliers, transporters and producers anywhere and anytime to highlight the propelling power or witchery of digital flows.

7. Configured by social consumption: towards a theory of supply chain operations under Industry 4.0

The evolving digital ecosystem of Industry 4.0 and, more particularly, the changing market environment in the wake of the COVID-19 pandemic has prompted the search for a theory of supply chain operations in this book. After the introduction (Chapter 1), our approach spread over five chapters has been to pursue a historical discourse on the supply chain both as a concept and a practice through the lens of consumption and technological evolution.

Our historical probe led us back to the start of Industry 1.0, where we traced the production-consumption cycles through the successive industrial revolutions (i.e. Industries 2.0, 3.0 and 4.0) in Chapter 2, noting the iconoclastic changes brought about by Industry 4.0. We stepped back from the production-consumption cycle in Chapter 3 to examine how those cycles morph from one revolution to the next, identifying the lynchpin role of technology in fostering logistics and supply chain efficiencies to fortify four waves of consumption (i.e. Consumerism 1.0, 2.0, 3.0 and 4.0).

We returned to the digital ecosystem of Industry 4.0 technology in Chapter 4 to gain a deeper glimpse of the visions, promises and challenges of those mind-boggling intelligent artefacts. Then we tried to make sense of their implications on supply chain operations against the backdrop of the incessant interactions between consumers and these artefacts, which spurs the rise of social consumption.

The unanticipated descent into COVID-19 lockdowns has accentuated these virtual interactions because many physical activities were forced to adopt a mirror online presence. This provided us with an opportunity to explore and assess the effects of Industry 4.0 technologies on supply chain operations to facilitate consumption under the partial absence of physical interactions in Chapter 5. Our analysis of consumption change and supply chain adjustments under the COVID-19 pandemic convinces us that supply chain performance under the digital ecosystem of Industry 4.0 (or Supply Chain 4.0) is built upon consumer connectivity. We drew on this observation to identify six types of productribution networks in Chapter 6, rationalizing that network connectivity will power supply chains' competitive advantage under the hegemony of the Industry 4.0 digital ecosystem.

This chapter connects the salient findings of Chapters 2 through 6 to amplify our underlying argument that changes in supply chain operations have been shaped by evolving patterns of consumption socialized by technological advancements. We argue that as human activities transcend from the physical to the virtual world under the digital connectivity of Industry 4.0, supply chain operations will be configured by social consumption.

REFLECTIONS

Logistics was revealed in Chapter 2 as a 'necessary evil' with its genesis in industrialization. As industrialization progressed from Industry 1.0 through to Industry 4.0, businesses increasingly needed the continuous upgrading of logistics, and subsequently supply chains, to bring goods faster to market. Yet the function of logistics was not considered to be 'value adding'. Indeed, organizations have treated logistics typically as an 'adjunct' activity – an indispensable, non-value-adding operation, the cost of which ought to be minimized.

During Industry 3.0 the supply chain concept was born out of the drive towards improving cost-efficiency. This task involved reducing logistical costs by increasing the speed of flows under the conventional brick-and-mortar retailing process. There was a pressing need to link a range of disparate logistical operations together to enhance the flow of goods from manufacturers through distributors to retailers.

'Supply chain management', as noted in Chapter 2, was first coined in 1982 by Keith Oliver. The term was intended to denote the 'chain of supply' that united fragmented corporations, which had involved, separately, the sourcing of raw materials, manufacturing, distribution and retailing of finished goods to consumers (Lambert et al., 1998). Viewing the logistics of sourcing and procurement, manufacturing, storage, transport, distribution and retailing as a chain of linked functions allowed these distinctive activities to be organized and staged as a 'flow of goods' process. This operation resulted in less cost and fewer risks. Thus, supply chain operations, as such, were conceived as a set of logistical functions organized to facilitate consumption.

Speed to market became a competitive norm under the brick-and-mortar retailing system. This precept reiterated the need to continuously increase the logistical efficiency of the conventional retailing channel. With production framed on a make-to-forecast strategy, supply chain operators were focused upon achieving speed to market both to fuel consumption rates and to gain a competitive edge.

Retailers made up the market and, as noted in Chapter 3's account of the evolution of consumerism, were the sole interface between the product supply chains and the consumers under brick-and-mortar retailing. Consumers converged on retailers under the conventional brick-and-mortar retailing regime. Access to supply chain and logistics infrastructure became critical – transport and communications hubs, notably container ports, aerotropolises and Internet hubs, were progressively incorporated into multilayered global gateways typified by Amsterdam, Hong Kong, Los Angeles, New York, Singapore and Tokyo.

Telephone and mail orders expanded the retailing landscape, offering an alternative to brick-and-mortar retailing, bypassing the retailers and creating an additional interface between the product supply chains and the consumers. As typified by Dell's 'make-to-order' mode, described in Chapter 3, products were able to flow from manufacturers and/or suppliers direct to consumers that met their exact specifications.

The advent of the Internet added yet another alternative to the brick-and-mortar retailing market, giving rise to e-commerce and creating multichannel retailing and the 'goods to flow' strategy. Invention of the mobile phone further augmented the 'alternative to brick-and-mortar' retailing market – suppliers and consumers can connect anywhere without being constrained by the location-grounded landline.

The birth of the smart phone, particularly the launch of the iPhone in 2007 and the Apple App Store in 2008, revolutionized e-commerce, giving rise to m-commerce and omnichannel retailing. This has been characterized as 'Triple-A shopping': shop anything, anytime, anywhere. Triple A shopping moves the consumer purchasing journey into the new era and the retailing industry 'toward a concierge model geared toward helping consumers, rather than only on transactions and deliveries' (Brynjolfsson et al., 2013: 24).

Aimed at offering consumers a seamless flow of experience between the e-commerce showroom and the brick-and-mortar store, omnichannel retailing promoted 'dynamic fulfilment'. This has led to warehouses doubling up as showrooms and display centres, while retail outlets also function as mini-warehouses and retail showrooms. Thus, warehousing and showcasing, as illustrated by IKEA's operations, have merged under one roof (Hamstra, 2015). Although IKEA's original setup predated the advent of omnichannel retailing, it came to epitomize the purchasing process through the digital and app versions of its catalogue on smart phones and tablets, promoted through social media, notably Facebook, Pinterest and Twitter.

Concomitant with the emergence of flexible omnichannel retailing is the explosive growth of social media. Social networking replaces physical networking. E-commerce and m-commerce took on a new image – customer feedback became a robust authentic advertising channel and a primary organ for nurturing consumer connectivity beyond loyalty.

Industry 4.0 technologies, as outlined in Chapter 4, further transformed the m-commerce ecosystem. These technologies opened a host of possibilities to inject 'realism' into digital retailing: shopping for goods need not necessarily entail a visit to the High Street.

The virtual showroom offers more shopping excitement for the consumer, especially the greater 'look' than that offered by the physical showroom, except there is no opportunity for the physical tasting of products like food or trying on clothing. Supported by the explosive growth of digital platforms and the growing dominance of social media, the comments of peers take centre stage. Social commerce becomes all the rage. The consumers' purchasing journey becomes an integral part of the digital social fabric. Drawing upon social media most steps of the way, a typical journey is outlined in Figure 7.1.

Also, Industry 4.0 technologies offer vast opportunities to supply chains to transform their operations. Indeed, supply chains have striven to keep pace with the myriad of possibilities that have unfolded from social commerce exploding upon digital platforms to emulate the seamless experience promise afforded by omnichannel retailing. As outlined in Chapter 4, this process has led not only to the use of drones and autonomous vehicles but also the popularization of consumer logistics.

The unanticipated arrival of the COVID-19 pandemic accelerated the transformation of supply chain operations, accentuating the criticality of e-commerce and m-commerce, heightening the superiority of the virtual showrooms. These developments have put global supply chains to the acid test of adaptability and flexibility. For example, automobile manufacturers during the pandemic became producers of ventilators, and beer distilleries turned into sanitizer manufacturers. Business imagination was also stretched to develop options for contactless last-mile deliveries during lockdowns. This resulted in car-boot deliveries and the age-old method of lowering baskets from apartment windows to collect goods. After shutting down Uber Rush in 2018 after a four-year operation, Uber (2020) launched two new types of services – Uber Direct and Uber Connect – offering businesses and individuals on-demand pick-ups and deliveries of pre-paid local goods by shared economy couriers (Dickey, 2018). These outcomes have prompted Christopher Craighead and others (2020) to coin the term 'transiliency' to describe the need for supply chain managers to restore some processes during a pandemic and jettison others.

As featured in Chapter 5, the COVID-19 pandemic also prompted businesses to recognize the importance of staff and customer care. Customer satisfaction can only be achieved if staff welfare is supported because customer care breeds customer satisfaction. The mandatory physical isolation and distancing arising

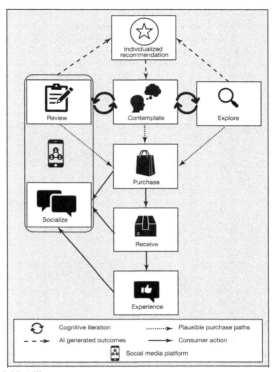

Note: AI – artificial intelligence.

Figure 7.1   A social shopping purchasing journey

from the COVID-19 lockdown and travel restrictions have also amplified the advantages of digital consumer connectivity.

Digital consumer connectivity, discussed in Chapter 6, has been built from either digital platform-mediated business networks typified by Amazon, Alibaba, UPS Store and 7-Eleven or the digital platform-mediated social networks characterized by Facebook and TikTok. As illustrated by Uber Eats and Airbnb, businesses who own these social networks are accorded almost limitless 'power' with few assets. Thus, these platform-mediated business and social networks have become global corporations, commanding enormous power through their networks of consumer connectivity.

Digital consumer connectivity has allowed businesses to transition from a service to a solution approach by working collaboratively with their customers to save costs, create needed services and grow. Indeed, digital consumer

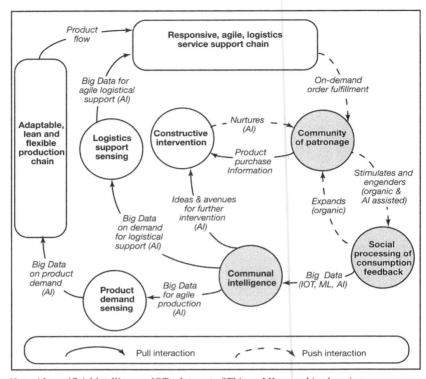

Note: AI – artificial intelligence; IOT – Internet of Things; ML – machine learning.

Figure 7.2   Value network of Supply Chain 4.0

connectivity has become the lynchpin of supply chain success under the Industry 4.0 ecosystem.

Social commerce has taken hold and artificial intelligence, Big Data analytics and the Internet of Things have continued to make inroads into Supply Chain 4.0 operations. This penetration has prompted us to argue that the value network of Supply Chain 4.0 will hinge on how well businesses can leverage artificial intelligence. In turn, Big Data analytics and the Internet of Things will constructively intervene in the socialization process of consumer purchases to provide unprecedented customer care and engender a community of patronage – the primary premise of the concierge model (Brynjolfsson et al., 2013: 24). Through artificial intelligence, the communal intelligence generated could be selectively extracted to progressively enhance and fine-tune three specific mechanisms in Supply Chain 4.0 operations: constructive intervention, logistics support sensing and product demand sensing.

'Constructive intervention' will target the growth of the 'community of patronage' to expand as well as solidify consumer connectivity. 'Product demand sensing' will inform the structuring of an adaptable, lean and flexible production chain to produce needed products on demand. 'Logistics support sensing' will provide directions on configuring a responsive, agile logistics service support chain within a specific operations context to meet on-demand order fulfilment. These conceptual underpinnings of the Supply Chain 4.0 Value Network are depicted in Figure 7.2.

Our conceptual underpinnings are underscored by what Nike, Alibaba and Pinduoduo are already doing. They milk the vast trails of consumers' digital footprints on their apps to determine what goods should be made or to alter how goods have been made, including using technology-aided planting techniques to increase specific types of fruit and vegetable yields on farms. Henry Tricks (2021) labels this operation 'mass craftmanship', also referred to as 'consumer to manufacturer' in China.

CONFIGURED BY SOCIAL CONSUMPTION

Industry 4.0 has given rise to Supply Chain 4.0. What has not been obvious is that while technology is providing businesses with the impetus to redefine and resynchronize their supply chain operations, technology is also constantly being reshaped by consumers through a continuous process of social interactions (see Chapter 4). Supply chain operators wanting to harness the prowess of technology need to appreciate and draw wisdom from the social shaping of technology. This book has argued that the dynamism of supply chain operations sits at the heart of the three interacting elements in Figure 7.3: technological advancements, business process changes and consumer purchase journeys.

Guided by that view, we have reviewed the historical evolution of supply chain operations through the unification of disparate logistics functions that emerged five decades ago. Our review has shown that these dissimilar logistics functions, viewed primarily as adjunct activities, have grown from being necessary evils to becoming recognized as an essential support function with the coining of supply chains. With supply chain activities continuing to be recognized as an indispensable component of business processes, supply chain operations have recently evolved into a corporate strategic resource. With the advent of Industry 4.0 technologies, we ask the critical question: What does supply chain management entail under Industry 4.0?

Our review journey has been reinforced by the events that have unfolded following the unanticipated arrival of the COVID-19 pandemic and the global responses to curb its spread. These outcomes have convinced us that supply

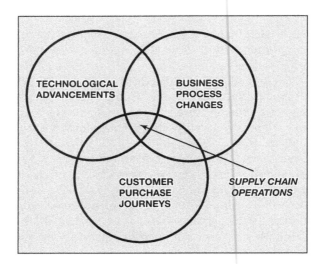

Figure 7.3   Nexus of supply chain operations

chain management under Supply Chain 4.0 will be staged as two interconnected smart layers: a digital value network centred upon social commerce
sitting atop two dynamically adaptive on-demand operational processes of
production and distribution in the physical space (Figure 7.4).

Social commerce (or social consumption) in the digital value network
will be anchored, as noted, by three specific mechanisms in Supply Chain
4.0 operations: 'constructive intervention', 'logistics support sensing' and
'product demand sensing'. In turn, the three key mechanisms of Supply Chain
4.0 operations will be powered by three smart hubs: the 'customer solution
hub', the 'customer experience hub' and the 'business process hub'. The three
hubs will be fuelled by Big Data produced from social commerce seated on
a platform-mediated network powered by machine learning.

The two dynamically adaptive on-demand operational processes will
provide the physical consumption support and will comprise an 'adaptable,
lean and flexible production chain' and a 'responsive, agile logistics service
support chain' to form a dynamic *productribution* network (see Chapter 6).
This is our vision of the operations of Supply Chain 4.0, where the physical
productribution network will coalesce with the intelligent social commerce
network.

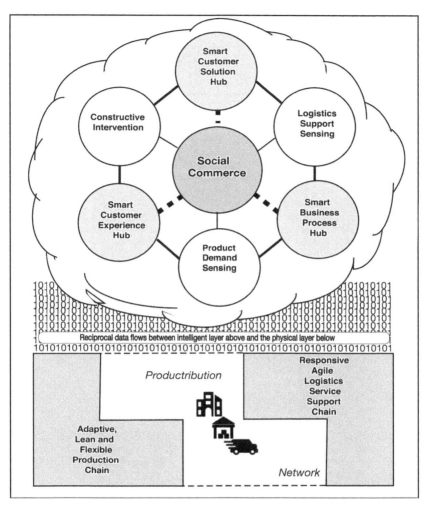

Figure 7.4   Supply Chain 4.0: Smart Productribution Network

Bibliography

3D Hubs (2019). *3D Printing Trends Q1 2019: Industry Highlights and Market Forecasts Including Special on 3D Printing in Automotive*. New York and Amsterdam: 3DHubs Manufacturing LLC and 3D Hubs B.V.

3D Hubs (2020). *3D Printing Trends 2020: Industry Highlights and Market Trends*. New York and Amsterdam: 3DHubs Manufacturing LLC and 3D Hubs B.V.

7-Eleven (2021). 'Enjoy app exclusive deals', 7eleven.com. Available at www.7eleven .com.au/my-7-eleven.html?gclid=EAIaIQobChMConnectivityqLr7wIV7xxyC h32cwPgEAAYASAAEgIlp_D_BwE&gclsrc=aw.ds (accessed 7 April 2021).

ACCC (2021). 'Dominance of Apple and Google's app stores impacting competition and consumers', Australian Competition and Consumer Commission, 18 April. Available at www.accc.gov.au/media-release/dominance-of-apple-and-google%E2 %80%99s-app-stores-impacting-competition-and-consumers (accessed 30 July 2021).

Accenture (2020). 'Building supply chain resilience: What to do now and next during COVID-19', Accenture.com, 17 March. Available at www.accenture.com/au-en/ about/company/coronavirus-supply-chain-impact (accessed 12 February 2021).

Actility (2019). 'Volvo Group implements an IoT tracking solution in its trucks plant, using Actility LoRaWAN GPS trackers and network management', Press release, 7 September. Available at www.actility.com/volvo-group-implements-in -its-trucks-plant-an-iot-tracking-solution-using-lorawan-gps-trackers-and-network -management-from-actility/ (accessed 19 November 2020).

Adhi, Praveen, Andrew Davis, Jai Jayakumar and Sarah Touse (2020). 'Reimagining stores for retail's next normal', McKinsey & Company, 22 April. Available at www .mckinsey.com/industries/retail/our-insights/reimagining-stores-for-retails-next -normal (accessed 22 February 2021).

Alam, Shahriar Tanvir, Sayem Ahmed, Syed Mithun Ali, Sudipa Sarker, Golam Kabir and Asif ul-Islam (2021). 'Challenges to COVID-19 vaccine supply chain: Implications for sustainable development goals', *International Journal of Production Economics*, 239: 108193.

Alfalla-Luque, Rafaela and Carmen Medina-López (2009). 'Supply Chain Management: Unheard of in the 1970s, core to today's company', *Business History*, 51(2): 202–221.

Ali, Imran, Sattar Satie and Vinh Thai (2021). 'Adopting Industry 4.0 technologies in agri-food supply chains: An exploratory investigation of drivers and barriers', in Emel Aktas, Michael Bourlakis, Ioannis Minis and Vasileios Zeimpekis (eds), *Improving Supply Chains with Analytics and Industry 4.0 Technologies*. London: Kogan Page, pp. 209–233.

Alibaba Cloud (2021). 'Alibaba Cloud's global infrastructure', Alibaba Cloud.com. Available at www.alibabacloud.com/global-locations (accessed 20 April 2021).

Alicke, Knut, Jürgen Rachor and Andreas Seyfert (2016). 'Supply Chain 4.0 – the next-generation digital supply chain', McKinsey.com, 27 October. Available at

www.mckinsey.com/business-functions/operations/our-insights/supply-chain-40-
-the-next-generation-digital-supply-chain# (accessed 20 October 2020).

Alicke, Knut, Richa Gupta and Vera Trautwein (2020). 'Resetting supply chains for the next normal', McKinsey & Company, 21 July. Available at www.mckinsey.com/business-functions/operations/our-insights/resetting-supply-chains-for-the-next-normal (accessed 23 February 2021).

Aljazeera (2021). 'Could a shipping crisis derail economic recovery from COVID-19?', *Inside Story*. Available at www.aljazeera.com/program/inside-story/2021/6/16/could-a-shipping-crisis-derail-economic-recovery-from-covid-19 (accessed 18 June 2021).

Amaranto, Glenita, Natali Chun and Anil Deolalikar (2010). 'Who are the middle class and what values do they hold? Evidence from the World Values Survey', *ADB Economics Working Paper Series No. 229*. Tokyo: Asian Development Bank. Available at https://think-asia.org/handle/11540/1566 (accessed 11 August 2020).

Ambrose, Jillian (2021). 'Brexit and Covid blamed as Asia-UK shipping occasioning rates increase fourfold', *Guardian*, 9 January. Available at www.theguardian.com/business/2021/jan/08/brexit-and-covid-blamed-as-asia-uk-shipping-rates-increase-fourfold (accessed 14 February 2021).

André, Jean-Claude (2019). *Industry 4.0: Paradoxes and Conflicts*. London: International Society for Technology in Education and Wiley.

Arcand, Rob (2019). 'The story of the very first thing securely sold on the Internet', Noisey: VICE.com, 15 August. Available at www.vice.com/en/article/bjwxzd/the-first-thing-sold-online-was-a-sting-cd (accessed 23 June 2021).

Aryapadi, Manik, Vishwa Chandra, Asutosh Dekhne, Kenza Haddioui, Tim Lange and Kumar Venkataraman (2020a). 'Five actions retail supply chains can take to navigate the coronavirus pandemic', McKinsey & Company, 1 April. Available at www.mckinsey.com/industries/retail/our-insights/five-actions-retail-supply-chains-can-take-to-navigate-the-coronavirus-pandemic (accessed 23 February 2021).

Aryapadi, Manik, Ashutosh Dekhne, Wolfgang Fleischer, Claudia Graf and Tim Lange (2020b). 'Supply chain of the future: Key principles in building an omnichannel distribution network', McKinsey & Company, January. Available at www.mckinsey.com/~/media/McKinsey/Industries/Retail/Our%20Insights/Future%20of%20retail%20operations%20Winning%20in%20a%20digital%20era/McK_Retail-Ops-2020_FullIssue-RGB-hyperlinks-011620.pdf (accessed 8 August 2020).

Asthana, Rahul (2018). 'Making sense of Supply Chain 4.0: What, exactly, can "digital transformation" improve upon?', *Industry Week*, 2 November. Available at www.industryweek.com/supply-chain/article/22026620/making-sense-of-supply-chain-40 (accessed 20 October 2020).

Atluri, Venkat, Aamer Baig and Satya Rao, eds (2018). 'Tech-enabled transformation: The million dollar opportunity for industrials', McKinsey & Company, September. Available at www.mckinsey.com/~/media/McKinsey/Business%20Functions/McKinsey%20Digital/Our%20Insights/Tech%20enabled%20transformation/Tech-enabled-transformation-The-trillion-dollar-opportunity-for-industrials.pdf (accessed 10 March 2021).

Atluri, Venkat, Aamer Baig, Rasagya Kabra and Satya Rao (2020). 'The industrial CEO's plan for the digital recovery', McKinsey & Company, 8 November. Available at www.mckinsey.com/industries/advanced-electronics/our-insights/the-industrial-ceos-plan-for-the-digital-recovery# (accessed 9 June 2020).

Australian Associated Press (2021). 'COVID shapes Aussie shopping habits: Study', *The Canberra Times*, 10 July. Available at www.canberratimes.com.au/story/ 7334528/covid-shapes-aussie-shopping-habits-study/ (accessed 10 July 2021).

Australian Government (2018a). *German–Australian Cooperation on Industrie 4.0: Platform Industrie 4.0*. Canberra: Prime Minister's Industry 4.0 Taskforce. Available at www.industry.gov.au/sites/default/files/2019-03/german-australian-cooperation -on-industrie-4.0.pdf (accessed 7 May 2020).

Australian Government (2018b). *Industry 4.0*. Canberra: Department of Industry, Science, Energy and Resources, Australian Government. Available at www.industry .gov.au/funding-and-incentives/industry-40 (accessed 7 May 2020).

Australian Government (2021). *Vulnerable Supply Chains: Productivity Commission Study Report, July 2021*. Canberra: Australian Government Productivity Commission. Available at www.pc.gov.au/inquiries/completed/supply-chains#report (accessed 22 August 2021).

AWS (2021). 'Global infrastructure: The most secure, extensive, and reliable global cloud infrastructure, for all your applications', *Amazon Web Services*. Available at https://aws.amazon.com/about-aws/global-infrastructure/ (accessed 2 April 2021).

Azzi, Rita, Rima Kilany Chamoun and Maria Sokhn (2019). 'The power of a blockchain-based supply chain', *Computers and Industrial Engineering*, 135: 582–592.

Baertlein, Lisa (2021). 'Echoing Amazon: Walmart, Target try local package delivery', *Reuters*, 19 May. Available at www.reuters.com/business/retail-consumer/echoing -amazon-walmart-target-try-local-package-delivery-2021-05-19/ (accessed 5 July 2021).

Baig, Aamer, Bryce Hall, Paul Jenkins, Eric Lamarre and Brian McCarthy (2020). 'The COVID recovery will be digital', *McKinsey Digital*. Available at www.mckinsey .com/business-functions/mckinsey-digital/our-insights/the-covid-19-recovery-will -be-digital-a-plan-for-the-first-90-days (accessed 10 March 2021).

Baird, Nikki (2020). 'Retail in the 2020s: The death of consumerism?', *Forbes*, 28 February. Available at www.forbes.com/sites/nikkibaird/2020/02/28/the-20s-retail -decade-the-death-of-consumerism/?sh=1b3758d44952 (accessed 25 February 2021).

Bala, Raj, Bob Gill, Dennis Smith, David Wright and Kevin Ji (2020). 'Magic quad-rant for cloud infrastructure and platform services', *Gartner*, 1 September – ID G00441742. Available at www.gartner.com/en/documents/2020/3989743-magic -quadrant-for-cloud-infrastructure-and-platform-ser1 (accessed 21 April 2021).

Balakrishnan, Tara, Michael Chui, Bryce Hall and Nicholaus Henke (2020). 'The state of AI in 2020', McKinsey.com, 17 November. Available at www.mckinsey.com/ business-functions/mckinsey-analytics/our-insights/global-survey-the-state-of-ai-in -2020 (accessed 30 December 2020).

Ballou, Ronald H. (2007). 'The evolution and future of logistics and supply chain management', *European Business Review*, 19(4): 332–348.

Baraniuk, Chris (2021). 'Covid-19: How the UK vaccine rollout delivered success, so far', *BMJ*, 18 February. Available at https://doi.org/10.1136/bmj.n421 (accessed 29 May 2021).

Barenji, Ali Vatankhah, Zhi Li, W.M. Wang, George Q. Huang and David A. Guerra-Zubiaga (2020). 'Blockchain-based ubiquitous manufacturing: A secure and reliable cyber-physical system', *International Journal of Production Research*, 58(7): 2200–2221.

Barre, Jack (2020). 'If Uber's food-delivery business isn't profitable now, when can it be?', *Intelligencer*, 10 August. Available at https://nymag.com/intelligencer/2020/08/if-uber-eats-isnt-profitable-now-when-can-it-be.html (accessed 12 April 2021).

BBC (2020a). 'Coronavirus: Much of "the world's factory" still shut', BBC.com, 7 February. Available at www.bbc.com/news/business-51439400 (accessed 10 February 2021).

BBC (2020b). 'Coronavirus: iPhone manufacturer Foxconn to make masks', *BBC News*, 7 February. Available at www.bbc.com/news/business-51410700 (accessed 7 February 2021).

BBC (2020c). 'Life after lockdown: How China went back to work', *BBC News*, 30 April. Available at www.bbc.com/worklife/article/20200430-is-china-going-back-to-normal-coronavirus-covid-19 (accessed 15 July 2021).

BBC (2020d). 'TikTok threatens legal action against Trump US ban', *British Broadcasting Corporation*, 7 August. Available at www.bbc.com/news/business-53660860 (accessed 30 June 2021).

BBC (2021). 'Covid vaccine: How many people in the UK have been vaccinated so far?', *BBC News*, 4 September. Available at www.bbc.com/news/health-55274833 (accessed 6 September 2021).

Becker, Annie, ed. (2008). *Electronic Commerce: Concepts, Methodologies, Tools, and Applications*. Hershey, PA: IGI Global.

Behrendt, Andreas, Enno de Boer, Tarek Kasah, Bodo Köerber, Niko Mohr and Gérard Richter (2021). 'Insights into the Internet of Things: A manufacturers guide to scaling IoT', *McKenzie Digital*, 5 February. Available at www.mckinsey.com/featured-insights/internet-of-things/our-insights (accessed 3 March 2021).

Ben-Daya, Mohamed, Elkafi Hassini and Zied Bahroun (2019). 'Internet of Things and supply chain management: A literature review', *International Journal of Production Research*, 57(15–16): 4719–4742.

Berg, Jeff, Eric Buesing, Vinay Gupta and Raelyn Jacobson (2020). 'Customer-care organizations: Moving from crisis management to recovery', McKinsey & Company, 3 April. Available at www.mckinsey.com/business-functions/operations/our-insights/customer-care-organizations-moving-from-crisis-management-to-recovery (accessed 1 March 2021).

Bernhofen, Daniel M., Zouheir El Sahli and Richard Kneller (2016). 'Estimating the effects of the trade', *Journal of International Economics*, 9: 36–50.

Berthene, April (2020). 'Shoppers buy more on line compared with before the pandemic', *Digital Commerce 360*, 8 June. Available at www.digitalcommerce360.com/2020/06/08/shoppers-buy-more-online-compared-with-before-the-pandemic/ (accessed 17 October 2020).

Betti, Francisco, Enno de Boer and Yves Giraud (2020). 'The Fourth Industrial Revolution and manufacturing's great reset', McKinsey & Company, 14 September. Available at www.mckinsey.com/business-functions/operations/our-insights/the-fourth-industrial-revolution-and-manufacturings-great-reset (accessed 5 March 2021).

Bhargava, Shruti, Bo Finneman, Jennifer Schmidt and Emma Spagnuolo (2020). 'The young and the restless: Generation Z in America', McKinsey & Company, 20 March. Available at www.mckinsey.com/industries/retail/our-insights/the-young-and-the-restless-generation-z-in-america (accessed 24 July 2020).

Biagi, Susan (2020). 'Rogue Ales uses IoT for efficient supply chain tracking', *IOT Integrator*, 20 January. Available at www.theiotintegrator.com/industrial

-manufacturing/rogue-ales-uses-iot-for-efficient-supply-chain-tracking (accessed 9 November 2020).

Binder, Rachel (2021). 'Last-mile on the mind', *CB Insights*, 20 May.

Biswas, Baidyanath and Robit Gupta (2019). 'Analysis of barriers to implementing, blockchain industry and service sectors', *Computers and Industrial Engineering*, 136: 225–241.

Boczkowski, Pablo J. (2004). 'The mutual shaping of technology and society in videotex newspapers: Beyond the diffusion and social shaping perspectives', *The Information Society*, 20(4): 255–267.

Boothby, Bryce (2021). 'The omnichannel alphabet soup: Structuring the unstructured', *MPO: Customer Chain Control*, 22 February. Available at https://blog.mpo .com/omnichannel-alphabet-soup (accessed 26 February 2021).

Boughner, Zeba and Kandice McQueen (2020). 'Where is my container, where is my cargo, and where is my coffee?', *TradeLens*, 28 October. Available at www .tradelens.com/post/where-is-my-container-where-is-my-cargo-and-where-is-my -coffee?partnerref=social (accessed 3 November 2020).

Bowles, Ruthie (2021). 'Organized chaos: Behind the scenes of Amazon's inventory management system', Logiwa.com, 28 June. Available at www.logiwa.com/blog/ amazon-inventory-management-system (accessed 30 June 2021).

Brady, Dianne with Edward Barriball and Susan Lund (2020). 'COVID-19 and supply-chain recovery: Planning for the future', McKinsey & Co., podcast, 9 October. Available at www.mckinsey.com/business-functions/operations/our -insights/covid-19-and-supply-chain-recovery-planning-for-the-future (accessed 17 May 2021).

Briglia, Casey (2020). 'Why customer engagement is important', *Gartner*, 20 August. Available at www.gartner.com/en/digital-markets/insights/why-customer -engagement-is-important (accessed 9 June 2021).

Brynjolfsson, Erik, Yu Jeffrey Hu and Mohammad S. Rahman (2013). 'Competing in the age of omnichannel retailing', *MIT Sloan Management Review*, 54(4): 23–29.

Buesing, Eric, Becca Kleinstein and Joshua Wolff (2018). 'Elevating customer satisfaction and growth through service to solutions', McKinsey & Company, 16 March. Available at www.mckinsey.com/business-functions/operations/our-insights/ elevating-customer-satisfaction-and-growth-through-service-to-solutions (accessed 1 March 2021).

C2VA (2020). 'A guide to marketing on China's social media platforms', *Click2ViewAsia*, 12 August. Available at https://click2view.asia/a-guide-to -marketing-on-china-social-media-platforms/ (accessed 27 June 2021).

Callaghan, Shaun, Martin Lösch, Stefan Rickert and Warren Teichner (2020). 'At the heart of a crisis: How consumer-health companies can lead in the time of the coronavirus', in McKinsey & Company (ed.), *Jumpstarting the Recovery: Navigating the Return across Industries*, McKinsey Publishing, May, pp.14–21.

Callahan, Sean (2020). 'So long 2010s: Reflecting on a decade in marketing and what's next', LinkedIn Marketing Solutions, blog, 8 January. Available at https:// business.linkedin.com/marketing-solutions/blog/b2b-content-marketing/2020/so -long--2010s--reflecting-on-a-decade-in-marketing-and-whats-ne (accessed 24 May 2021).

Carey, Conner (2021). 'The evolution of the iPhone: Every model from 2007–2020', *iPhoneLife Magazine*, 8 April. Available at www.iphonelife.com/content/evolution -iphone-every-model-2007-2016 (accessed 31 July 2021).

Cassidy, John (2002). *Dot.Con: The Greatest Story Ever Sold*. New York: Harper Collins.

CBI (2021a). 'Here's a list of 117 bankruptcies in the retail apocalypse and why they failed', *CB Insights*, 19 September. Available at www.cbinsights.com/research/retail -apocalypse-timeline-infographic (accessed 7 June 2021).

CBI (2021b). *State of Retail Tech Q1 21 Report: Investment and Sector Trends to Watch*. New York: CB Insights.

Chaffey, Dave (2021). 'Amazon marketing strategy: Business case study, revenue model and culture of customer metrics: History of Amazon.com marketing objectives', *Smart Insights*, 4 May. Available at www.smartinsights.com/digital -marketing-strategy/online-business-revenue-models/amazon-casestudy/ (accessed 11 June 2021).

Chang, Rachel, Kevin Varley, Michael Munoz, Felix Tam and Malavika Kaur Makol (2021). 'The Covid resilience ranking: The best and worst places to be as Delta wrecks reopening plans', Bloomberg.com, 26 August. Available at www.bloomberg .com/graphics/covid-resilience-ranking/ (accessed 2 September 2021).

Chapman, Lizette (2020). 'Uber Eats ditches seven countries, subsidiary Careem cuts staff', *Bloomberg*, 5 May. Available at www.bloombergquint.com/technology/uber -eats-ditches-seven-countries-where-food-delivery-lags (accessed 13 January 2022).

Charm, Tamara, Ravi Dhar, Stacey Haas, Jenny Liu, Nathan Novemsky and Warren Teichner (2020). 'Understanding and shaping consumer behavior in the next normal', McKinsey & Company, 24 July. Available at www.mckinsey.com/business -functions/marketing-and-sales/our-insights/understanding-and-shaping-consumer -behavior-in-the-next-normal (accessed 31 August 2020).

Charm, Tamara, Anne Grimmelt, Hyunjin Kim, Kelsey Robinson, Nancy Lu, Mayank, Mianne Ortega Yvonne Staack and Naomi Yamakawa (2021). 'Consumer sentiment and behavior continue to reflect the uncertainty of the COVID-19 crisis', McKinsey & Company, 26 October. Available at www.mckinsey.com/business-functions/ marketing-and-sales/our-insights/a-global-view-of-how-consumer-behavior-is -changing-amid-covid-19 (accessed 8 May 2021).

Chopra, Sunil (2018). 'The evolution of omni-channel retailing and its impact on supply chains', *Transport Research Procedia*, 30: 4–13.

Chottani, Aisha, Greg Hastings, John Murnane and Florian Neuhaus (2018). 'Distraction or disruption? Autonomous trucks gain ground in US logistics', McKinsey & Company, 20 December. Available at www.mckinsey.com/industries/travel-logistics -and-infrastructure/our-insights/distraction-or-disruption-autonomous-trucks-gain -ground-in-us-logistics (accessed 15 February 2021).

Christopher, Martin (2021). 'Supply Chain 4.0: Enabling market-driven strategies', in Emel Aktas, Michael Bourlakis, Ioannis Minis and Vasileios Zeimpekis (eds), *Improving Supply Chains with Analytics and Industry 4.0 Technologies*. London: Kogan Page, pp. 1–15.

Chua, Beng-Huat, ed. (2000). *Consumption in Asia: Lifestyles and Identities*. London: Routledge.

Coe, Neil M., Phillip F. Kelly and Henry W.C. Yeung (2007). *Economic Geography: A Contemporary Introduction*. Malden, MA: Blackwell.

Cogito (2020). 'Elevate human connections in real time with Cogito: Augment your workforce with the AI coaching system for the contact center', Cogito.com, 11 November. Available at https://cogitocorp.com/ (accessed 2 March 2021).

Columbus, Louis (2015). 'Ten ways Big Data is revolutionizing supply chain man- agement', *Forbes*, 13 July. Available at www.forbes.com/sites/louiscolumbus/

2015/07/13/ten-ways-big-data-is-revolutionizing-supply-chain-management/?sh=4 (accessed 9 November 2020).

Costello, John P. and Rebecca Walker Reczek (2020). 'Providers versus platforms: Marketing communications in the sharing economy', *Journal of Marketing*, 84(6): 22–38.

Crafts, Nicholas (2004). 'Productivity growth in the Industrial Revolution: A new growth accounting perspective', *Journal of Economic History*, 64(2): 521–535.

Craighead, Christopher W., David J. Ketchen, Jr. and Jessica L. Darby (2020). 'Pandemics and supply chain management research: Toward a theoretical toolbox', *Decision Sciences*, 51(4): 838–866.

Crandall, Richard E. (2017a). 'Industry 1.0 to 4.0: The evolution of smart factories', *SCM Now Magazine*, September/October. Available at www.apics.org/apics-for-individuals/apics-magazine-home/magazine-detail-page/2017/09/20/industry-1.0-to-4.0-the-evolution-of-smart-factories (accessed 28 April 2020).

Crandall, Richard E. (2017b). 'Upgrading smart 4.0: The evolution of smart factories', *SCM Now Magazine*, September/October. Available at www.apics.org/apics-for-individuals/apics-magazine-home/magazine-detail-page/2017/09/20/upgrading-smart-manufacturing-with-industry-4 (accessed 3 August 2020).

Cross, Tim (2020). 'An understanding of AI's limitations is starting to sink in', *The Economist*, 11 June. Available at www.economist.com/technology-quarterly/2020/06/11/an-understanding-of-ais-limitations-is-starting-to-sink-in (accessed 18 October 2020).

CRR (2021a). 'The crisis in retailing; Closures and job losses', Centre for Retail Research, May. Available at www.retailresearch.org/retail-crisis.html (accessed 7 June 2021).

CRR (2021b). 'Who's gone bust in retail? Who's gone bust in UK retailing in 2019–2021?', Centre for Retail Research, May. Available at www.retailresearch.org/whos-gone-bust-retail.html (accessed 7 June 2021).

Csikszentmihalyi, Mihaly (1990). *Flow – the Psychology of Optimal Experience.* New York: Harper and Row.

Cudahy, Brian J. (2006). *Box Boats: How Container Ships Changed the World.* New York: Fordham University Press.

Curry, David (2021a). 'Most popular apps (2020)', *Business of Apps*, 6 July. Available at www.businessofapps.com/data/most-popular-apps/ (accessed 14 August 2021).

Curry, David (2021b). 'Uber Eats revenue and usage statistics (2021)', *Business of Apps*, 19 March. Available at www.businessofapps.com/data/uber-eats-statistics/ (accessed 12 April 2021).

Daleiden, Joseph L. (1999). *The American Dream: Can It Survive the 21st Century?* Amherst: Prometheus Books.

Danziger, Pamela (2019). 'Marketing disrupted: Evolve from the 4Ps to the 4Es of marketing', *Unity Marketing*, 23 July. Available at https://pameladanziger.com/marketing-disrupted-evolve-from-the-4ps-to-the-4es-of-marketing/ (accessed 24 February 2021).

Davey, Joseph Dillion (2012). *The Shrinking American Middle Class: The Social and Cultural Implications of Growing Inequality.* New York: Palgrave Macmillan.

Davis, Steve and Precious Matsoso (2020). 'COVID-19 as a digital pandemic', *Think Global Health*, 7 July. Available at www.thinkglobalhealth.org/article/covid-19-digital-pandemic (accessed 17 July 2020).

De Haas, Henning, John Bang Mathiasen, Søren Skjold Andersen and Torben Tambo (2021). 'In search of a human dimension of Supply Chain 4.0: Stipulating learning as a lever for the future supply chain organization', in Emel Aktas, Michael Bourlakis, Ioannis Minis and Vasileios Zeimpekis (eds), *Improving Supply Chains with Analytics and Industry 4.0 Technologies*. London: Kogan Page, pp. 261–281.

Dekhne, Ashutosh, Greg Hastings, John Murnane and Florian Neuhaus (2019). 'Automation in logistics: Big opportunity, bigger uncertainty', McKinsey & Company, 24 April. Available at www.mckinsey.com/industries/travel-logistics -and-infrastructure/our-insights/automation-in-logistics-big-opportunity-bigger -uncertainty (accessed 28 April 2021).

Del Rey, Jason (2019). 'How robots are transforming Amazon warehouse jobs – for better and worse', *Vox*, 11 December. Available at www.vox.com/recode/2019/12/ 11/20982652/robots-amazon-warehouse-jobs-automation (accessed 31 May 2021).

Deloitte (2020). 'COVID-19's impact on the aerospace and defense sector: Guidance for aerospace and defense executives', Deloitte.com. Available at www2.deloitte .com/global/en/pages/about-deloitte/articles/covid-19/understanding-covid-19 -impact-on-aerospace-and-defense.html (accessed 10 March 2021).

Desai, Jignesh and Ezhil Mani (2020). 'How to rethink, and redefine retail stores', CIO.com, 28 April. Available at www.cio.com/article/3540299/how-to-rethink-and -redefine-retail-stores.html (accessed 15 March 2021).

Desai, Parag, Ali Potia and Brian Salsberg (2013). *Retail 4.0: The Future of Retail Grocery in a Digital World*. Singapore: McKinsey's Asia Consumer and Retail Practice.

Dick, H.W. (1985). 'The rise of a middle class and the changing concept of equity in Indonesia: An interpretation', *Indonesia*, 39(April): 71–92.

Dickey, Megan Rose (2018). 'Uber RUSH is shutting down', *Tech Crunch*, 31 March. Available at https://techcrunch.com/2018/03/30/uberrush-is-shutting-down/ (accessed 17 August 2021).

Diebner, Rachel, Elizabeth Silliman, Kelly Ungerman and Maxence Vancauwenberghe (2020). 'Adapting customer experience in the time of coronavirus', McKinsey & Company, 2 April. Available at www.mckinsey.com/business-functions/marketing -and-sales/our-insights/adapting-customer-experience-in-the-time-of-coronavirus (accessed 2 March 2021).

Dobosz, John (2021). 'Amazon and Walmart slug it out for retail supremacy as pandemic boosts sales for both GIANTS', *Forbes*, 13 May. Available at https://editorpen.com/ finance/market/amazon-and-walmart-slug-it-out-for-retail-supremacy-as-pandemic -boosts-sales-for-both-giants/ (accessed 1 July 2021).

Donovan, Arthur and Joseph Bonney (2006). *The Box That Changed the World: Fifty Years of Container Shipping – an Illustrated History*. East Windsor, NJ: Commonwealth Business Media.

Doshi, Rush (2020). 'The United States, China and the contest for the fourth industrial revolution', Prepared statement before the United States Senate Committee on Commerce, Science and Transportation Subcommittee, 30 July. Available at www.commerce.senate.gov/services/files/6880BBA6-2AF0-4A43-8D32 -6774E069B53E (accessed 1 August 2020).

DPDHL (2016). *Robotics in Logistics: A DPDHL Perspective on Implications and Use Cases for the Logistics Industry*. Troisdorf: DHL Customer Solutions and Innovation. Available at www.dhl.com/content/dam/downloads/g0/about_us/ logistics_insights/dhl_trendreport_robotics.pdf (accessed 19 July 2021).

Durkin, Patrick (2020). 'Daily delivery ends as posties switch to parcels', *Financial Review*, 21 April. Available at www.afr.com/companies/retail/daily-delivery-ends -as-posties-switch-to-parcels-20200421-p54lqq (accessed 18 October 2020).

DW (2021). 'COVID: EU pulls out all stops to boost vaccine rollout', *Deutsche Welle*, 17 April. Available at www.dw.com/en/covid-eu-pulls-out-all-stops-to-boost -vaccine-rollout/a-57117948 (accessed 2 September 2021).

Eadicicco, Lisa (2017). 'This is why the iPhone upended the tech industry', *Time*, 29 June. Available at https://time.com/4837176/iphone-10th-anniversary/ (accessed 13 August 2021).

Eberts, Stephanie, Tyler Potter, Jacquelyn Howard and Jake Werbeck (2021). 'How Starbucks improved supply chain operations with service management: Featuring insights for the Starbucks', Webinar, Starbucks, chaired by Karen Jenkins, 25 February. Available at www.youtube.com/watch?v=FKDm_iJohP4 (accessed 12 June 2021).

EC (2020). 'Developments and forecasts of growing consumerism', Brussels: European Commission. Available at https://ec.europa.eu/knowledge4policy/foresight/topic/ growing-consumerism/more-developments-relevant-growing-consumerism_en (accessed 12 January 2022).

The Economist (2021a). 'After the pandemic boom, online retail sales are slowing: But shoppers are still in splurging mood', *The Economist*, 20–21 May.

The Economist (2021b). 'The future of e-commerce: The great mall of China', *The Economist*, 2 January.

The Economist (2021c). 'E-commerce profits may become harder to make: The Amazons and Alibabas are not as impregnable as they might seem', Special Report: The Retail Renaissance – the Future of Shopping, *The Economist*, 13 March.

Ellis, Simon (2020). *IDC White Paper: Solving the Pandemic Pharma Supply Chain Struggle*. North Reading, MA: Tracelink. Available at https://go.tracelink.com/ Discover-How-to-Solve-the-COVID-19-Supply-Chain-Struggle-Thank-You.html (accessed 24 March 2021).

F&F (2020). 'Global m-commerce market size will reach USD 3,901 million by 2026: Facts and Factors'. *Facts and Factors*, 23 December. Available at www .globenewswire.com/news-release/2020/12/23/2149983/0/en/Global-M-Commerce -Market-Size-Will-Reach-USD-3-901-Million-by-2026-Facts-Factors.html (accessed 28 January 2021).

Facebook (2021). 'Facebook Marketplace directory'. Available at www.facebook.com/ marketplace/directory/ (accessed 24 June 2021).

Factorachian, Hajar and Hadi Kazemi (2021). 'Impact of Industry 4.0 on supply chain performance', *Production Planning and Control*, 32(1): 63–81.

Fahrni, Stefan, Christian Jansen, Michael John, Tarek Kasah, Bodo Körber and Niko Mohr (2020). 'Coronavirus: Industrial IoT in challenging times', McKinsey & Company, 22 April. Available at www.mckinsey.com/~/media/McKinsey/ Industries/Advanced%20Electronics/Our%20Insights/Coronavirus%20Industrial %20IoT%20in%20challenging%20times/Coronavirus-industrial-iot-in-challenging -times.pdf?shouldIndex=false (accessed 3 March 2021).

Farachi, Gary (2020). Personal communication, 5 May.

Fast Radius (2018). 'Fast Radius named one of the "nine best factories in the world" by the World Economic Forum', Fast Radius.com, September. Available at www .fastradius.com/news/fast-radius-named-one-of-the-nine-best-factories-in-the-world -by-the-world-economic-forum/ (accessed 10 April 2020).

Fast Radius (2021). 'Fast Radius', Fast Radius.com. Available at www.fastradius.com/ (accessed 7 April 2021).

Ferrantino, Michael J. and Emine Elcin Koten (2019). 'Understanding Supply Chain 4.0 and its potential impact on global value chains', in *Global Value Chain*

Development Report 2019: Technological Innovation, Supply Chain Trade, and Workers in a Globalized World. Washington, DC: World Bank Group and World Trade Organization, pp. 103–119.

Fetherstonhaugh, Brian (2009). 'The 4P's are out, the 4E's are in', *Ogilvy and Mather*, 19 April. Available at www.ogilvy.com/on-our-minds/articles/the_4e_-are_in.aspx (accessed 24 February 2021).

Fiedler, Lars, Eric Hazan, Brian Ruwadi and Kelly Ungerman (2020). 'The reinvention of retail: Everybody needs to rethink both digital and in-store sales', *Periscope @ McKinsey*, August. Available at www.mckinsey.com/business-functions/marketing -and-sales/solutions/periscope/our-insights/surveys/reinventing-retail (accessed 28 January 2021).

Fink, Larry (2020). '"Climate risk is investment risk": BlackRock exiting thermal coal investments', S&P Global.com, 14 January. Available at www.spglobal.com/ marketintelligence/en/news-insights/trending/ielAyMF1ZEZZHhP1MVhWBQ2 (accessed 3 March 2021).

Fisher, Marshall L., Santiago Gallino and Joseph Jiaqi Xi (2019). 'The value of rapid delivery in online retailing', *Journal of Marketing Research*, 56(5): 732–748.

Forger, Gary (2018). 'NextGen supply chain interview: Tom Ward', *Supply Chain Management Review*, 15 August. Available at www.scmr.com/article/nextgen _supply_chain_interview_tom_ward (accessed 25 November 2020).

Forrester (2000). 'eMarketplaces will lead US Business eCommerce to $2.7 trillion in 2004, according to Forrester', Forrester.com, 7 February. Available at https://go .forrester.com/press-newsroom/emarketplaces-will-lead-us-business-ecommerce-to -2-7-trillion-in-2004-according-to-forrester/ (accessed 12 January 2020).

Francis, Tracy and Fernanda Hoefei (2018). '"True Gen": Generation Z and its implications for companies', McKinsey & Company, 12 November. Available at www.mckinsey.com/industries/consumer-packaged-goods/our-insights/true-gen -generation-z-and-its-implications-for-companies (accessed 24 July 2020).

Francks, Penelope (2009). *The Japanese Consumer: An Alternative Economic History of Modern Japan.* Cambridge: Cambridge University Press.

Frazzon, Enzo M., Carlos M.T. Rodriguez, Marina M. Pereira, Matheus C. Pires and Iracyanne Uhlmann (2019). 'Towards supply change management 4.0', *Brazilian Journal of Operations and Production Management*, 16(2): 180–191.

Freeman, Oliver (2020). 'Accenture: How robust is your supply chain?', *Supply Chain Digital*, 14 September. Available at www.supplychaindigital.com/technology-4/ accenture-how-robust-your-supply-chain (accessed 12 February 2021).

Freshippo (2021). 'What is Freshippo?', *Alibaba Group*, 15 March. Available at www .youtube.com/watch?v=STX7t8Q38s4 (accessed 12 June 2021).

Furlong, Joanna (2017). 'RFID for retail: Know the pros and cons', business.com, 14 July. Available at www.business.com/articles/rfid-for-retail (accessed 23 July 2021).

Garfinkle, Norton (2006). *The American Dream vs the Gospel of Wealth: The Fight for a Productive Middle-Class Economy.* New Haven, CT: Yale University Press.

GE (2020). 'Additive manufacturing: Aviation and aerospace industry', *GE Additive*. Available at www.ge.com/additive/additive-manufacturing/industries/aviation -aerospace (accessed 9 October 2020).

Geocowets, George A. (1979). 'Physical distribution management', Special Issue: Physical Distribution Management, *Defense Transportation Journal*, 35(4), 5–8, 10–12.

George, Katy and Enno de Boer (2020). 'The future of production: How digital factories lead in the fourth industrial revolution', McKinsey & Company, 1

March. Available at www.mckinsey.com/featured-insights/world-economic-forum/ knowledge-collaborations/the-future-of-production (accessed 3 March 2021).

Gerckens, Claus, Abhiram Ramprasad and Martin Wrulich (2020). 'Can connectivity help narrow the growing retailer gap?', *McKinsey Digital*, 10 September. Available at www.mckinsey.com/business-functions/mckinsey-digital/our-insights/digital -blog/can-connectivity-help-narrow-the-growing-retailer-gap (accessed 29 March 2021).

Gerdeman, Dina and Clayton Christensen (2016). 'Author interview: Clayton Christensen: *The Theory of Jobs to Be Done*', Working Knowledge: Business Research for Business Leaders, Harvard Business School, 3 October.

Gezgin, Enis, Xin Huang, Prakash Samal and Ildefonso Silva (2017). 'Digital transformation: Raising supply chain performance to new levels', McKinsey.com, 17 November. Available at www.mckinsey.com/business-functions/operations/our -insights/digital-transformation-raising-supply-chain-performance-to-new-levels (accessed 21 October 2020).

Gialos, Anastasios and Vasileios Zeimpekis (2021). 'Defining and testing system parameters for enhancing vision picking technology in warehouse operations', in Emel Aktas, Michael Bourlakis, Ioannis Minis and Vasileios Zeimpekis (eds), *Improving Supply Chains with Analytics and Industry 4.0 Technologies*. London: Kogan Page, pp. 113–149.

Gilmour, Peter (1974). *Physical Distribution Management in Australia*. Melbourne: Cheshire Publishing.

Glockner, Holger, Kai Jannek, Johannes Mahn and Björn Theis (2014). *Augmented Reality in Logistics: Changing the Way We See Logistics – a DHL Perspective*. Troisdorf: DHL Customer Solutions and Innovation.

Glucksman, Morgan (2017). 'The rise of social media influencer marketing on lifestyle branding: A case study of Lucie Fink', *The Elon Journal*, 8(2): 77–87.

Glynn, Fergal (2018). 'What is voice picking?', *River Systems*, 10 May. Available at https://6river.com/what-is-voice-picking/ (accessed 16 October 2020).

GM (2020). 'Ventec Life Systems and GM Partner to mass produce critical care ventilators in response to COVID-19 pandemic', *GM Corporate Newsroom*, 27 March. Available at https://media.gm.com/media/us/en/gm/news.detail.html/content/ Pages/news/us/en/2020/mar/0327-coronavirus-update-6-kokomo.html (accessed 18 October 2020).

Goodman, Peter S., Alexandra Stevenson, Niraj Chokshi and Michael Corkery (2021). '"I've never seen anything like this": Chaos strikes global shipping', *New York Times*, 6 March. Available at www.nytimes.com/2021/03/06/business/global -shipping.html (accessed 11 June 2021).

Goodwin, Tom (2015). 'The battle is for the customer interface', *TechCrunch*, 4 March. Available at https://techcrunch.com/2015/03/03/in-the-age-of-disintermediation-the -battle-is-all-for-the-customer-interface/ (accessed 28 July 2021).

Goodwin, Tom (2018). 'The battle for consumers gets physical (instead of virtual)', *TechCrunch*, 4 March. Available at https://techcrunch.com/2018/01/25/the-battle -for-consumers-gets-physical-instead-of-virtual/ (accessed 28 July 2021).

Grain Brokers Australia (2021). 'Global container crisis disrupts food supply', *The Land*, 11 February.

Granzin, Kent L. and Kenneth D. Bahn (1989). 'Consumer logistics: Conceptualization, pertinent issues and a proposed program for research', *Journal of the Academy of Marketing Science*, 17(1): 91–101.

Grijpink, Ferry, Eric Kutcher, Alexandra Ménard, Sree Ramaswamy, Davide Schiavotto, James Manyika, Michael Chui, Rob Hamill and Emir Okan (2020). 'Connected world: An evolution in connectivity beyond the 5G revolution', McKinsey Global Institute, 20 February. Available at www.mckinsey.com/industries/technology -media-and-telecommunications/our-insights/connected-world-an-evolution-in -connectivity-beyond-the-5g-revolution (accessed 29 March 2021).

Grothaus, Michael (2020). 'Walmart is looking more like Amazon thanks to the COVID-19 pandemic', *Fast Company*, 17 November. Available at www .fastcompany.com/90576402/walmart-is-looking-more-like-amazon-thanks-to-the -covid-19-pandemic (accessed 1 June 2021).

Guardian (2021). 'Retail is at death's door – and tinkering with business rates won't save it', *Guardian*, 31 January. Available at www.theguardian.com/business/ 2021/jan/31/retail-is-at-deaths-door-and-tinkering-with-business-rates-wont-save-it (accessed 18 March 2021).

Haddon, Heather (2021). 'Starbucks faces shortage of cups, syrup as eased Covid-19 boosts sales', *Wall Street Journal*, 9 June. Available at www.wsj.com/articles/ starbucks-runs-short-on-cups-and-syrup-as-covid-19-eases-11623287198 (accessed 14 June 2021).

Hahn, Gerd J. (2020). 'Industry 4.0: A supply chain innovation perspective', *International Journal of Production Research*, 58(5): 1425–1441.

Hamstra, Mark (2015). 'IKEA creates omnichannel shopping experience from favorited items in app', *Mobile Commerce Daily* (now *Retail Dive*). Available at www .retaildive.com/ex/mobilecommercedaily/ikea-boosts-content-functionality-for -catalog-app (accessed 27 April 2021).

Hänninen, Mikko, Stephen K. Kwan and Lasse Mitronen (2021). 'From the store to omnichannel retail: Looking back over three decades of research', *International Review of Retail, Distribution and Consumer Research*, 31(1): 1–35.

Hariharan, Anu and Nic Dardenne (2020). 'How Pinduoduo's success serves as a model for the rise of social ecommerce', *TECHINASIA*, 17 June. Available at www .techinasia.com/pinduoduo-rise-social-ecommerce (accessed 26 May 2021).

Harrington, Lisa (2020). 'Digitalization business brief – Warehousing 4.0: The age of the smart DC'. Available at www.dhl.com/content/dam/dhl/global/dhl-supply chain/ documents/pdf/SCI_Warehousing-4-Brief.pdf (accessed 19 July 2021).

Harris, Anna, Susan Kelly and Sally Wyatt (2016). *CyberGenetics: Health Genetics and New Media*. London: Routledge.

Haselmayr, Melanie (2021). '7 reasons why your business needs a mobile app', *All Business*. Available at www.allbusiness.com/7-reasons-business-needs-mobile-app -19179-1.html (accessed 5 April 2021).

Hatch, Walter and Kozo Yamamura (1996). *Asia in Japan's Embrace: Building a Regional Production Alliance*. Cambridge: Cambridge University Press.

Hausmann, Ludwig, Ankit Mittal and Gabriela Rome (2021). 'Lessons from growth outperformers in logistics', McKinsey & Company, 13 January. Available at www .mckinsey.com/business-functions/strategy-and-corporate-finance/our-insights/ lessons-from-growth-outperformers-in-logistics (accessed 28 April 2021).

Hayes, Khaleel (2022). 'Benefits of ERP: Advantages and disadvantages of an Enterprise Resource Planning system', *Select Hub*. Available at www.selecthub .com/enterprise-resource-planning/erp-advantages-and-disadvantages/ (accessed 13 January 2022).

Headrick, Daniel R. (2009). *Technology: A World History*. Oxford: Oxford University Press.

Hegarty, Nicole, Joanna Prendergast and Anthony Scully (2020). 'Coronavirus demand sees rum, gin distillers donate ethanol and switch to hand sanitiser production', *ABC News*, 25 March. Available at www.abc.net.au/news/2020-03-25/coronavirus-sees -distillers-push-to-meet-hand-sanitiser-demand/12085426 (accessed 18 October 2020).

Heskett, James L., Robert M. Ivie and Nicholas A. Glaskowsky, Jr. (1964). *Business Logistics: Management of Physical Supply and Distribution*. New York: Ronald Press Company.

Hesse, Markus (2002). 'Logistics real estate markets: Indicators of structural change, linking land use and freight transport', *42nd Congress of the European Regional Science Association: 'From Industry to Advanced Services – Perspectives of European Metropolitan Regions'*, 27–31 August, Dortmund, European Regional Science Association.

Heutger, Matthias and Markus Kückelhaus (2020). *Logistics Trend Radar*, 5th Edition. Bonn: Deutsche Post DHL Group. Available at www.dhl.com/cn-en/home/insights -and-innovation/insights/logistics-trend-radar.html (accessed 10 November 2020).

Hinds, Simon (2019). 'Supply chain 4.0: Managing a digital transformation', McKinsey & Company, 22 August. Available at www.mckinsey.com/business-functions/ operations/our-insights/operations-blog/supply-chain-40-managing-a-digital -transformation (accessed 23 April 2019).

Hirsch-Kreinsen, Hartmut (2016). '"Industry 4.0" as promising technology: Emergence, semantics and ambivalent character', *Arbeitspapier*, 48(October): 1–27. Arbeiten aus der Wirtschafts- und Sozialwissenschaftlichen. Fakultät der Technischen Universität Dortmund (Work from the Economic and Social Sciences. Faculty of the Technical University of Dortmund).

Hirsch-Kreinsen, Hartmut (2019). '"Industry 4.0": A path-dependent', *Arbeitspapier*, 56(January): 1–20. Arbeiten aus der Wirtschafts- und Sozialwissenschaftlichen. Fakultät der Technischen Universität Dortmund (Work from the Economic and Social Sciences. Faculty of the Technical University of Dortmund).

Hitachi (2021). 'Customer engagement marketing manager', *Hitachi ABB Power Grids*, 23 March. Available at www.hitachiabb-powergrids.com/au/en/career/jobs/ details/HQ51185464_E6 (accessed 9 June 2021).

HKTDC (2021). 'COVID windfall for Taiwan's PC sector', *Hong Kong Trade Development Council Research*, 17 February. Available at https://hkmb.hktdc.com/ en/1X0ALABV/market-spotlight/COVID-windfall-for-Taiwan%E2%80%99s-PC -sector (accessed 20 March 2021).

Höber, Björn and Mario Schaarschmidt (2017). 'Transforming from service providers to solution providers: Implications for provider–customer relationships and customer-induced solution innovation', *International Journal of Technology Management*, 73(1/2/3): 65–90.

Hodd, Malcolm (ed.) (1970). *Containerisation International Year Book 1970*. London: National Magazine.

Hoekstra, Janny C. and Peter S.H. Leeflang (2020). 'Marketing in the era of COVID-19', *Italian Journal of Marketing*: 249–260. Available at https://link .springer.com/article/10.1007/s43039-020-00016-3 (accessed 11 June 2021).

Hofmann, Erik, Henrik Sternberg, Haozhe Chen, Alexander Pflaum and Günter Prockl (2019). 'Guest editorial: Supply chain management and Industry 4.0: Conducting research in the digital age', *International Journal of Physical Distribution and Logistics Management*, 49(10): 945–955.

Hogg, Richard (2020). 'Is technology the cure for future supply chain disruption', *Supply Chain Digital*, 1 June. Available at www.supplychaindigital.com/supply -chain-2/technology-cure-future-supply-chain-disruption (accessed 12 February 2021).

Holder, Josh (2021). 'Tracking coronavirus vaccinations around the world', *New York Times*, 28 April. Available at www.nytimes.com/interactive/2021/world/covid -vaccinations-tracker.html (accessed 4 May 2021).

Holloway, Nigel, ed. (1991). *Japan in Asia*. Hong Kong: Review Publishing.

Howe, Neil and William Strauss (2000). *Millennials Rising: The Next Great Generation* (cartoons by R.J. Matson). New York: Vintage Books.

Huang, Xin, Alex Sawaya and Daniel Zipser (2020). 'How China's consumer companies managed through the COVID-19 crisis: A virtual roundtable', McKinsey & Company, 27 March. Available at www.mckinsey.com/industries/retail/our -insights/how-chinas-consumercompanies-managed-through-the-covid-19-crisis-a -virtual-roundtable (accessed 15 February 2021).

Hullum, Chet (2019). 'How Rogue Ales makes a great beer from wet hops, clean water and innovation', *IOT@Intel*, 6 February. Available at https://blogs.intel.com/ iot/2018/02/06/how-rogue-ales-makes-a-great-beer-from-wet-hops-clean-water-and -innovation/#gs.5mt6tj (accessed 12 July 2021).

Hummels, David L. (2007). 'Transportation costs and international trade in the second era of globalization', *Journal of Economic Perspectives*, 21(3): 131–154.

Hwang, Jinsoo, Dohyung Kim and Jinkyung Jenny Kim (2020). 'How to form behavioral intentions in the field of drone food delivery services: The moderating role of the COVID-19 outbreak', *International Journal of Environmental Research and Public Health*, 17(23): 9117.

Hyperledger (2020). 'Revolutionizing the supply chain: Bringing traceability and accountability to the supply chain through the power of Hyperledger's Sawtooth's distributed ledger technology', Hyperledger, CC-by 4.0. Available at https:// sawtooth.hyperledger.org/examples/seafood.html (accessed 16 November 2020).

IATA (2021). *WATS 2020 – World Air Transport Statistics*. Montreal: International Air Transport Association.

IDB and WEF (2019). *White Paper: Supply Chain 4.0: Global Practices and Lessons Learned for Latin America and the Caribbean*. Cologne and Geneva: World Economic Forum.

IDC (2021). 'Worldwide semiconductor revenue grew 5.4% in 2020 despite COVID-19 and further growth is forecast in 2021, according to IDC', *International Data Corporation*, 2 February. Available at www.idc.com/getdoc.jsp?containerId= prUS47424221 (accessed 4 March 2021).

Ikeshita, Yuma and Shiho Miyajima (2020). '7-Eleven rethinks "convenience" in Japan's new normal', *Nikkei Asia*, 19 July. Available at https://asia.nikkei.com/ Business/Retail/7-Eleven-rethinks-convenience-in-Japan-s-new-normal (accessed 24 June 2021).

ILS (2018). 'Total number of sites', *Internet Live Statistics*. Available at www .internetlivestats.com/total-number-of-websites/ (accessed 13 January 2021).

Insight Works (2018). 'Voice picking vs. barcode scanning: Which is the best choice for your warehouse?', *ERP Software Blog*, 29 January. Available at www .erpsoftwareblog.com/2018/01/voice-picking-vs-barcode-scanning-best-choice -warehouse/ (accessed 16 November 2020).

Insights Team (2018). 'Logistics 4.0: How IoT is transforming the supply chain', *Forbes Insights*, 14 June. Available at www.forbes.com/sites/insights-inteliot/

2018/06/14/logistics-4-0-how-iot-is-transforming-the-supply-chain/#f347797880fc (accessed 20 October 2020).

Intel (2018). 'It's hop harvest time: Here's how Rogue Farms, Intel keep fresh hops fresh on their journey', *Craft Brewing Business*, 29 August. Available at www. craftbrewingbusiness.com/ingredients-supplies/heres-how-rogue-farms-keeps-fresh -hops-fresh-on-their-journey/ (accessed 12 July 2021).

Investopedia Staff (2020). 'Consumerism', *Investopedia*, 20 September. Available at www.investopedia.com/terms/c/consumerism.asp (accessed 29 December 2020).

Investopedia Team (2021). 'Amazon's vs. Alibaba's business models: What's the difference?', *Investopedia*, 16 December. Available at www.investopedia.com/articles/ investing/061215/difference-between-amazon-and-alibabas-business-models.asp (accessed 12 January 2022).

Iqbal, Mansoor (2021). 'TikTok revenue and usage statistics (2021)', *BusinessofApps*, 24 May. Available at www.businessofapps.com/data/tik-tok-statistics/ (accessed 30 June 2021).

Iqbal, Mansoor (2022a). 'Deliveroo revenue and usage statistics (2022)', *BusinessofApps*, 11 January. Available at www.businessofapps.com/data/deliveroo -statistics/#2 (accessed 13 January 2022).

Iqbal, Mansoor (2022b). 'Uber revenue and usage statistics (2022)', *BusinessofApps*, 11 January. Available at www.businessofapps.com/data/uber-statistics/ (accessed 13 January 2022).

IRMA (2017). *Digital Multimedia: Concepts, Methodologies, Tools, and Applications*. Hershey, PA: Management Association, Information Resources IGI Global.

Jaconi, Mile (2014). 'The "on-demand economy" is revolutionizing consumer behavior – here's how', *Insider*, 14 July. Available at www.businessinsider.com/the-on -demand-economy-2014-7?IR=T (accessed 11 May 2021).

Jaffrelot, Christophe and Peter van der Veer, eds (2008). *Patterns of Middle Class Consumption in India and China*. Los Angeles: Sage.

JD.com (2016). 'JD.com's drone delivery program takes flight in rural China', JD.com, 11 November. Available at https://corporate.jd.com/whatIsNewDetail?contentCode =6IhXLeeSAFLjLLlyuZatDA (accessed 9 October 2020).

Jeske, Martin, Maritz Gruner and Frank Weil (2014). *Big Data in Logistics: A DHL Perspective about How to Move beyond the Hype*. Troisdorf: DHL Customer Solutions and Innovation.

Jia, Kai and Martin Kenney (2021). 'The Chinese platform business group: An alternative to the Silicon Valley model?', *Journal of Chinese Governance*. Available at https://doi.org/10.1080/23812346.2021.1877446 (accessed 24 May 2021).

Jillson, Calvin C. (2016). *The American Dream: In History, Politics and Fiction*. Lawrence, KS: University Press of Kansas.

Johnson, K.M. and H.C. Garnett (1971). *The Economics of Containerisation*. London: Allen and Unwin.

Joshi, Naveen (2019). 'Retail 4.0: How the retail sector will evolve in the fourth industrial revolution', *BBN Times*, 22 March. Available at www.bbntimes.com/ technology/retail-4-0-how-the-retail-sector-will-evolve-in-the-fourth-industrial -revolution (accessed 3 June 2021).

Joshi, Sanjay, ed. (2010). *The Middle Class in Colonial India*. New Delhi: Oxford University Press.

Kaas, Hans-Werner, Andreas Tschiesner, Dominik Wee and Matthias Kässer (2015). 'How carmakers can compete for the connected consumer', McKinsey & Company, 1 September. Available at www.mckinsey.com/industries/automotive-and-assembly/

our-insights/how-carmakers-can-compete-for-the-connected-consumer (accessed 29 March 2021).

Kagermann, Henning (2015). 'Change through digitization – value creation in the age of Industry 4.0', in Horst Albach, Heribert Meffert, Andreas Pinkwart and Ralf Reichwald (eds), *Management of Permanent Change*. Wiesbaden: Springer Gable, pp. 23–48.

Kalaria, Chirag (2019). 'Demand sensing – NextGen supply chain technology', *Medium.com*, 10 August. Available at https://medium.com/@chiragkalaria/demand -sensing-nextgen-supply-chain-technology-6229dbc960e2 (accessed 15 February 2021).

Kasarda, John (2000). 'Logistics and the rise of the aerotropolis', *Real Estate Issues*, 25(4): 43–48.

Kasarda, John and Greg Lindsay (2011). *Aerotropolis: The Way We'll Live Next*. London: Allen Lane.

Kearney (2015). 'Digital supply chains: Increasingly critical for competitive edge': European Kearney/WHU Logistics Study. Kearney/Estudio de logística WHU. Available at www.es.kearney.com/operations-performance-transformation/article/ ?/a/digital-supply-chains-increasingly-critical-for-competitive-edge (accessed 22 October 2020).

Kelly, Greg (2020). 'Connectivity with the consumer: The Honest Company's formula for growth', McKinsey & Company, 4 August. Available at www.mckinsey.com/ industries/consumer-packaged-goods/our-insights/connectivity-with-the-consumer -the-honest-companys-formula-for-growth (accessed 29 March 2021).

Kelly, Makena (2021). 'Biden revokes and replaces Trump orders banning TikTok and WeChat: But the apps still aren't out of hot water', *The Verge*, 9 June. Available at www.theverge.com/2021/6/9/22525953/biden-tiktok-wechat-trump-bans-revoked -alipay (accessed 5 July 2021).

Kench, James (2021). 'Supply Chain 4.0: The cyber-security challenge', in Emel Aktas, Michael Bourlakis, Ioannis Minis and Vasileios Zeimpekis (eds), *Improving Supply Chains with Analytics and Industry 4.0 Technologies*. London: Kogan Page, pp. 92–112.

Kersten, Wolfgang, Mischa Seiter, Birgit von See, Niels Hackius and Timo Maurer (2017). *Trends und strategien in logistic und supply chain management – Chancen der digitalen Transformation*. Hamburg: DVV Media Group GmbH.

Kharas, Homi and Kristofer Hamel (2018). 'A global tipping point: Half the world is now middle class or wealthier', *Brookings*, 27 September. Available at www .brookings.edu/blog/future-development/2018/09/27/a-global-tipping-point-half-the -world-is-now-middle-class-or-wealthier/ (accessed 24 July 2020).

Kidd, Alan J. (1985). 'The middle class in nineteenth century Manchester', in Alan J. Kidd and K.W. Roberts (eds), *City, Class and Culture: Studies of Social Policy and Cultural Production in Victorian Manchester*. Manchester: Manchester University Press, pp. 1–24.

Kim, Aimee, Paul McInerney, Thomas Rüdiger Smith and Naomi Yamakawa (2020). 'What makes the Asia-Pacific's generation Z different', McKinsey & Company, 29 June. Available at www.mckinsey.com/business-functions/marketing-and-sales/our -insights/what-makes-asia-pacifics-generation-z-different (accessed 24 July 2020).

Kincade, D.H., N. Cassill and N. Williamson (1993). 'The Quick Response Management System: Structure and components for the apparel industry', *Journal of the Textile Institute*, 84(2): 147–155.

Kinder, Molly and Laura Stateler (2020). 'Amazon and Walmart have raked in billions in additional profits during the pandemic, and shared almost none of it with their workers', *Brookings*, 22 December. Available at www.brookings.edu/blog/the-avenue/2020/12/22/amazon-and-walmart-have-raked-in-billions-in-additional-profits-during-the-pandemic-and-shared-almost-none-of-it-with-their-workers/ (accessed 1 June 2021).

Kitchin, Rob (2014). 'Big Data, new epistemologies and paradigm shifts', *Big Data and Society*, 1(1): 1–12.

Knowles, Simon (2019). 'Five ways 3D printing will impact the global supply chain', *Maine Pointe*, 6 March. Available at www.mainepointe.com/practical-insights/five-ways-3d-printing-will-impact-the-global-supply-chain (accessed 13 October 2020).

Kolb, Darl G., Kristine Dery, Marlene Huysman and Anca Metiu (2020). 'Connectivity in and around organizations: Waves, tensions and trade-offs', *Organization Studies*, 41(12): 1589–1599.

Kruman, Yuri (2019). *What Millennials Really Want from Work and Life*. New York: Business Expert Press.

La Londe, Bernard J. (1969). 'Integrated distribution management: The American perspective', *Journal of the Society for Long Range Planning*, 2(2): 61–71.

LaBerge, Laura, Clayton O'Toole, Jeremy Schneider and Kate Smaje (2020). 'How COVID-19 has pushed companies over the technology tipping point – and transformed business forever', McKinsey & Company, 5 October. Available at www.mckinsey.com/business-functions/strategy-and-corporate-finance/our-insights/how-covid-19-has-pushed-companies-over-the-technology-tipping-point-and-transformed-business-forever (accessed 9 May 2021).

Lambert, Douglas M., Martha C. Cooper and Janus D. Pagh (1998). 'Supply Chain management: Implementation and research opportunities', *International Journal of Logistics Management*, 9(2): 1–19.

Lambert, Lance (2020). '75% of companies report coronavirus has disrupted their supply chains', *Fortune*, 12 March. Available at https://fortune.com/2020/03/11/75-of-companies-report-coronavirus-has-disrupted-their-supply-chains/ (accessed 12 February 2021).

Lambert, Mark R., ed. (1987). *Containerisation International Year Book 1987*. London: National Magazine.

Leurent, Helena, Enno de Boer and Diego Hernandez Diaz (2018). 'The fourth industrial revolution and the factories of the future', *World Economic Forum*, 10 August. Available at www.weforum.org/agenda/2018/08/3-lessons-from-the-lighthouses-beaming-the-way-for-the-4ir/ (accessed 14 June 2021).

Levenson, Michael (2020). 'Anheuser-Busch and distilleries race to make hand sanitizer amid coronavirus pandemic', *New York Times*, 19 March. Available at www.nytimes.com/2020/03/19/us/distilleries-virus-hand-sanitizer.html (accessed 17 February 2021).

Levinson, Marc (2006). *The Box: How the Shipping Container Made the World Smaller and the World Economy Bigger*. Princeton, NJ: Princeton University Press.

Levinson, Marc (2016). *The Box: How the Shipping Container Made the World Smaller and the World Economy Bigger*, 2nd Edition. Princeton, NJ: Princeton University Press.

Libert, Barry, Yoram (Jerry) Wind and Megan Beck (2014). 'What Airbnb, Uber, and Alibaba have in common', *Harvard Business Review*, 20 November. Available at https://hbr.org/2014/11/what-airbnb-uber-and-alibaba-have-in-common (accessed 12 August 2014).

Lieb, Robert and John Miller (2002). 'The use of third-party logistics services by large US manufacturers: The 2000 Survey', *International Journal of Logistics Research and Applications*, 5(1): 1–12.

Lindsay, John (2007). 'The rise of the aerotropolis', *Fast Company*, 6 January. Available at www.fastcompany.com/57081/rise-aerotropolis (accessed 13 January 2020).

LL (2020). 'One hundred ports 2019', *Lloyds List*. Available at https://lloydslist.maritimeintelligence.informa.com/one-hundred-container-ports-2019 (accessed 18 August 2021).

Lohr, Steve (1998). 'Microsoft on trial: The overview; Microsoft goes to court', *New York Times*, 19 October. Available at www.nytimes.com/1998/10/19/business/microsoft-on-trial-the-overview-microsoft-goes-to-court.html (accessed 13 January 2021).

Loxton, Mary, Robert Truskett, Brigette Scarf, Laura Sindone, George Baldry and Yinong Zhao (2020). 'Consumer behaviour during crises: Preliminary research on how coronavirus has manifested consumer panic buying, herd mentality, changing discretionary spending and the role of the media in influencing behaviour', *Journal of Risk and Financial Management*, 30 July. Available at www.mdpi.com/1911-8074/13/8/166 (accessed 15 February 2021).

Lukashevich, Stanislav (2020). 'Why have Starbucks failed in Australia but succeeded in China?', *Linkedin.com*, 6 May. Available at www.linkedin.com/pulse/why-starbucks-failed-australia-succeeded-china-stanislav-lukashevich-/ (accessed 6 September 2021).

Lummus, Rhonda R. and Robert J. Vokurka (1999). 'Managing the demand chain through managing the information flow: Capturing "moments of information"', *Production and Inventory Management Journal*, 40(1): 16–20.

Ma, Zhaolin (2016). 中国制造2025强国之路与工业4.0实战：重构智慧型产业，开启产业转型新时代 [Zhōngguó zhìzào 2025 qiángguó zhī lù yǔ gōngyè 4.0 Shízhàn: Zhòng gòu zhìhuì xíng chǎnyè, kāiqǐ chǎnyè zhuǎnxíng xīn shídài] (Made in China 2025 – The Actual Combat of Industry 4.0 and the Road to a Powerful Country: Reconstructing Smart Industries and Opening a New Era of Industrial Transformation). Beijing, CN: Ren min you dian chu ban she.

Makarian, Josh (2021). 'Top 10 social media platforms ranked by monthly annual users', *Teris*, 16 February. Available at https://teris.com/top-10-social-media-platforms-ranked-by-monthly-annual-users-social-media-ediscovery/ (accessed 13 April 2021).

Makris, Dimitrios, Zaza Nadja Lee Hansen and Omera Khan (2019). 'Adapting to supply chain 4.0: An explorative study of multinational companies', *Supply Chain Forum: An International Journal*, 20(2): 116–131. Available at www.tandfonline.com/doi/full/10.1080/16258312.2019.1577114 (accessed 21 June 2021).

Marr, Bernard (2019). 'What is the Artificial Intelligence of Things? When AI meets IoT', *Forbes*, 20 December. Available at www.forbes.com/sites/bernardmarr/2019/12/20/what-is-the-artificial-intelligence-of-things-when-ai-meets-iot/?sh=2225d51cb1fd (accessed 17 November 2020).

Matthews, Neil (2020). 'Improving supply chain visibility through RFID', *Supply Chain*, 17 May. Available at https://supplychaindigital.com/supply-chain-risk-management/improving-supply-chain-visibility-through-rfid (accessed 3 June 2021).

McCarthy, E. Jerome (1960). *Basic Marketing: A Managerial Approach*. Homewood, IL: R.D. Irwin.

McCloskey, Deidre N. (2016). *Bourgeois Equality: How Ideas, Not Capital or Institutions, Enriched the World*. Chicago, IL: University of Chicago Press.

McCormack, Gavan (1996). *The Emptiness of Japanese Affluence*. Armonk, NY: M.E. Sharpe.

McKinsey & Company (2020). 'The path to the next normal; Leading with *resolve* through the coronavirus pandemic', McKinsey & Company, May. Available at www.mckinsey.com/~/media/McKinsey/Featured%20Insights/Navigating %20the%20coronavirus%20crisis%20collected%20works/Path-to-the-next-normal -collection.pdf (accessed 8 August 2021).

Mendis, Dinusha, Jan Bernd Nordemann, Rosa Maria Ballardini, Hans Brorsen, Maria del Carmen Calatrava-Moreno, Julie Robson and Phill Dickens (2020). *The Intellectual Property Implications of the Development of Industrial 3D Printing*. Brussels: European Commission.

Mentzer, John T., Roger Gomes and Robert E. Krapfel, Jr. (1989). 'Physical distribution service: A fundamental marketing concept?', *Journal of the Academy of Marketing Science*, 17(1): 53–62.

Miao, Ying (2017). *Being Middle Class in China: Identity, Attitudes and Behaviour*. London: Routledge.

Miled, Zina Ben, Jeremy Archbold and Brooke Renee Cochenour (2021). 'Predicting distribution transit times: A case study of outbound logistics', in Emel Aktas, Michael Bourlakis, Ioannis Minis and Vasileios Zeimpekis (eds), *Improving Supply Chains with Analytics and Industry 4.0 Technologies*. London: Kogan Page, pp. 189–208.

Mishra, Ruchi, Rajesh Kumar Singh and Bernadett Koles (2020). 'Consumer decision-making in omnichannel retailing: Literature review and future research agenda', *International Journal of Consumer Studies*. Available at https://doi.org/10 .1111/ijcs.12617 (accessed 23 June 2021).

Morgan, Blake (2018). '5 examples of how AI can be used across the supply chain', *Forbes*, 17 September. Available at www.forbes.com/sites/blakemorgan/2018/09/ 17/5-examples-of-how-ai-can-be-used-across-the-supply-chain/?sh=423f4a63342e (accessed 9 October 2020).

Morris-Suzuki, Tessa (1988). *Beyond Computopia: Information, Automation, and Democracy in Japan*. London: Kegan Paul.

Murphy, Hannah (2021). 'TikTok takes on Facebook with US ecommerce push', *Financial Times*, 8 February. Available at www.ft.com/content/629c1c17-3daa-46af -8177-1814baaa2bed (accessed 1 July 2021).

Myong, Elizabeth (2019). 'Walmart to test self-driving delivery from warehouse to warehouse', *CNBC*, 19 June. Available at www.cnbc.com/2019/06/19/walmart -to-test-self-driving-delivery-from-warehouse-to-warehouse.html (accessed 20 November 2020).

Mysore, Mihir and Ophelia Usher (2020). 'Responding to coronavirus: The minimum viable nerve center', McKinsey & Company, 16 March. Available at www.mckinsey .com/business-functions/risk/our-insights/responding-to-coronavirus-the-minimum -viable-nerve-center (accessed 23 February 2021).

NCSA (2021). 'NCSA Mosiac™', *National Centre for Supercomputing Applications*. Available at www.ncsa.illinois.edu/enabling/mosaic (accessed 20 July 2021).

Nerad, Jack R. (2020). 'How car companies are producing medical personal protective equipment (PPE) due to coronavirus', J.D. Power, 24 March. Available at www .jdpower.com/cars/shopping-guides/how-car-companies-are-helping-to-produce -medical-personal-protective-equipment-ppe (accessed 17 February 2021).

Neubert, Jonas and Cornelia Scheitz (2021). 'Exploring the supply chain of the Pfizer/BioNTech and Moderna COVID-19 vaccines', jonasneubert.com, 10 January. Available at https://blog.jonasneubert.com/2021/01/10/exploring-the-supply-chain-of-the-pfizer-biontech-and-moderna-covid-19-vaccines/ (accessed 10 March 2021).

Nguyen, Truong, Li Zhou, Virginia Spiegler, Petros Ieromonachou and Yong Lin (2018). 'Big Data analytics in supply chain management: A state-of-the-art literature review', *Computers and Operations Research*, 98(October): 254–264.

NHS (2021). 'Map of vaccination sites – 26 July', National Health Service. Available at www.england.nhs.uk/coronavirus/hospital-hubs-and-local-vaccination-services/ (accessed 6 September 2021).

Nicola, John (2019). 'Executing a digital strategy is table stakes and there is no turning back', Multichannel Merchant, 26 July. Available at https://multichannelmerchant.com/blog/executing-a-digital-strategy-is-table-stakes-and-there-is-no-turning-back/ (accessed 22 February 2021).

Notteboom, Theo, Thanos Pallis and Jean Paul Rodrigue (2021). 'Disruptions and resilience in global container shipping and ports: The COVID-19 pandemic versus the 2008–2009 financial crisis', *Maritime Economics and Logistics*, 23(January): 179–210.

Ota, Tushar, Sachi Ghai, Prasanna Venkatesan and Aditya Bagri (2017). *Disruptions in Retail through Digital Transformation: Reimagining the Store of the Future*. Mumbai: Deloitte Touche Tohmatsu India LLP.

Pahwa, Aashish (2021). 'Everything you need to know about Facebook Marketplace', Feedough, 18 June. Available at www.feedough.com/facebook-marketplace/ (accessed 13 January 2022).

Papagiannis, Helen (2020). 'How AR is redefining retail in the pandemic', *Harvard Business Review*, 7 October. Available at https://hbr.org/2020/10/how-ar-is-redefining-retail-in-the-pandemic (accessed 16 March 2021).

Paris, Costas and Stella Yifan Xie (2021). 'COVID-19 closure at Ningbo's port is latest snarl in global supply chains', *Wall Street Journal*, 20 August. Available at www.wsj.com/articles/covid-19-closure-at-chinas-ningbo-port-is-latest-snarl-in-global-supply-chains-11629451800 (accessed 23 August 2021).

Parker, Geoffrey G., Marshall W. Van Alstyne and Sangeet Paul Choudary (2016). *Platform Revolution: How Networked Markets Are Transforming the Economy – and How to Make Them Work for You*. New York: W.W. Norton & Company.

Partner, Simon (1999). *Assembled in Japan: Electrical Goods and the Making of the Japanese Consumer*. Berkeley, CA: University of California Press.

PBSUC and NZTSC (1964). *New Zealand Overseas Trade: Report on Shipping Ports Transport and Other Services*. Producer Boards' Shipping Utilisation Committee New Zealand and New Zealand Trade Streamlining Committee. Wellington: Government Printer.

PCO (2021). 'Manufacturing network', *Pfizer Centre One*. Available at www.pfizercentreone.com/manufacturing-network (accessed 2 February 2021).

Perussi, Jéssica Bruna, Fernando Gressler and Robson Seleme (2019). 'Supply Chain 4.0: Autonomous vehicles and equipment to meet demand', *International Journal of Supply Chain Management*, 8(4): 33–41.

Petri, Peter A. and David Dollar (2020). 'The US–China tech-rivalry shapes the economic relationship', *Brookings Institution: Dollars and Sense Podcast*, 8 June. Available at www.brookings.edu/podcast-episode/the-us-china-tech-rivalry-shapes-the-economic-relationship/ (accessed 14 June 2020).

Pinches, Michael, ed. (1999). *Culture and Privilege in Capitalist Asia*. London: Routledge.

Pladson, Kristina (2021). 'The COVID-19 vaccines: Where do they come from? Where will they go?', DW.com., 6 January. Available at www.dw.com/en/the-covid-19-vaccines-where-do-they-come-from-where-will-they-go/a-56134178 (accessed 1 February 2021).

Ponnambalam, S.G., Nachiappan Subramanian, Manoj Kumar Tiwari and Wan Azhar Yusoff, eds (2019). *Industry 4.0 and Hyper-Customized Smart Manufacturing Supply Chains*. Hershey, PA: Business Science Reference.

Pooler, Michael and Thomas Hale (2020). 'Coronavirus and globalisation: The surprising resilience of container shipping', *Financial Times*, 13 September. Available at www.ft.com/content/65fe4650-5d90-41bc-8025-4ac81df8a5e4 (accessed 13 February 2021).

Prahalad, C.K. and Venkat Ramaswamy (2004a). 'Co-creating unique value with customers', *Strategy and Leadership*, 32(3): 4–9.

Prahalad, C.K. and Venkat Ramaswamy (2004b). 'Co-creation experiences: The next practice in value creation', *Journal of Interactive Marketing*, 18(3): 5–14.

Prainsack, Barbara (2014). 'Understanding participation: The "citizen science" of genetics', in Barbara Prainsack, Gabrielle Werner-Felmayer and Silke Schicktanz (eds), *Genetics as Social Practice: Transdisciplinary Views on Science and Culture*. Farnham: Ashgate Publishing, pp. 1–27. Available at www.researchgate.net/publication/236850804 (accessed 20 April 2021).

Prainsack, Barbara (2020). 'The political economy of digital data: Introduction to the Special Issue', *Policy Studies*, 41(5): 439–446.

Ptolemy Project (2018). *Cyber-Physical Systems*. Berkeley, CA: University of California Press. Available at https://ptolemy.berkeley.edu/projects/cps/ (accessed 6 May 2020).

QIRI (2020). 年中国汽车行业发展现状分析 正成为全球汽车销售增长引擎及行业投资热点\ [2020 Nián zhōngguó qìchē hángyè fāzhǎn xiànzhuàng fēnxī zhèng chéngwéi quánqiú qìchē xiāoshòu zēngzhǎng yǐnqíng jí hángyè tóuzī rèdiǎn] (Analysis of the development status of China's auto industry in 2020 is becoming a global auto sales growth engine and industry investment hotspot). Beijing: Qianzhan Industry Research Institute. Available at https://bg.qianzhan.com/report/detail/300/200811-ad9df62c.html (accessed 9 March 2020).

Queiroz, Maciel, M. and Samuel Fosso Wamba (2021). 'The role of digital connectivity in supply chain and logistics systems: A proposed SIMPLE framework', in *Conference on e-Business, e-Services and e-Society I3E 2020: Responsible Design, Implementation and Use of Information and Communication Technology*, pp. 79–88. Available at https://link.springer.com/chapter/10.1007/978-3-030-44999-5_7 (accessed 17 March 2021).

Rabb, Martin and Belinda Griffin-Cryan (2017). 'Digital transformation of supply chains: Creating value – when digital meets physical', Capgemini Consulting, 30 July. Available at www.capgemini.com/consulting/wp-content/uploads/sites/30/2017/07/Digital_Transformation_of_Supply_Chains.pdf (accessed 21 October 2020).

Rae, John B. (1965). *The American Automobile: A Brief History*. Chicago, IL: Chicago University Press.

Raybould, Trevor (1984). 'Aristocratic landowners and the Industrial Revolution: The Black Country experience c. 1760–1840', *Midland History*, 9(1): 59–86.

Recknagel, Robert (2020). 'The supply chain manager's guide to Industry 4.0', *flexis AG*. Available at https://pages.flexis.com/lp/guide-to-industry-4-0 (accessed 13 January 2022).

Remes, Jaana and Steve Saxon (2021). 'What going on with shipping rates?', McKinsey & Company, 20 August. Available at www.mckinsey.com/industries/travel-logistics-and-infrastructure/our-insights/whats-going-on-with-shipping-rates (accessed 23 August 2021).

Ren, Rebecca (2021). 'TikTok is ramping up its e-commerce push', *Pingwest*, 5 March. Available at https://en.pingwest.com/a/8368 (accessed 30 June 2021).

Repko, Melissa and Noah Higgins Dunn (2021). 'The Covid vaccine's long journey: How doses get from the manufacturer's plant to your arm', *CNBC*, 6 January. Available at www.cnbc.com/2021/01/06/covid-vaccine-how-doses-get-from-the -manufacturing-plant-to-your-arm.html (accessed 1 February 2021).

Research and Markets (2020). 'Global Autonomous Trucking Market Report 2020: COVID-19 pandemic has underlined the need for autonomous trucks – forecast to 2040', *Research and Markets*, 20 October. Available at www.prnewswire.com/news -releases/global-autonomous-trucking-market-report-2020-covid-19-pandemic-has -underlined-the-need-for-autonomous-trucks---forecast-to-2040-301155917.html (accessed 18 February 2021).

RIA (2020). 'Honeywell Intelligrated – robotic integrator in Mason, Ohio, USA', *Robotics Online*, Robotics Industry Association. Available at www.robotics.org/ robotics/testimonial-interview-honeywell-intelligrated (accessed 25 November 2020).

Rifkin, Jeremy (2016). *One Belt One Road: Ushering in the Green Internet Plus Third Industrial Revolution in China, the European Union and Eurasia.* Available at http:// pinguet.free.fr/rifkin15.pdf (accessed 7 May 2018).

Rimmer, Peter J. (1992). 'Japan resort archipelago: Regions of fun, pleasure, relaxation and recreation', *Environment and Planning A*, 24(11): 1599–1625.

Rimmer, Peter J. (1994). 'Japanese investment in golf course development: Australia– Japan Links', *International Journal of Urban and Regional Research*, 18(2): 234–255.

Rimmer, Peter J. (1995). 'Industrialisation and the role of the state: Newly industrial- izing economies', in Richard Le Heron and Sam Ock Park (eds), *The Asian Pacific Rim and Globalization*. Aldershot: Ashgate, pp. 17–36.

Rimmer, Peter J. (2014). *Asian-Pacific Rim Logistics: Global Context and Local Policies*. Cheltenham, UK and Northampton, MA, USA: Edward Elgar Publishing.

Rimmer, Peter J. (2020). 'Aviation and COVID-19: Flying to the next normal', *Journal of International Trade, Logistics and Law*, 6(2): 119–136.

Rimmer, Peter J. and Howard Dick (2009). *The City in Southeast Asia: Patterns, Processes and Policy*. Singapore and Honolulu, HI: NUS Press and University of Hawai'i Press.

Rimmer, Peter J. and Howard Dick (forthcoming). 'Shrinking the Pacific? Container, jet and Internet', in Paul D'Arcy (general ed.), Matt Masuda and Ryan Jones (eds), *Cambridge History of the Pacific*, Volume 2. Cambridge: Cambridge University Press.

Rimmer, Peter J. and Booi Hon Kam (2018). *Consumer Logistics: Surfing the Digital Wave*. Cheltenham, UK and Northampton, MA, USA: Edward Elgar Publishing.

Ritchie, Hannah (2020). 'Google mobility trends: How has the pandemic changed the movement of people around the world?', *Our World in Data*, 2 June. Available at https://ourworldindata.org/covid-mobility-trends (accessed 4 May 2021).

Ritchie, Hannah, Esteban Ortiz-Ospina, Diana Beltekian, Edouard Mathieu, Joe Hasell, Bobbie Macdonald, Charlie Giattino, Cameron Appel and Max Roser (2021). 'Statistics and research: Coronavirus (COVID-19) vaccinations', *Our World in Data*. Available at https://ourworldindata.org/covid-vaccinations (accessed 4 May 2021).

Ritzer, George and Nathan Jurgenson (2010). 'Production, consumption, prosumption: The nature of capitalism in the age of the digital "prosumer"', *Journal of Consumer Culture*, 10(1): 13–36.

RO (2020). 'Australian stores closure list', *Retail Oasis*, November. Available at www.retailoasis.com/retail-blog/retail-store-closures (accessed 8 June 2021).

Robb, Kirsten and Ashlynne McGee (2020). 'Waiting on a parcel from Australia Post? This is why it is taking so long', *ABC News*, 22 April. Available at www.abc.net.au/news/2020-04-22/waiting-on-a-parcel-from-australia-post-why-its-taking-so-long/12172772 (accessed 18 October 2020).

Roberts, Tess, ed. (2021). *Additive Manufacturing Trend Report: 3D Printing Market Grows in the Year of the COVID-19*. Telford: Protolabs.

Robison, Richard and David S.G. Goodman (eds) (1996). *The New Rich in Asia: Mobile Phones, McDonalds and Middle-Class Revolution*. London, UK: Routledge.

Rodgers, H.B. (1960). 'The Lancashire cotton industry in 1840', *Transactions and Papers (Institute of British Geographers)*, 28: 135–153.

Rodgers, H.B. (1962). 'The suburban growth of Victorian Manchester', *Journal of the Manchester Geographical Society*, 58: 1–12. Available at www.mangeogsoc.org.uk/pdfs/centenaryedition/Cent_17_Rodgers.pdf (accessed 15 July 2020).

Rodrigue, Jean-Paul (2020a). *The Geography of Transport Systems*, 5th Edition. New York: Routledge.

Rodrigue, Jean-Paul (2020b). 'The distribution network of Amazon and the footprint of freight', *Journal of Transportation Geography*, 88: 102825.

Rogers, Everett M. and Judith K. Larsen (1984). *Silicon Valley Fever: Growth of High-Technology Culture*. New York: Basic Books.

Rojko, Andreja (2017). 'Industry 4.0 concept: Background and overview', *International Journal of Interactive Mobile Technologies*, 11(5): 77–90. Available at https://online-journals.org/index.php/i-jim/article/view/7072 (accessed 22 April 2020).

Rosenberg, David (2002). *Cloning Silicon Valley: The Next Generation High-Tech Hot Spots*. Harlow: Pearson Education.

Rosencrance, Linda (2021). 'IoT remote monitoring helps enterprises traverse COVID-19 and beyond', *IoT World Today*, 26 February. Available at www.iotworldtoday.com/2021/02/26/iot-remote-monitoring-helps-enterprises-traverse-covid-19-and-beyond/ (accessed 9 July 2021).

Rummelt, Richard P. (2008). 'Strategy in a "structural break"', *McKinsey Quarterly*, 11 December. Available at www.mckinsey.com/business-functions/strategy-and-corporate-finance/our-insights/strategy-in-a-structural-break (accessed 7 May 2020).

Safdar, Khadeeja (2019). 'Nike's strategy to get a lot more personal with its customers: The company is also using its apps to create a different kind of shopping experience', *Wall Street Journal*, 14 May. Available at www.wsj.com/articles/nikes-strategy-to-get-a-lot-more-personal-with-its-customers-11557799501 (accessed 30 August 2021).

Samuel, Lawrence R. (2014). *The American Middle Class: A Cultural History*. New York: Routledge.

Sanders, Julian (2018). 'Regulation for artificial intelligence and robotics in transportation, supply chain management, and logistics', *Network Industries Quarterly*, 20(2): 1–10. Available at www.network-industries.org/2018/06/27/regulation-for -artificial-intelligence-and-robotics-in-transportation-logistics-and-supply-chain -management/ (accessed 25 March 2021).

SAP (2019). 'Demand sensing in SAP IBP: What does demand sensing do?', Systems Applications and Product Integrated Development Planning, Walldorf, Baden-Württemberg, 19 July. Available at www.youtube.com/watch?v= OsL6Gt0W3Yc (accessed 17 February 2021).

Saran, Cliff (2020). 'A tech reboot of retail', *Computer Weekly*, 14 December. Available at www.computerweekly.com/feature/A-tech-reboot-of-retail (accessed 21 July 2021).

SAS (2019). 'SAS offers Nestlé analytics solutions to improve demand planning process and accuracy', *SAS Analytics*, 29 April. Available at www.sas.com/ en_us/news/press-releases/2019/april/nestle-analytics-manufacturing-sgf19.html (accessed 11 June 2021).

Saxenian, AnnaLee (1994). *Regional Advantage: Culture and Competition in Silicon Valley and Route 128*. Cambridge, MA: Harvard University Press.

Saxenian, AnnaLee (2006). *The New Argonauts: Regional Advantage in a Global Economy*. Cambridge, MA: Harvard University Press.

Schwab, Klaus (2016). 'The fourth industrial revolution: What it means, how to respond', *World Economic Forum*, 14 January. Available at www.weforum.org/ agenda/2016/01/the-fourth-industrial-revolution-what-it-means-and-how-to -respond/ (accessed 3 August 2020).

Schwarztman, Roberta (2020). 'Amazon vs. Alibaba: A quick comparison', *California Business Journal*. Available at https://calbizjournal.com/amazon-vs-alibaba-a-quick -comparison (accessed 28 March 2021).

Seddighi, Hamed and Hamid Moradlou (2021). 'The impact of sharing economy incentives and Industry 4.0 technologies on humanitarian logistics: Insights from the Iran floods of 2019', in Emel Aktas, Michael Bourlakis, Ioannis Minis and Vasileios Zeimpekis (eds), *Improving Supply Chains with Analytics and Industry 4.0 Technologies*. London: Kogan Page, pp. 233–260.

SensorTower (2021). 'Nike, Inc.', *SensorTower*, 28 August. Available at https:// sensortower.com/ios/publisher/nike-inc/301521406 (accessed 30 August 2021).

Seraphin, Sean (2020). 'Top 3 omnichannel strategies retailers are using during COVID-19', *RIS News*, 29 September. Available at https://risnews.com/top-3 -omnichannel-strategies-retailers-are-using-during-covid-19 (accessed 17 February 2021).

Shackelford, Scott (2016). 'How to fix an Internet of Broken Things', *Christian Science Monitor*, 26 October. Available at www.csmonitor.com/World/Passcode/Passcode -Voices/2016/1026/Opinion-How-to-fix-an-internet-of-broken-things (accessed 15 December 2020).

Shah, Nidhi (2016). 'The evolution of mobile apps – 1994 through 2016', *Arkenea*, 18 March. Available at https://arkenea.com/blog/evolution-of-mobile-apps/ (accessed 10 August 2021).

Sharif, Amir, Liz Breen and Sankar Silvarajah (2021). 'AstraZeneca vaccine: How to fix supply issues', *The Conversation*, 19 March. Available at https://theconversation .com/astrazeneca-vaccine-how-to-fix-supply-issues-157450 (accessed 13 June 2021).

Sheff, Laura (2020). '2020 Gartner Magic Quadrant for Cloud Infrastructure and Platform Services', *bmc blogs*, 17 September. Available at www.bmc.com/blogs/ gartner-magic-quadrant-cips-cloud-infrastructure-platform-services/ (accessed 3 April 2021).

Shehadi, Sebastian (2021). 'Covid vaccine production mapped: The regions left behind', *Investment Monitor*, 21 April. Available at https://investmentmonitor .ai/business-activities/manufacturing/covid-vaccine-regions-left-behind (accessed 2 September 2021).

Sheng, Jie, Joseph Amankwah-Amoah, Zaheer Khan and Xiaojun Wang (2020). 'COVID-10 pandemic in the new era of Big Data analytics: Methodological innovations and future research directions', *British Journal of Management/Early View*, 20 November. Available at https://onlinelibrary.wiley.com/doi/full/10.1111/1467-8551 .12441 (accessed 15 February 2021).

Sherman, Eric (2020). '94% of the Fortune 1000 are seeing coronavirus supply chain disruptions: Report', *Fortune*, 21 February. Available at https://fortune.com/2020/ 02/21/fortune-1000-coronavirus-china-supply-chain-impact/ (accessed 12 February 2021).

Shih, Willy C. (2020). 'Global supply chains in a post-pandemic world', *Magazine* (September–October), *Harvard Business Review*. Available at https://hbr.org/2020/ 09/global-supply-chains-in-a-post-pandemic-world (accessed 29 July 2021).

Siemens (2021). 'Digital connectivity for industry', Siemens.com. Available at https:// new.siemens.com/global/en/products/automation/topic-areas/digital-connectivity .html (accessed 25 February 2021).

Silver, Laura (2019). 'Smartphone ownership is growing rapidly around the world, but not always equally', Pew Research Center, 5 February. Available at www .pewresearch.org/global/2019/02/05/smartphone-ownership-is-growing-rapidly -around-the-world-but-not-always-equally/ (accessed 16 January 2021).

Smykay, Edward W., Donald J. Bowersox and Frank H. Mossman (1961). *Physical Distribution Management*. New York: Macmillan.

Sneader, Kevin and Shubham Singhal (2020). 'From thinking about the next normal to making it work: What to stop, start, and accelerate', McKinsey & Company, 15 May. Available at www.mckinsey.com/featured-insights/leadership/from-thinking-about -the-next-normal-to-making-it-work-what-to-stop-start-and-accelerate (accessed 2 March 2021).

Sniderman, Brenna, Monika Mahto and Mark J. Cotteleer (2016). *Industry 4.0 and Manufacturing Ecosystems*. New York: Deloitte University Press. Available at https://dupress.deloitte.com/content/dam/dup-us-en/articles/manufacturing -ecosystems-exploring-world-connected-enterprises/DUP_2898_Industry4.0Man ufacturingEcosystems.pdf (accessed 28 April 2020).

Solvoyo (2014). 'Omnichannel fulfillment: Distributed vs distributed', Solvoyo.com, 23 December. Available at www.solvoyo.com/omni-channel-fulfillment-dynamic -vs-distributed/ (accessed 24 February 2021).

Somerton, Clare (2020). 'Datafication', in Laurie A. Schintler and Connie L. McNeely (eds), *The Encylopedia of Big Data*. Cham: Springer, pp. 1–15. Available at https:// link.springer.com/referencework/10.1007/978-3-319-32001-4#bibliographic-info (accessed 19 July 2021).

Song, Sungeon (2019). 'Korean manufacturing's digital transformation must escape "pilot purgatory"', McKinsey & Company, 8 August. Available at www.mckinsey .com/featured-insights/asia-pacific/korean-manufacturings-digital-transformation -must-escape-pilot-purgatory (accessed 6 March 2021).

Spadafora, John (2020). 'Pitney Bowes Parcel Shipping Index reports global parcel volume exceeds 100 billion for first time ever', *Business Wire*, 12 October. Available at www.businesswire.com/news/home/20201012005150/en/Pitney-Bowes-Parcel -Shipping-Index-Reports-Continued-Growth-as-Global-Parcel-Volume-Exceeds -100-billion-for-First-Time-Ever (accessed 13 May 2021).

Speedel (2020). 'Quantum computing: The impact of Quantum on the supply chain', Speedel.com, 13 October. Available at www.speedel.co.uk/the-impact-of-quantum -computing-on-the-supply-chain/ (accessed 17 November 2020).

Speringer, Markus and Judith Schnelzer (2019). 'Differentiation of Industry 4.0 models: The 4th industrial revolution from different regional perspectives in the Global North and Global South', in *Innovations for Development: Towards Sustainable, Inclusive, and Peaceful Societies*. Vienna: Regional Academy on the United Nations. Available at www.ra-un.org/publications (accessed 5 May 2020).

Statista (2020a). 'E-commerce worldwide – statistics and facts', *Statista Research Department*, 26 October. Available at www.statista.com/topics/871/online -shopping/ (accessed 26 January 2021).

Statista (2020b). 'Number of 7-Eleven stores worldwide as of January 2020, by country', *Statista*, January. Available at www.statista.com/statistics/269454/number -of-7-eleven-stores-worldwide-in-2010-by-country/ (accessed 7 April 2021).

Statista (2021a). 'Number of mobile app downloads worldwide from 2016 to 2020', *Statista Research Department*, 6 July. Available at www.statista.com/statistics/ 271644/worldwide-free-and-paid-mobile-app-store-downloads/ (accessed 30 July 2021).

Statista (2021b). 'Selected countries with the largest number of Starbucks stores worldwide as of September 2020', *Statista Research Department*, 27 September. Available at www.statista.com/statistics/306915/countries-with-the-largest-number -of-starbucks-stores-worldwide/ (accessed 21 August 2021).

Statista (2021c). 'Number of apps available in leading app stores as of 1st quarter 2021', *Statista*, 6 July. Available at www.statista.com/statistics/276623/number-of -apps-available-in-leading-app-stores/ (accessed 10 August 2021).

Statista (2021d). 'Statistics and facts about mobile app usage', *Statista*, 12 July. Available at www.statista.com/topics/1002/mobile-app-usage/ (accessed 10 August 2021).

Sterman, Yoav, Ezri Tarazi, Ofer Berman, Yuval Gur, Haim Parnas, Rami Tareef and Shmuel Arwas (2020). 'Safety on demand: A case study for the design and manufacturing-on-demand of personal protective equipment for healthcare workers during the COVID-19 pandemic', *Safety Science*, 136(April). Available at https:// pubmed.ncbi.nlm.nih.gov/33519093/ (accessed 16 February 2021).

Strauss, Patrick (2021). 'Driving better customer experience in digital supply chains', in Emel Aktas, Michael Bourlakis, Ioannis Minis and Vasileios Zeimpekis (eds), *Improving Supply Chains with Analytics and Industry 4.0 Technologies*. London: Kogan Page, pp. 16–32.

Steins, Dietmar, Stephen O'Connor, Annika Neumair, Timur Lips, Adrien Dedieu and Joerg Marienfeld (2021). *Automotive: A Shifting Landscape*. Bonn: DHL Supply Chain. Available at www.dhl.com/content/dam/dhl/global/dhl-supply-chain/ documents/pdf/SC_Automotive_Trend_Report_2021_EN_.pdf (accessed 23 July 2021).

Sundarakani, Balan, Rukshanda Kamran, Piyush Maheshwari and Vipul Jain (2021). 'Designing a hybrid cloud for a supply chain network of Industry 4.0: A theoretical framework', *Benchmarking: An International Journal*, 28(5): 1524–1542.

Sundararajan, Arun (2019). 'Commentary: The twilight of brand and consumerism? Digital trust, cultural meaning, and the quest for connection in the sharing economy', *Journal of Marketing*, 83(5): 32–35.

Tankovska, H. (2021a). 'Most popular global mobile messaging apps 2021', *Statista*, 10 February. Available at www.statista.com/statistics/258749/most-popular-global-mobile-messenger-apps/#:~:text=As%20of%20January%202021%2C%20two,popular%20mobile%20social%20apps%20worldwide.%20(last%20visited%20Feb%2020,%202021) (accessed 13 April 2021).

Tankovska, H. (2021b). 'Percentage of global population using Facebook as of January 2020, by region', *Statista*, 27 January. Available at www.statista.com/statistics/241552/share-of-global-population-using-facebook-by-region/ (accessed 19 April 2020).

Tankovska, H. (2021c). 'Leading countries based on Facebook audience size as of January 2021', *Statista*, 9 February. Available at www.statista.com/statistics/268136/top-15-countries-based-on-number-of-facebook-users/ (accessed 13 April 2021).

Tany, Tony (2018). 'Demand sensing and demand shaping – a new way of demand forecasting', *LinkedIn*, 31 March. Available at www.linkedin.com/pulse/demand-sensing-shaping-new-way-forecasting-tony-tany (accessed 15 February 2021).

TeleGeography (2011). *TeleGeography 2010*. Washington, DC: Primetrica.

TeleGeography (2021). Personal communication, 5 May.

Temperton, James (2018). 'Such a dumb myth', *Twitter*, 23 January. Available at https://twitter.com/jtemperton/status/955748426205089792?lang=en (accessed 28 July 2021).

Thorby, Chris (2007). 'Freight forwarders and logistics: Evolution and revolution', in John Fossey (ed.), *CI 40th Anniversary 2007*. London: Containerisation International, pp. 21–28.

Thrift, Nigel (2006). 'Re-inventing invention: New tendencies in capitalist commodification', *Economy and Society*, 35(2): 279–306.

Tian, Yan and Concetta Stewart (2006). 'History of E-Commerce', in Medhi Khosrow-Pour (ed.), *Encyclopedia of E-Commerce, E-Government and Mobile Commerce*. Hershey, PA: IGI Global, pp. 559–564.

TikTok (2021). 'TikTok Shop seller on-boarding', *TikTok Shop: Seller University*. Available at https://seller-id.tiktok.com/university/article?knowledge_id=10000741 (accessed 1 July 2021).

Tocci, Meghan (2020). 'History and evolution of the smartphones', *Simple Texting*, 19 August. Available at https://simpletexting.com/where-have-we-come-since-the-first-smartphone (accessed 16 January 2021).

Topleva, Silviya (2018). 'Industry 4.0: Transforming economy through value added', *Asian Journal of Economic Modelling*, 6(1): 37–46.

Tran, William (2018). 'Insights from Hype vs Reality Emerging Technology Survey', *LinkedIn*, 12 October. Available at www.linkedin.com/pulse/insights-from-hype-vs-reality-emerging-technology-survey-william-tran/ (accessed 1 March 2021).

Tran-Dang, Hoa, Nicolas Krommenacker, Patrick Charpentier and Dong-Seong Kim (2020). 'The Internet of Things for logistics: Perspectives, application review, and challenges', *IETE Technical Review*, DOI: 10.1080/02564602.2020.1827308.

Tranos, Emmanouil (2011). 'The topology and emerging urban geographies of the Internet backbone and aviation networks in Europe: A comparative study', *Environment and Planning A*, 43(2): 378–392.

Tranos, Emmanouil (2013). *The Geography of the Internet: Cities, Regions and Internet Infrastructure in Europe*. Cheltenham, UK and Northampton, MA, USA: Edward Elgar Publishing.

Tricks, Henry (2021). 'How to know what customers want', Special report: The retail renaissance – the future of shopping, *The Economist*, 13 March.

Trivago (2021). 'Annual report 2020'. Available at https://ir.trivago.com/financial-information/annual-reports (accessed 6 April 2021).

Tulgan, Bruce and Carolyn A. Martin (2001). *Managing Generation Y: Global Citizens Born in the Late Seventies and Early Eighties*. Amherst, MA: HRD Press.

Uber (2020). 'Moving more of what matters with delivery', *Uber Newsroom*, 19 April. Available at www.uber.com/newsroom/moving-more-of-what-matters-with-delivery/ (accessed 27 June 2021).

United States Senate (2020). *The Logistics of Transporting a COVID-19 Vaccine*. US Senate Committee on Commerce, Science and Transportation, Commerce Subcommittee on Transport and Safety, Washington, DC, 10 December. Available at www.commerce.senate.gov/2020/12/the-logistics-of-transporting-a-covid-19-vaccine (accessed 2 February 2021).

UPS (2021). *SEC Filing Details Form 10-K, Annual Report 2020*. Securities and Exchange Commission, 20 February. Available at www.investors.ups.com/financials/sec-filings (accessed 7 April 2021).

UPS Store (2021). '3D printing locations', The upsstore.com. Available at www.theupsstore.com/print/3d-printing/locations (accessed 14 April 2020).

USDHHS (2020). 'Operation Warp Speed vaccine distribution process', Coronavirus US, Department of Health and Human Services, Washington, DC. Available at www.hhs.gov/coronavirus/explaining-operation-warp-speed/index.html (accessed 15 March 2021).

USSEC (2020). *Uber Technologies, Inc. for Fiscal Year Ending 30 December 2019*. Washington, DC: United States Security and Exchange Commission. Available at www.sec.gov/Archives/edgar/data/1543151/000119312519103850/d647752ds1.htm (accessed 11 April 2021).

USSEC (2021a). 'Form 10-K: *Annual report for fiscal year ended 31 December, 2020*, AMAZON.COM, INC.', United States Securities and Exchange Commission, Washington, DC. Available at www.sec.gov/ix?doc=/Archives/edgar/data/1018724/000101872421000004/amzn-20201231.htm#i75de98b9097f40f-3b5884e541f532421 (accessed 20 April 2021).

USSEC (2021b). 'Form 20-F: Alibaba Group Holdings Limited', United States Securities and Exchange Commission, Washington, DC. Available at https://sec.report//Document/1577552/000110465920082409/baba-20200331x20f.htm#ITEM3KEYINFORMATION_740987 (accessed 20 April 2021).

USSEC (2021c). '7 Eleven Inc', United States Securities and Exchange Commission, Washington, DC, 30 April. Available at https://sec.report/CIK/0000092344 (accessed 22 July 2021).

USSEC (2021d). 'Form 10-K Uber Technologies, Inc. for fiscal year ending 30 December 2020', United States Securities and Exchange Commission, Washington, DC. Available at https://fintel.io/doc/sec-uber-technologies-inc-10k-2021-march-01-18687-92 (accessed 13 April 2021).

USSEC (2021e). 'Form 20-F Trivago N.v. Annual and transition report of foreign private issuers [Sections 13 or 15(d)]', United States Securities and Exchange Commission, Washington, DC, 5 March. Available at https://sec.report/Document/0001683825-21-000008/ (accessed 6 April 2021).

Valdes-Dapena, Peter (2020). 'Ford is working with 3M and GE to make respirators and ventilators', *CNN Business*, 24 March. Available at https://edition.cnn.com/2020/03/24/business/ford-3m-ge-ventilators-coronavirus-duplicate-2/index.html (accessed 18 October 2020).

Van Asch, Thomas, Wouter Dewulf, Franziska Kupfer, Ivan Cárdenas and Eddy Van de Voorde (2020). 'Cross-border e-commerce logistics: Strategic success factors for airports', *Research in Transportation Economics*, 79(C), 10.1016/j.retrec.2019.100761.

Van Dijck, José (2009). 'Users like you? Theorizing agency in user-generated content', *Media, Culture and Society*, 31(1): 41–58.

Van Dijck, José and Thomas Poell (2013). 'Understanding social media logic', *Media and Communications*, 1(1): 2–14.

Van Dijck, José and Thomas Poell (2016). 'Understanding the promises and premises of online health platforms', *Big Data and Society*, 3(1): 1–11.

Varotsis, Alkaios Bournias (2019). '3D printing vs. CNC machining', *Hubs*, 4 September. Available at www.hubs.com/knowledge-base/3d-printing-vs-cnc-machining/ (accessed 29 July 2021).

Venkumar, Ponnusamy (2019). 'Supply and demand management during industrial evolutions: Present and future outlook', in S.G. Ponnambalam, Nachiappan Subramanian, Manoj Kumar Tiwari and Wan Azhar Wan Yusoff (eds), *Industry 4.0 and Hyper-Customized Smart Manufacturing Supply Chains*. Hershey, PA: Business Science Reference, pp. 263–293.

Verhoef, Peter C., P.K. Kannan and J. Jeffrey Inman (2015). 'From multi-channel retailing to omni-channel retailing: Introduction to the Special Issue on multi-channel retailing', *Journal of Retailing*, 91(2): 174–181.

Violino, Simona, Simone Figorilli, Corrado Costa and Federico Pallottino (2020). 'Internet of beer: A review on smart technologies from mash to pint', *Foods*, 9: 950. Available at www.mdpi.com/journal/foods (accessed 12 July 2021).

Vogel, Ezra F. (1979). *Japan as No. One: Lessons for America*. Cambridge, MA: Harvard University Press.

Vogel, Ezra F. (1991). *The Four Little Dragons: The Spread of Industrialization in East Asia*. Cambridge, MA: Harvard University Press.

Vogel-Heuser, Birgit and Dieter Hess (2016), 'Guest Editorial Industry 4.0 – prerequisites and visions', *IEEE Transactions on Automation Science and Engineering*, 13(2): 411–413.

Vorderer, Peter and Matthias Kohring (2013). 'Permanently online: A challenge for media and communication research', *International Journal of Communication*, 7(1): 188–196.

Vorderer, Peter, Nicola Kromer and Frank M. Schneider (2016). 'Permanently online – permanently connected: Explorations into university students' use of social media and mobile smart devices', *Computers in Human Behavior*, 63(October): 694–703.

Wadhwa, Balbir, Kenny Rajan, Scott Francis and Manas Srivastava (2020). 'Supply chain tracking and traceability with IoT-enabled blockchain on AWS', *AWS Partner Network Blog*, 16 September. Available at https://aws.amazon.com/blogs/apn/supply-chain-tracking-and-traceability-with-iot-enabled-blockchain-on-aws/ (accessed 22 December 2020).

Walker, Martyn (2021). 'Blockchain in the supply chain', in Emel Aktas, Michael Bourlakis, Ioannis Minis and Vasileios Zeimpekis (eds), *Improving Supply Chains with Analytics and Industry 4.0 Technologies*. London: Kogan Page, pp. 33–60.

Walmart (2018). 'Walmart to invest in Flipkart Group, India's innovative eCommerce company', *Walmart.com*, 9 May. Available at https://corporate.walmart.com/newsroom/2018/05/09/walmart-to-invest-in-flipkart-group-indias-innovative-ecommerc e-company (accessed 7 June 2021).

Walmart Staff (2017). '5 ways Walmart uses Big Data to help customers', *Walmart*, 7 August. Available at https://corporate.walmart.com/newsroom/innovation/201708 07/5-ways-walmart-uses-big-data-to-help-customers (accessed 9 November 2020).

Wang, Yubin, Jingjing Wang and Xiaoyang Wang (2020). 'COVID-19, supply chain disruption and China's hog market: A dynamic analysis', *China Agricultural Economic Review*, 20(3): 427–443.

Webster, Karen and Adam Kumar (2020). 'DHL: What happens when robots run the warehouse', *Paymts.com*, 3 March. Available at www.pymnts.com/news/delivery/2020/dhl-strengthening-fulfillment-weak-link/ (accessed 25 November 2020).

Wee, Dominik, Matthias Kässer, Michele Bertoncello, Kersten Heineke, Gregir Eckhard, Julian Hölz, Florian Saupe and Thibaut Müller (2015). 'Competing for the connected customer – perspectives on the opportunities created by car connectivity', McKinsey & Company, September. Available at www.mckinsey.com/~/media/ mckinsey/industries/automotive%20and%20assembly/our%20insights/how%20 carmakers%20can%20compete%20for%20the%20connected%20consumer/competing_for_the_connected_customer.ashx (accessed 30 March 2021).

WEF (2017). *Impact of the Fourth Industrial Revolution on Supply Chains*. Cologne and Geneva: World Economic Forum. Available at www.weforum.org/whitepapers/impact-of-the-fourth-industrial-revolution-on-supply-chains (accessed 4 March 2021).

Weinberg, Neil (2020). 'How Amazon launched the warehouse robotics industry', *TechTarget*, 7 August. Available at https://searchaws.techtarget.com/feature/ How-Amazon-launched-the-warehouse-robotics-industry (accessed 9 October 2020).

Welsh, Taylor (2020). 'Industry 4.0: Connected customers; customized experiences', *Datumize*, 15 October. Available at https://blog.datumize.com/industry-4.0-connecte d-consumers-customized-experiences (accessed 9 May 2021).

WHO (2021). 'COVAX: Working for global equitable access to COVID-19 vaccines', World Health Organization. Available at www.who.int/initiatives/act-accelerator/ covax (accessed 23 August 2021).

WHO Council (2021). 'Governing health for the common good', *Council Brief No.1*, *WHO Council on the Economics of Health for All*, World Health Organization, 9 June. Available at www.marilynwaring.com/files/20210609-CouncilBrief-no1.pdf (accessed 23 August 2021).

Wilding, Richard (2020). 'Biochemistry wins the Covid19 battle but logistics and supply chain will win the war'. Available at www.richardwilding.info/logistic s-winning-the-covid19-vaccine-war.html (accessed 13 June 2020).

Williamson, Deborah Aho (2020). 'TikTok users around the world 2020: eMarketer forecasts and other essential stats', *Insider Intelligence: eMarketer*, 14 December. Available at www.emarketer.com/content/tiktok-users-around-world-2020 (accessed 1 July 2021).

Winseck, Dwayne (2017). 'The geopolitical economy of the global Internet infrastructure', *Journal of Information Policy*, 7: 228–267.

Wood, Zoe (2020). 'Shops warn of Christmas stock shortages as PPE shipments clog key UK port', *Guardian*, 14 November. Available at www.theguardian.com/

business/2020/nov/14/shops-warn-of-christmas-stock-shortages-as-ppe-shipments -clog-key-uk-port (accessed 14 February 2021).

Woods Agency (2017). 'Beyond 2020: The era of conscious consumption', Woods Agency. Available at www.woodsagency.nz/blogs/beyond-2020 (accessed 13 May 2021).

World Courier (2020). 'COVID-19: Contact-free procedures for pick-up and deliveries', *AmerisourceBergen*, 6 April. Available at www.worldcourier.com/insights/covid-19-contact-free (accessed 17 February 2021).

WP (2021). 'Uber Eats', *Wikipedia*. Available at https://en.wikipedia.org/wiki/Uber_ Eats (accessed 21 April 2021).

WPR (2021). 'Facebook users by country 2021', *World Population Review*. Available at https://worldpopulationreview.com/country-rankings/facebook-users-by-country (accessed 13 April 2021).

WTC (2021). *The Future Shopper Report 2021*. London: Wunderman Thompson Commerce. Available at https://insights.wundermanthompsoncommerce.com/hubfs/NL/2021/The-Future-Shopper-2021-NL.pdf?hsCtaTracking=f400cfdf-06f 0-4676-a11f-0f5aa6a70e8e%7C8fee9ef5-418a-4f66-b734-57a946800734 (accessed 13 July 2021).

Wu, Lifang, Xiaohang Yue, Alan Jin and David C. Yen (2016). 'Smart supply chain management: A review and implications for future research', *International Journal of Logistics Management*, 27(2): 395–417.

Xiao, Carol (2019). 'How Pinduoduo successfully gained market share through social E-commerce?', *Target China*, 1 November. Available at https://targetchina.com.au/article/how-pinduoduo-successfully-gained-market-share-through-social-co mmerce/ (accessed 18 August 2021).

Xu, Kevin (2020). 'Where are the data centers: AWS, Alibaba Cloud, Azure, GCP', interconnected blog, 5 March. Available at https://interconnected.blog/data-cente r-coverage-aws-alibaba-azure-gcp/ (accessed 3 April 2021).

Xu, Li Da, Eric L. Xu and Ling Li (2018). 'Industry 4.0: State of the art and future trends', *International Journal of Production Research*, 56(8): 2941–2962.

Xu, Marc, Brett Ferrand and Martyn Roberts (2008). 'The last mile of e-commerce: Unattended delivery from the consumers and eTailers' perspectives', *International Journal of Electronic Marketing and Retailing*, 2(1): 20–38.

Yin, Yong, Kathryn E. Stecke and Dongni Li (2018). 'The evolution of production systems from Industry 2.0 through Industry 4.0', *International Journal of Production Research*, 56(1–2): 848–861.

Yoon, Saemoon (2020). '17 ways technology could change the world by 2025', *World Economic Forum*, 23 June. Available at www.weforum.org/agenda/2020/0 6/17-predictions-for-our-world-in-2025/ (accessed 20 November 2020).

Zhou, Baohua (2019). 'Fear of missing out, feeling of acceleration, and being permanently online: A survey study of university students' use of mobile apps in China', *Chinese Journal of Communication*, 12(1): 66–83.

Zlady, Hannah (2021). 'The shipping crisis is getting worse. Here's what that means for holiday shopping', *CNN Business*, 23 August. Available at https://edition.cnn.com/2021/08/23/business/global-supply-chains-christmas-shipping/index.html (accessed 25 August 2021).

Index